Selecting and Organizing

STATE
GOVERNMENT
PUBLICATIONS

By
Margaret T. Lane

D1008178

American Library Association
CHICAGO AND LONDON 1987

Designed by Charles Bozett

Composed by Impressions, Inc.
   in Baskerville on a
   Penta-driven Autologic APS-μ5
   Phototypesetting system

Printed on 50-pound Glatfelter
   a pH-neutral stock, and bound
   in 10-point Carolina cover stock
   by BookCrafters

Library of Congress Cataloging-in-Publication Data

Lane, Margaret T.
   Selecting and organizing state government publications.

   Bibliography: p.
   Includes index.
   1. Libraries—Special collections—Government
publications. 2. United States—Government publications
(State governments)—Bibliography—Methodology.
3. Acquisition of government publications. I. Title.
Z688.G6L35   1987   025.2′834   87-1341
ISBN 0-8389-0477-7

CONTENTS

FIGURES

TABLES

ACKNOWLEDGMENTS

Friends in all fifty states have shared information, advice, and copies of state publications with me for more than forty years. It is difficult to select names for individual recognition. I hope this book will partially repay my indebtedness to all state documents librarians, past and present.

Three prominent documents librarians who helped during the writing of this text must be mentioned. Kathleen Heim, Louisiana State University, a library school dean who remains a documents librarian at heart, read several drafts of the manuscript and helped revise the text and the tables. Marilyn Moody, Iowa State University, and David Parish, State University of New York at Geneseo, both experts in state publications, gave the manuscript a careful reading and provided thoughtful corrections and suggestions. Betty Lou Roundtree and Betty Jo Finley read and advised on parts of the text.

Herbert Bloom, my editor at ALA, saw the need for a state publications text and encouraged me. Helen Cline and Harriett Banner patiently guided the text through production. Zelda Long and Jo Ann Wimberly gave substantial help in assembling materials and putting the manuscript together. I am also indebted to Laura Cotton, Pat Kersey, and Paul Landry, who gave technical advice. Marjorie B. Tolbert and Marcilene Dutton helped me with many last-minute details. I extend special thanks to those whom I have named and to many unnamed state documents librarians throughout the country.

1 INTRODUCTION

The arrival of the 1980s was accompanied by the "new federalism," presenting a challenge to state documents librarians. The reapportioning of governmental powers, with more functions exercised by the states, emphasized and underlined the federal nature of our government and the importance of the individual states.

The states are central to the form of government in the United States. This is confirmed by the very name of our nation: "The United States of America." As President Reagan said in his first inaugural address, "All of us need to be reminded that the Federal Government did not create the States; the States created the Federal Government.[1]

As governmental powers relating to the social, economic, and political functions of our society are returned to the states, the states will become increasingly important in our daily lives. The idea that decentralization will promote prosperity and progress is inherent in the idea of the "new federalism." The renewed significance of the states in the lives of individuals makes the actions and activities of state government of vital interest to the public. "Perhaps the new federalism will have a silver lining as a positive motivation for state programs, subsequently, and their publications," observed David Parish, a state documents specialist.[2]

Access to information about one's own state government is essential in a democracy. The United States form of government recognizes the right of the public *to know*. This right extends to governments at all levels— national, state and local. The right to monitor the activities of government is guaranteed by the federal Constitution, by state constitutions, and by federal and state laws. Freedom of the press, guaranteed by the Bill of Rights, permits and encourages journalists to report to the people. Open meeting laws and government in the sunshine are sometimes objected to by officials who are the focus of scrutiny, but both are necessary to assure the accountability of government agencies. Public records acts provide

1. Inaugural Address of President Ronald Reagan, January 20, 1981, *Weekly Compilation of Presidential Documents* 17, no.4 (January 26, 1981): 2.
2. David Parish, "The New Federalism: A Boon for State Documents," *Government Publications Review* 12 (July–August 1985): 383.

access to working files of government bodies. Promulgation and reporting requirements make known to all the actions of our governments. By these means citizens are encouraged to monitor government activities.

That state government officials are interested in information is evidenced by the proliferation of government research agencies, legislative councils, and reference bureaus. These agencies are concerned not only with home-state information but also with comparative information from other states. Out-of-state information on governmental actions and activities is useful for new programs or as a basis for comparison. For example, if one state has a well-developed land-use plan, other states may use it as a model or starting point for their own plan.

Many state agencies have a mission to inform, to regulate, to warn, and to advise the public. They perform these tasks by preparing and distributing publications. This information, in a democracy, must be accessible and available to all. Although such information is state-specific, it is often similar from state to state.

Information produced by the federal and local governments likewise has an impact on our lives, but this is a separate topic. Only state government information is being considered in this book.

Range of Publications

What is needed to open a marriage counseling business? What state agencies provide services to the handicapped? Can a certain physician in a state be located by only the physician's name? What innoculations are required for a student to enter a particular school system? What occupations are prohibited to convicted felons? How much money did the state spend last year? The most accurate and up-to-date answers to these questions are found in state publications. This is not to say that the published answer is always the best. One should remember that there are times when published information must be confirmed by consultation with the publishing source.

Appreciation for state documents is enhanced by a realization of the areas in which state governments publish. The range of topics addressed in state documents is wide—from armadillos (a Texas topic) to zinc (a Colorado concern). Some topics vary from state to state. For example, polar bears might well be a subject never treated in southern state publications; however, other animals are subjects about which state wildlife commissions and state university zoology departments often publish. The variances in areas of concern are based largely on geographical or demographical factors and are fewer than the areas of common interest. Listings of state activities by subject have entries for all fifty states, with minor exceptions, such as mining and minerals. Community health is a topic common to all the states.

Christine Britten, a reference librarian in a public library, has extolled the virtues of state documents and their scope, ending with the admonition, "think 'bonsai, beekeeping, canning, farming, space travel, pollution . . . people.' Documents are for everyone."[3]

Role of Libraries

Use of state publications and the role of libraries go hand in hand. Libraries acquire, organize, preserve and service state publications. For certain information (especially state publications), maintenance and preservation in libraries are essential.

Recent studies have shown that current information is most used by scholars.[4] The general public seeking information about hunting seasons, the farmer needing advice on fertilizers and weed killers, the manufacturer concerned about pollution control standards, and the property owner studying flood control plans also need the latest and most current information. In many libraries, particularly public libraries, it is current information that is sought and the library performs a needed service by providing a collection of state documents that contains only the latest information. However, for any kind of historical survey, for comparisons, for chronological reporting, and even for resurrecting ideas that flourished before their time, older state publications, as found in libraries, are essential sources of information.

In addition to making state publications and the information therein available to citizens in the state in which the publications originate, libraries have a role in making publications available beyond the state. The state in which a publication originates is the one most likely to have a copy in a library collection and available for interlibrary loan. And states do need to borrow from one another: a state that has a well-written school bus drivers' guide or that has studied the pros and cons of a state lottery has a publication with potential value to other states. Constitutional convention studies, reports of commissions on water rights, and election returns all provide information that can be used outside the state in which it originates.

Large research libraries collect certain types of state publications for all the states so that basic information relating to every state is at hand. First among these frequently collected publications are the checklists of state publications now issued by most states. "Blue books," a type of hand-

3. Christine Britten, "What Do You Do with Them? Put Your Documents Where Their Service Is," *Wisconsin Library Bulletin* 73 (January–February 1977): 33.

4. Peter Hernon, *Use of Government Publications by Social Scientists* (Norwood, N.J.: Ablex Publishing, 1979); Gary Purcell, "Reference Use of State Government Information in Public Libraries," *Government Publications Review* 10 (March–April 1983): 173–87.

book issued in many states, contain basic information on state history, public officials, and governmental organization. Statistical abstracts, another concise source of state information, are also collected on a nationwide basis. One of the purposes of David Parish's *State Government Reference Publications* is to identify these categories of publications that can profitably and conveniently be made available in large research libraries and to list the publications in each category for each state.

That libraries are a vital source of state government information is a basic premise of this text. Libraries are a connecting link between state agencies and the general public. The role of librarians as managers of information in concrete forms (particularly print and microformats) is well established. Publications received in libraries are made accessible and available to many users. The newer forms in which state information is available (computer databases are the prime example) are not as widely accessible and available to libraries or to the general public. Thus, the discussion here deals more with state publications, or state documents as they are sometimes called, than with state information.

Libraries as the primary link between access and availability and as the facilitators of the use of state publications are acknowledged here as state-of-the-art facts. Although getting documents to libraries is not synonymous with getting documents to the ultimate user, it is a step in the right direction. According to Cherns and Hernon, depository library programs, such as those described in Chapter 5, may not be the most efficient medium for dissemination of government information and perhaps a "government information specialist" is needed (a proposal advanced by Weech).[5] Still these programs are a type of safety net.[6] Although government information is available through the Freedom of Information Act and public records acts, that availability is not as conducive to public participation as that provided by depository libraries. Expansion of the role of libraries to provide both state publications and state information is the challenge of the eighties. Every library must have state documents; even the smallest library needs the state manual or roster, the state constitution, and the official map of the state. Many small libraries also need their state's statistical abstract and checklist.

5. J. J. Cherns, *Official Publishing: An Overview* (N.Y.: Pergamon Press, 1979), 295; Peter Hernon, "Introduction," *Drexel Library Quarterly* 16 (October 1980): 4–5; Terry Weech, "New Technology and State Government Sources," in *New Technology and Documents Librarianship; Proceedings of the Third Annual Library Government Documents and Information Conference*, ed. Peter Hernon (Westport, Conn.: Meckler Publishing, 1983), 85–86.

6. Office of Management and Budget, *Management of Federal Information Services* OMB Circular A-130 (December 12, 1985) in *Federal Register* 50 (December 24, 1985): 52748. AE 2.106.

Scope of Work

For documents specialists with years of experience in handling documents, this book collects in one place much of the background information needed for managing a documents collection or providing reference service for state documents. For the newcomer to state documents, this text serves as an introduction to the field of state documents providing an overview of the administration and use of state documents in libraries. Although this book is about state documents, it is not about individual state documents but rather about the collection, bibliographic control, and use of state documents in general. Sources for this text include writings from the state documents literature (and some books and articles on federal documents), documents newsletters, information taken from ALA GODORT State and Local Documents Task Force meetings and publications, and student papers, as well as the personal files and experiences of the author.

After a general chapter on the characteristics of state documents and a brief historical survey, this text begins, as state documents do, with state agencies. A chapter on the distribution practices of state agencies follows, and then the remainder of the text deals with libraries, especially acquisition methods and user services. Notwithstanding the current thinking that documents should be "mainstreamed" and completely integrated with other library materials, the administration of separate state documents collections, including processing, cataloging, and classifying, is discussed as many libraries do have separate state documents collections or are depository libraries for state documents.

Sources

There are a number of bibliographies, guides, and other tools which must be cited over and over in a text on state documents. Some of these are referred to in abbreviated form in this text—a shortened title for the *Monthly Checklist* or a reference by author or compiler. They are given here for ready reference in Table 1.

The *Monthly Checklist of State Publications,* the comprehensive, all-state checklist, and the *Manual on the Use of State Publications,* long a basic text and bibliographic source, are two such examples. Some state documents librarians refer to the *Manual* by the last name of its compiler, Wilcox.

The *Documents on Documents Collection* or *Docs on Docs,* also requires frequent citation. It is a collection of materials produced in the administration of state documents programs, assembled and organized by the ALA GODORT State and Local Documents Task Force. The collection is a source of examples of legislation, manuals, flyers, and workshop mate-

Table 1. *Frequently Cited Works and Abbreviations*

Book of the States	*Book of the States.* Lexington, Ky.: Council of State Governments, 1935+ Biennial.
Bowker	Bowker, Richard R. *State Publications: A Provisional List of the Official Publications of the Several States of the United States from Their Organization.* New York: Publishers' Weekly, 1908. 1 v. in 4.
Documents on Documents Collection, or *Docs on Docs*	Lane, Margaret T., comp. *Documents on Documents Collection, 1973–1979 and 1980–1983.* Chicago: American Library Association, Government Documents Round Table, State and Local Documents Task Force, 1984 and 1985. (ERIC ED 247 940 and ED 263 923).
Hasse	Hasse, Adelaide R. *Index of Economic Material in Documents of the States of the United States.* Pub. no. 85. Washington: Carnegie Institution of Washington, D.C. [1907–22].
Monthly Checklist	*Monthly Checklist of State Publications.* Washington, D.C.: GPO. v. 1+, 1910+. Monthly
Palic	Palic, Vladimir M. *Government Publications: A Guide to Bibliographic Tools.* 4th ed. Washington, D.C.: Library of Congress, 1975. (LC1.6/4:G74).
Parish	Parish, David W. *State Government Reference Publications: An Annotated Bibliography.* 2d ed. Littleton, Colo.: Libraries Unlimited, 1981.
S&LDTF *State Publications*	Lane, Margaret T., comp. *State Publications: Depository Distribution and Bibliographical Programs.* State and Local Documents Task Force, Government Documents Round Table, American Library Association: Texas State Publications Clearinghouse, Documents Monograph Series, nos. 2 and 2A. [Austin]: Texas State Library, 1981. No. 2 is ERIC ED 195 283.
Wilcox	Wilcox, Jerome K., ed. *Manual on the Use of State Publications.* Chicago: American Library Association, 1940. 342 p.

rials. Ten years' worth of items are available in ERIC, and the current materials are circulated through interlibrary loan. For materials from the collection cited in this text, note references include the *Docs on Docs* identification numbers used in the guides to the collection. A detailed description of this collection is included in Chapter 5.

Another important source is the ALA GODORT State and Local Documents Task Force *State Publications: Depository Distribution and Bibliographical Programs*, a compilation of informal state reports. The second volume of the set completes the coverage of the states and should not be overlooked. This compilation provided data for several state documents studies (see Chapter 5) and has been frequently cited by other authors.

David Parish has contributed two hardcover books to the field of state documents, in addition to articles and regular columns. His first work, now in its second edition, is on reference publications. His *Subject Bibliographies* is also a reference tool.

Other state documents works referred to by author are Palic for the chapter on state, territorial and local government bibliographic tools, and Bowker and Hasse, whose documents listings have become part of state documents bibliographical history.

Appendix B is a bibliography of state documents readings. Most of these suggested readings are general articles applicable to all the states. A few articles limited to a single state, such as Dallas Shaffer's account of the Nebraska experience in securing depository legislation, are included.

State Documents as a Starting Place

"Official publications" is the broad term used to describe governmentally produced publications without designating the issuing government. Librarians can become acquainted with official publications, or documents as they are often called, by starting with state documents. Federal documents are so numerous and varied that they may intimidate the novice; on the other hand, local documents (city and county) may be too few, too difficult to obtain, and too seldom under bibliographic control for a beginning documents librarian to understand. State government is closer to home and less complex than the federal government; yet state government includes enough different agencies and a sufficient quantity of publications to justify study. This is not true of most of our smaller cities. Nevertheless, federal publications, and more particularly federal procedures, should not be overlooked or neglected by state documents librarians. Some documents questions and problems are the same regardless of the level of government. A few examples of parallel characteristics across levels of government are compared in Table 2.

The number of publications issued by any level of government is always an estimate because it is not possible to say that all publications have come to the attention of any one central agency. Although the Library Services Program of the Government Printing Office has an acquisitions unit, no one can assert that all publications come to its attention. At the state level,

Table 2. Comparison of Bibliographic and Distribution Characteristics across Levels of Government

	FEDERAL	STATE	LOCAL
Printed bibliographic data	*Monthly Catalog*	*Monthly Checklist*	*The Index to Current Urban Documents*
Number of publications listed	26,757 (*MC* 12/85)	28,168 (*MCL* 12/85)	Not available
Online bibliographic data	GPO MARC tapes	Formerly IHS	LOGIN
Government printer	GPO	A few states, California, Nebraska	Not available
Depository distribution system	GPO since 1895	Most states since 1950	Not available
Number of depository libraries	1,391[a]	1,097[b]	Not available
Number of publications distributed	54,882[c]	120,101[d]	Not available
Texts to aid use[c]	Morehead Hernon/McClure	Parish Wilcox	Nakata

[a]*Administrative Notes* 6 (October 1985): 6.

[b]Moody survey for S&LDTF (unpublished).

[c]*Administrative Notes* 7 (March 1986): 9.

[d]Documents at Library of Congress: *Annual Report, 1984, of the Librarian of Congress*, 62.

[e]Joe Morehead, *Introduction to United States Public Documents*, 3rd ed. (Littleton, Colo.: Libraries Unlimited, 1983); Peter Hernon and Charles R. McClure, *Public Access to Government Information: Issues, Trends, and Strategies* (Norwood, N.J.: Ablex Publishing, 1984); David W. Parish, *State Government Reference Publications*, 2nd ed. (Littleton, Colo.: Libraries Unlimited, 1981); Jerome K. Wilcox, *Manual on the Use of State Publications* (Chicago: American Library Association, 1940); Yuri Nakata, Susan J. Smith, and William B. Ernst, Jr., *Organizing a Local Government Documents Collection* (Chicago: American Library Association, 1979).

the same difficulty in acquiring all publications exists, and no definitive answer can be given on the number of publications. Most libraries are concerned with the publications of their own state, but there again it is not possible to be sure of the quantity of publications issued.

The depository programs of the federal government and of the various states differ in a number of ways. Major differences are (1) the way depository libraries are selected, (2) the lack of a printer or distributor at the state level, and (3) the size of the distribution program with respect to the number of depositories and the quantity of items distributed. State documents depositories are described in detail in Chapter 5.

Library texts that discuss the use of federal, state and local publications include numerous guides for federal documents. For state documents, Parish has the two bibliographies in print mentioned earlier, and the *Manual on the Use of State Publications* by Wilcox can be used for historical research. Yuri Nakata's *Organizing a Local Government Documents Collection* is a model text on local documents collections.[7]

Bibliographic access to official publications differs at different levels of government. Again, at the federal level there are well-developed tools—the *Monthly Catalog,* the GPO MARC tapes, and audiovisual aids. The *Monthly Checklist of State Publications* and the individual checklists provide bibliographic control in printed form at the state level. Currently there is no general online access at the state level except through the large bibliographic utilities or on a strictly state-of-origin level. Slide presentations explaining the use of state documents have been made in Nebraska and New Mexico, and Texas A&M has a videotape prepared for in-house staff training.

The federal government often provides examples for the states to follow in the adoption of innovative administrative practices and procedures relating to official publications. Because there are more federal publications, and more libraries interested in those publications, the federal government, with its greater resources, has led the way in such areas as microformat publishing, setting up advisory councils, publishing documents newsletters, and setting standards for depository libraries. Experienced documents librarians are cognizant of the benefits of comparing problems with librarians from other jurisdictions.

Although in many situations state documents librarians can learn more from one another than from federal government activities and publishing, there are few tools that provide parallel information for all the states. *State Government Reference Publications* by David Parish and the *Book of the States* are the two most helpful publications in providing this type of information, but they both have drawbacks. Parish, published in 1981, lists publications in nine categories, but is limited to reference tools, although the subject

7. Yuri Nakata, Susan J. Smith, and William B. Ernst, Jr., *Organizing a Local Government Documents Collection* (Chicago: American Library Association, 1979).

index provides a secondary approach. The *Book of the States* is a compilation that changes from year to year. The *Manual on the Use of State Publications* was a monumental achievement, but is now out of date.

State to state parallels exist because of many factors: the control of the federal government, ease of communication among the states, long-standing exchange of documents, and research that crosses state boundaries. State documents librarians often benefit from the similarities of state documents from state to state. In collection development, the usefulness of the statistical abstract for one state may be matched by a similar tool in another state. For checklist preparation, examples of how to list labor area market reports or how to indicate distribution patterns can be copied. In reference work, the development of new tools can be stimulated by the example of other states, and in cataloging, the similarity of problems from state to state can be observed in the bibliographic utilities.

Working Definitions

Defining *state publications* as publications issued by state agencies provides a convenient, working definition. *State agencies,* briefly defined, are units of the legislative, judicial, and executive branches of a state government. *State documents collection* may refer either to a collection of the publications of a single state, or to a multistate collection. *Depository library* is the term used to refer to a library designated to receive state publications in order to make them available to the public.

These broad definitions are refined on a state-by-state basis by practicing librarians who interpret them in accordance with state laws and regulations. Practices that have developed in the administration of the statutes and regulations, such as the depository distribution patterns and the scope of the state checklist, also influence the working definitions in a particular state. For example, California state documents librarians do not think of state university publications as state documents because their depository library law specifically excludes this type of publication. When state agencies are mentioned in New Hampshire, the reference may be only to the executive branch agencies because the New Hampshire checklist covers departmental publications but not legislative or judicial publications.

State publications is an alternative term for state documents, and the terms are used interchangeably. The term *state publications* avoids confusion in the minds of those who think of documents as legal instruments, such as contracts or marriage licenses, but is not necessarily intended to be broader in scope than *state documents.*

When the American Library Association's Committee on Public Documents was active in the 1930s, definitions were not a specific concern. Interest in creating definitions for the terms *state publication* and *state agency* is relatively recent and probably attributable to the drafting of legislation for the depository distribution of state publications. Legislation requires precision. Because depository library legislation places a burden on state agencies to supply copies of their publications, a clear statement becomes necessary. Librarians want state agencies to understand that the law applies to them and that all their publications are to be supplied for distribution.

The word *document* has a formal connotation, appropriate for referring to laws, legislative journals, and judicial opinions and was used for many years. Recently librarians began using the term *state publications* to encompass both formal documents as well as all types of publications from research studies to flyers, and also the new formats—maps, microforms, and recordings. More recently, the term *state information* has come into use to indicate that the data might not even be a publication, insofar as that word implies publishing.

These working definitions will be elaborated upon later, state publications in the next chapter, and state agencies in Chapter 3.

Conclusion

Some of the changes in recent years in the state documents field require special attention. Others are not unique to state documents and must be addressed as library concerns rather than state documents problems. The many new formats in which documents are available fall in the latter group and affect state documents librarians only peripherally. Documents librarians now use microform readers, printers and computer terminals, and other new technology, just as other librarians.

The increase in quantity of material does affect state documents librarians directly, both in acquiring the documents and in providing access to them. One of the major ways that states have attempted to solve the acquisition problem is by means of depository library programs that assign acquisition functions for the benefit of several libraries to a single institution. The fact that state depository system administrators often identify "getting the documents" as their primary frustration indicates the importance they attach to this function.

The new avenues of bibliographic control regulated by the new catalog code and fostered by the computer databases have had a significant impact in state documents work, particularly for state checklist editors. The *Anglo-American Cataloguing Rules,* both editions, required fundamental changes for documents as well as for other types of library materials. The prime example is in the choice of entry. The bibliographic utilities that accept cataloging data require adherence to the new codes as well as conformity to the MARC format. Increasingly the state checklists are being produced from cataloging data, by mechanical reproduction of the card (as for example, in Arkansas and North Carolina), or by manipulation of a database to produce the checklist (as for example, in California and Colorado). Without doubt, more and more states will begin using cataloging data for checklist entries, and as economical programs become available will produce the state documents checklist directly from cataloging tapes.

Continuing problems include perpetual worries about acquiring state documents and concern about whether *all* documents have been captured. In both instances, the only solution is constant vigilance, or more crassly expressed, nagging. A partial solution is realized in states having comprehensive depository library laws which are conscientiously administered. However, vigilance is still necessary. Closely related to the acquisition problem is the question of lack of use. One line of thought is that if a state document is worth publishing, it is worth maintaining in a library. However, if there is an archival collection of all state documents in the state, that collection might suffice, thus relieving other libraries of the burden of preservation for historical research.

Still another real, but unexpressed, hazard is the lack of a career path in state documents. Turnover in the state documents field hinders the development of an in-depth background. For many librarians, state documents work is a stepping stone in their career. It is a good starting point and provides an excellent background for more prestigious positions but does not include many individuals who have built their career solely around state documents.

The growing concern among librarians about the availability of information in general relates to the release of information from government agencies, censorship and also copyright. Documents librarians feel their responsibilities as guardians of the public's right to know. These concerns pertain to both state and federal documents librarians.

2

CHARACTERISTICS
AND HISTORY

A brief survey of the characteristics distinguishing state publications from other publications and a short history of the publications, organizations, and activities related specifically to state documents provide both background information for the librarian new to the field of state documents and a convenient recapitulation for the experienced practitioner. Certain characteristics that affect work with state publications and come to the fore again and again include official issuance, primary source materials, statehood as a beginning date, issuance in series, and relationship to archival records. These characteristics are embedded in the history of state documents.

Characteristics of State Documents

Some of the characteristics of state documents are delineated in the working definition of state documents or state publications given in the previous chapter.

DEFINITION OF STATE PUBLICATION

In order to meet various situations in different states, the definition must be worded to be as inclusive as needed and at the same time must distinguish that which is not desired.

State documents librarians have only recently become concerned about a definition for the terms *state document* or *state publication.* Several factors have prompted the need for a definition: (1) the joint issuance of publications by federal/state, state/local, and state/private agencies; (2) the development of new formats for issuing publications—mimeograph, audiovisual, microform, and database, among others; (3) the enlarged scope of state government and its increased complexity; and (4) the drafting of legislation for the distribution and handling of state publications.

Definitions may be useful in delineating publications issued cooperatively by more than one level of government. For the library patron who wants information, the source of the document has little meaning. For the librarian, joint issuance represents an area that can become a no-man's land unless the responsibility for acquisition of such materials is clearly allocated. Some of the definitions in depository legislation address this specifically by providing, as in the Texas legislation for example, "The term includes publications sponsored by or purchased for distribution by a state agency and publications released by private institutions, such as research and consulting firms, under contract with a state agency."[1]

The definition of state publication must reflect the availability of information in new formats. Processed, microformatted, and audiovisual publications are within a broad interpretation of the words *state publication*, but a carefully constructed definition will indicate clearly that these non-print types of information are encompassed.

The formality of a definition is necessary because of an increase in the number of state agencies. The existence of more numerous units of government requires more standardized means of communication.

Some states in their depository legislation definitions exclude certain types of agencies. California, for example, excludes the publications of the University of California. Careful attention must be directed to the acquisition of materials from such agencies.

Depository legislation, which has at its core the duty of state agencies to supply copies of their publications, raises major questions for state agencies on the scope of the definition for *state publication*, which must be resolved during the drafting of legislation.

There are several areas in which it is important to specify what is *not* needed. First is the familiar requirement arising in depository legislation to exclude correspondence, blank forms, and intraoffice memoranda. Sometimes even interoffice memoranda are excluded (Arkansas and Missouri are examples).

Second, current office files and records must be excluded. The advent of the office copier has, according to Paul Pross, a Canadian political scientist, been responsible for an increase in the number of publications. He says, "Many documents, which a few years ago would have been treated as records, are today being reproduced in limited quantities and receiving a small circulation to administrators, consultants, academics, and some librarians."[2]

The phrase "issued for public distribution" is sometimes used to exclude records but is too broad. It is subject to the interpretation that nothing is issued for public distribution unless a multitude of copies are issued. Two alternative ways around this are the solution given by Pross and the interpretation in the Oklahoma manual.

---

1. *Vernon's Annotated Revised Civil Statutes of the State of Texas* (St. Paul, Minn.: West Publishing, 1987), art. 5442a (Supplement, 1987).

2. A. Paul Pross and Catherine A. Pross, *Government Publishing in the Canadian Provinces* (Toronto: University of Toronto Press, 1972), 12.

Pross defined a government publication by the breadth of circulation afforded it.

> A government publication is created when a document prepared by or for an agency of government is reproduced and circulated to individuals and groups other than those advising or negotiating with the government concerning the subject matter of the document.[3]

The Oklahoma manual cautions that publications are collected for a variety of patrons and uses. "The targeted audience for publications is not relevant to the status of the materials as long as such publications are distributed outside of the agency."[4]

Today state documents librarians strive to define state documents to include all publications, even those issued in limited quantities. The definition for *official publications* devised by Pross specifically addressed this problem:

> Thus, a publication is defined not by the process by which it is reproduced, but by the breadth of circulation afforded it. Its circulation beyond the immediate confines of a government and those advising or doing business with authority removes a document from the status of record, and thus the concern of the records manager and the archivist, to the status of publication, and the purview of the general public and the librarian.[5]

Definitions are basic to quality control, standards, and broader understanding. Definitions may encompass (1) the three branches of government, the independent agencies, borderline or quasi-state agencies, and institutions; (2) all formats used in the transfer of information; and (3) all degrees of formality in the presentation of information, from mimeographed press releases to bound volumes.

OFFICIAL ISSUANCE

State documents are a subgroup of a larger class of materials known as *official publications;* that is, publications issued by an agency of government in the exercise of its prescribed functions. Thus, state documents are distinguished from commercial and nonprofit publications because they are publications issued by a governmental entity. State documents are differentiated from other official publications by the fact that they are issued by a state government. The level of government from which the

3. Ibid., 17.

4. Oklahoma Department of Libraries, Oklahoma Publications Clearinghouse, *Manual for Publications Officers* (Oklahoma City: The Library, November 1984), 14. In *Docs on Docs,* item OK 85:H.

5. Pross, *Government Publishing,* 17.

publications emanate makes them a separate category within official publications.

If one assumes that librarians are most familiar with federal publications (not an unreasonable assumption if library school curricula are examined), the several studies demonstrating parallels between federal and state publications are a useful device for increasing understanding of state publications.[6]

PRIMARY SOURCE MATERIALS

State documents, like federal documents, include several basic types of legal publications: acts of the legislature, decisions of the courts, regulations of executive agencies, and rules and decisions of administrative agencies. These are called *primary sources;* they are the recorded rules which will be enforced by the state. When the states were young, as when our federal government was new, most state publications were primary sources. As agencies in the executive branch of government have become more numerous, other types of publications—reports to the legislature, directories, research studies, and statistics, have multiplied and become more common.

STATEHOOD AS A BEGINNING DATE

For the state documents of a particular state there is an indisputable beginning date—the date of statehood. Strictly speaking, there can be no state documents before there is a state; but a less strict interpretation is often followed in bibliographies. Many state document bibliographies include documents published before statehood: for the colony (Virginia), the territory (Louisiana), the republic (Texas), the kingdom (Hawaii), and even Indian nations (Oklahoma). Vladimir Palic, in his lists of state publications from the individual states, recognizes the practice of including these earlier publications in bibliographies of state publications. For each state he gives the date of statehood and also earlier dates for acquisition by the United States and changes in status to territory and then to statehood.[7]

6. Marilyn Domas White, "Drawing Analogies Between State and Federal Documents: A Method for Increasing Access to State Publications," *Government Publications Review* 2 (Spring 1975): 111–25; *The State of State Documents: Past, Present, Future,* ed. Brenda F. Shelton Olds (Austin, Tex.: Legislative Reference Library, November 1976). Also in ERIC microfiche ED 142 174 and *Docs on Docs,* 1973–1979, item Region. 3; three studies done at Emporia State University by Tamsen Emerson on Colorado and by Don Batson and Jerald A. Merrick, both on Kansas.

7. Vladimir M. Palic, *Government Publications: A Guide to Bibliographic Tools,* 4th ed. (Washington, D.C.: Library of Congress, 1975).

ISSUANCE IN SERIES

One reason why documents published before statehood in a particular jurisdiction are included in state document bibliographies is that many state documents are serials. This significant characteristic of state documents is important for historians, who want not only the legislative acts from the time of statehood, but also the earlier acts of the colonial or territorial period. Modern day librarians striving to make the publications of state government available are also cognizant of this trait; for serial publications, completeness of the series is an important goal in research libraries.

TIMELINESS

State documents librarians asked to list important documents of their state usually respond with current titles. Most people are not historians; we live in the present and look forward to the future. Peter Hernon's research showed that social scientists, not including historians, use primarily documents published within the last three years.[8]

State documents are particularly useful for information that is timely in nature. Hunting seasons, port dockings, and tourist attractions are all publicized in magazines issued, often monthly, by state agencies. Statistics on health, employment, crime, and the economy are usually published first by the state, although they may subsequently be available in federal publications. For example, the time lag for vital statistics published by the federal government is three to five years.[9]

Historical Accounts in the Documents Literature

Many state documents librarians date their involvement with state documents librarianship from the early 1970s, about the time when the State Documents Task Force, a unit of the American Library Association's new Government Documents Round Table, was formed. The Task Force brought together on a regular, semiannual basis, an enthusiastic group of librarians with a common interest in state documents. For those active in the field before that time, the opportunities for meetings with colleagues were few; keeping abreast of current developments in other states came largely from the professional literature. Even writing as one with antebellum experience (World War II, that is), the present author must rely on published accounts to chronicle the early history of state documents librarianship.

8. Peter Hernon, *Use of Government Publications by Social Scientists* (Norwood, N.J.: Ablex Publishing, 1979), 112.

9. K. D. Sell, "Sources of State Vital Statistics Reports," *RQ* 16 (Fall 1976): 45.

For those interested in the evolution of the documents themselves, the account by William S. Jenkins, "Collecting and Using the Records of the States of the United States: Twenty-Five Years in Retrospection," describes the beginning of record keeping in the colonies.[10] Legislative journals printed the governors' messages to the legislatures and the departmental reports filed with the legislature. As these messages and reports became more numerous, they were relegated to an appendix in the journal; as the appendices became bulky, they were published in separate volumes known as "Public Documents," or "Collected Documents." Jenkins prepared a checklist of these documents volumes in 1947.[11] The similarity of these series to the federal Serial Set, which is also known as the congressional set, becomes apparent after reading Jenkins's account. The collected documents series, issued during various periods by all but five of the states, were discontinued during the period 1900 to 1934 in all but thirteen states. The demise of these collected documents series may be attributable to the desire of departments to handle the distribution of their own reports and to the duplication entailed by publication in a collected series. Peter Paulson gives rising costs of binding and preparation as the reason for discontinuance.[12]

The exchange and distribution of state publications were an early concern of the state librarians who organized the National Association of State Librarians in 1898. One of the principal objectives in organizing an annual meeting for this group was stated as "the development of uniform laws and policies to insure efficient distribution and preservation of domestic and foreign public documents through the State libraries."[13] The chronology prepared by A. F. Kuhlman, chairman of the American Library Association Public Documents Committee in 1934, records the highlights of the activities of this group for the years from 1887 to 1934.

Kuhlman's historical account concludes with a statement that the efforts of the Association over the years had been directed toward (1) securing exchange and distribution legislation; (2) defining principles that should guide the states in state documents work; and (3) building up an appreciation of the importance of adequate distribution of state documents. He made a proposal, endorsed by those present at the 1934 meeting, that in some states it would be appropriate to designate state university

10. William S. Jenkins, "Collecting and Using the Records of the States of the United States: Twenty-Five Years in Retrospection" (Chapel Hill, N.C.: University of North Carolina, 1960).

11. National Association of State Libraries, *Collected Public Documents of the States: A Check List*, comp. William S. Jenkins (Boston: NASL, 1947).

12. Peter J. Paulson, "Government Documents and Other Non-Trade Publications," *Library Trends* 18 (January 1970): 369.

13. A. F. Kuhlman, "A Proposal to Modify the System of Exchange and Distribution of State Publications in Certain States," in American Library Association, Committee on Public Documents, *Public Documents; Their Selection, Distribution, Cataloging, Reproduction and Preservation, 1934*, ed. A. F. Kuhlman (Chicago: the Committee, 1935), 58.

libraries as the official center for exchange and distribution of state documents as a supplementary service to that which the state law library or state historical library might be giving.[14]

A brief historical account of the bibliographical control of state publications through bibliographies and checklists is found in the introductory pages for the state chapter of the guide by Vladimir Palic. Palic mentions the work of the National Association of State Librarians and the activities of the Public Documents Committee of the American Library Association in the 1930s, and cites the books and articles necessary for a comprehensive study of retrospective state documents bibliography. With reference to the issuance of current checklists in the individual states, Palic reports, "Before the Second World War, only eight states published periodical checklists of their official publications; during the war, their number increased to 22, which doubled in the post-war period."[15] Ronald Haselhuhn reported in 1980, "all states publish or have authority to publish checklists."[16]

Milestones

Milestones in the history of state publications, supplementing the chronology made by Kuhlman and emphasizing the years since 1940, are discussed below to highlight publications, organizations, and events important to state documents librarianship.

BEFORE THE 1930s

Adelaide Hasse's thirteen-volume *Index of Economic Material in Documents of the States of the United States* (1907–22)[17] serves as one of two pillars of state documents bibliography for thirteen states. The other pillar, Richard Bowker's *State Publications* . . . . (1908)[18] is described by Palic as "still the best bibliographic source for the early official documents of the states."[19]

The Monthly Checklist of State Publications,[20] which began in 1910, is the only comprehensive, current listing of state publications and is the state counterpart of the federal *Monthly Catalog of United States Government Pub-*

14. Ibid., 66.

15. Palic, *Government Publications*, 82.

16. Ronald P. Haselhuhn, "Bibliographic Control and Distribution of State Documents," *RQ* 20 (Fall 1980): 20.

17. Adelaide R. Hasse, *Index of Economic Material in Documents of the States of the United States* . . . (Washington, D.C.: Carnegie Institution of Washington, 1907–22) 13 v.

18. Richard R. Bowker, *State Publications: A Provisional List of the Official Publications of the Several States of the United States from Their Organization* (New York: Publishers' Weekly, 1908). 1 v. in 4. The years 1884–90 and 1890–95 are in *American Catalog . . . July 1, 1876– Dec. 31, 1910* (New York: Bowker, 1941).

19. Palic, *Government Publications*, 81.

20. *Monthly Checklist of State Publications*, v.1+, 1910+ (Washington, D.C.: GPO).

lications. Only publications received at the Library of Congress are included, which gives rise to frequent comments that the listing is not complete. There is, however, nothing else that comes close to comprehensiveness. The annual index includes corporate and individual authors, titles, and subjects. A subject index has been added to the monthly issues beginning with the January 1987 issue.

THE 1930s

In 1931 the Public Document Clearing House and the Macdonald lists were started.[21] The Clearing House, created to circulate want and offer records for libraries to use in building their collections and sharing their duplicates, was short-lived. The "Macdonald lists," edited by Grace Macdonald, were checklists of session laws, legislative journals, etc., prepared to facilitate the work of the Clearing House. Working at the Rhode Island State Library for the Clearing House, Macdonald assembled bibliographic data for the checklists from Bowker and Hasse and from checklists verified by the individual states. Published under the imprint of the National Association of State Libraries, these checklists were particularly helpful in the 1950 Jenkins filming project.[22] Publications compiled by Meira Pimsleur in the AALL series superseded the Macdonald lists.[23]

The State Public Document Center Plan originated with the Social Science Research Council under the leadership of Leonard D. White.[24] It was transferred for implementation to the ALA Public Documents Committee in 1932 because it was essentially a library-oriented project. A. F. Kuhlman, then chairman of the Documents Committee, was completely familiar with the plan, having worked with the Council in its development. Kuhlman observed:

> This plan concerned itself primarily with the collection, preservation and organization for efficient research of the public documents and related source materials of each state by designating as document centers one or

21. Herbert O. Brigham, "Public Document Clearing House and Its Problems," American Library Association, Committee on Public Documents, *Public Documents, 1933,* 80–83. The "Macdonald lists," now of historical interest only, are included in Palic, *Government Publications,* under National Association of State Libraries together with supplementary works by other compilers.

22. U.S. Library of Congress, *A Guide to the Microfilm Collection of Early State Records,* prepared by the Library of Congress in association with the University of North Carolina; collected and compiled under the direction of William S. Jenkins, edited by Lillian A. Hamrick (Washington, D.C.: Library of Congress, Photoduplication Service, 1950) 1 v.; Supplement (1951), 130 p.

23. Meira G. Pimsleur, ed., *Checklists of Basic American Legal Publications,* American Association of Law Libraries Publications Series, no. 4 (South Hackensack, N.J.: Rothman, 1962+). Looseleaf.

24. A. F. Kuhlman, "Preserving Social Science Source Materials," *Bulletin of the American Library Association* 27 (March 1933): 128–32.

more libraries in each state that seemed particularly qualified to carry on this work, and that were willing to assume responsibility for it.[25]

Ten categories of materials to be collected were listed, the original and most important being public documents of the states. The other materials, all of which, like documents, were not copyrighted or available through the book market, included local publications and nongovernmental publications from both state and local organizations and newspapers. The program of action was unstructured and not prescriptive. Activities suggested for inclusion were (1) a conference or survey to determine existing resources and develop interest in preserving the materials, (2) inventories of holdings, (3) preparation of checklists of official publications, (4) introduction of legislation to make the documents center library a depository, or to centralize printing or exchange and distribution, (5) regional planning, (6) publicity directed toward state agencies and toward scholars, and (7) a clearinghouse for exchange of duplicates.

In some states, a qualified library pledged its participation immediately; in others, it was necessary to solicit cooperation. Perhaps because the State Documents Center plan was voluntary, without legal approbation or financial backing from state governments, it never became fully operational. Some libraries, such as the University of North Carolina library, assumed the responsibility for collecting and maintaining state documents and continued to collect as provided for in the plan. In other states, not even a start was made.

THE 1940s

Jerome K. Wilcox, chairman of the ALA Public Documents Committee, edited the *Manual on the Use of State Publications*, which was published in 1940.[26] The volume is still appropriately and affectionately referred to by his name. Though it is now out of date, it is not superseded. The amount of detail is astounding. For each type of publication or subject a listing of individual titles for each of the then forty-eight states is given. The major parts of the work are: importance, character and use; bibliographical aids; basic state publications; national associations of state officers and their publications; and printing and distribution.

The Wilcox *Manual*, more than a mere bibliographical tool, is important today for historical use and as a model for the organization of information about state documents.

25. A. F. Kuhlman, "The Need for a Check-list Bibliography of State Publications," in American Library Association, Committee on Public Documents, *Public Documents. State, Municipal, Federal, Foreign Policies and Problems Concerning Issuance, Distribution and Use, 1933*, ed. A. F. Kuhlman (Chicago: the Committee, 1934), 69.
26. Jerome K. Wilcox, *Manual on the Use of State Publications* (Chicago: American Library Association, 1940). 342 p.

The California depository library law, passed in 1945, broke new ground because it provided for a system of depository libraries rather than naming specific libraries as depositories.[27] The law was innovative in its provisions: the state printer was required to distribute printed documents to libraries that contracted for this service and state agencies were required to provide mimeographed publications for distribution. This distribution was automatic; that is, the libraries did not need to make individual requests for each item needed.

The statement of policy in the first section, "to make freely available to [California's] inhabitants all state publications by distribution to libraries throughout the state,"[28] was an early recognition of the need for easy and widespread public access to these materials.

Another project that endeavored to acquire and preserve state publications was called the Jenkins Project.[29] This effort, like the Kuhlman project, was spearheaded by one man—William Sumner Jenkins. Jenkins was a political scientist interested in the amendment process of the federal constitution. His research for the records of adoption of the federal constitutional amendments in the state legislative journals focused his attention on the value of these early state records. In cooperation with the Library of Congress, Jenkins located and filmed not only legislative journals but also executive records, court records, collected public documents, constitutions, and the proceedings of constitutional conventions. The variance in the ending dates for the film of the different series is accounted for by the holdings of the University of North Carolina, Jenkins' home institution. The guide to the microfilm rolls was prepared by Lillian Hamrick and published by the Library of Congress.

Jenkins should be remembered because his efforts helped make the text of rare, original state publications available through filming. While Hasse deserves credit for providing the early bibliographical control of early state documents, Jenkins deserves credit for preserving the text of these records. The two endeavors complement one another. Macdonald's preparation of the checklists for the materials that Jenkins filmed was an important factor in facilitating the work that Jenkins accomplished.

THE 1950s

With the beginning of the Center for Research Libraries (CRL) state documents collection in 1952, a major resource for scholars was created. The Center for Research Libraries is a nonprofit library for research libraries; it makes infrequently used materials available to its members

27. *West's Annotated California Codes, Government Code* (St. Paul, Minn.: West Publishing, 1980) sections 14900–14912.
28. Ibid., section 14900.
29. Jenkins, *Guide to the Microform Collection.*

through interlibrary loan. One of the areas to which CRL has always given special emphasis is state publications. The Center actively acquires *all* the publications of the fifty states with the exception of certain legal materials and quasi-state publications (publications of some entities only partially supported by state funds). The Center receives depository shipments from twenty-six states and has a policy of immediately ordering state publications requested by members. Deposits of pre-1952 documents from member libraries substantially augment the collection. The result is an all-state collection of national significance. For the years after 1952, the CRL collection is more comprehensive than that at the Library of Congress, where selection for retention is based on substantial subject or reference content.[30]

THE 1970s

Bernadine Hoduski organized the State and Local Documents Task Force as part of the American Library Association's Government Documents Round Table in 1972. The Task Force was originally the State Documents Task Force; it expanded to include local documents in 1978. The publications, programs, projects, and activities of the Task Force have been extensive; some qualify as milestones.

Two activities of the Task Force during the 1970s have had long-range significance. The first, a set of rules, "Guidelines for Minimum State Servicing of State Documents," was adopted by the Task Force, moved rapidly through the hierarchy of the American Library Association, and was adopted by the ALA Council in 1975.[31] These guidelines, reproduced in Appendix A, are discussed in detail in Chapter 5. The second, a program sponsored by the Task Force, entitled "Anglo-Am or Not?" was noteworthy because it sparked interest in what became the Name Authority Cooperative Project, in which individual states establish corporate headings in accordance with *Anglo-American Cataloguing Rules,* second edition, and LC practice. The discussion of this cooperative endeavor and some suggestions for participation can be found in Chapter 10.

The first edition of *State Government Reference Publications,* by David W. Parish, was published in 1974.[32] This was the first book-length listing of useful reference publications in the state documents field since *Wilcox* in 1940. It was arranged by state and included bibliographies, directories, and statistical works. The second edition of this work, published in 1981,

30. Center for Research Libraries, *Research Materials Available from the Center for Research Libraries* (Chicago: CRL, 1980).

31. American Library Association, Council, *Minutes, 1975,* 17–19, Council Document #21 (Exhibit 27); "Guidelines for Minimum State Servicing of State Documents," *Documents to the People* 3, no. 7 (September 1975): 32–33.

32. David W. Parish, *State Government Reference Publications: An Annotated Bibliography* (Littleton, Colo.: Libraries Unlimited, 1974), 236 p.

cited 1756 titles and is arranged first by bibliographic classification and then by state.[33] In both editions the titles are annotated.

The 1973/74 annual listing of Washington state publications was based on data retrieved from the cataloging database created at the Washington State Library in the Washington Library Network (WLN).[34] WLN, which has been renamed the Western Library Network, is a bibliographic utility similar to OCLC and RLIN (Research Libraries Information Network). Other states had earlier issued state checklists by means of a database created specifically for that purpose. The Washington list was the first to be produced from a cataloging database and using the MARC (machine-readable cataloging) format. The tags encoded in the MARC format enabled the library to produce a checklist with four distinct access points: (1) an author list, that is, arrangement by the cataloging main entry; (2) a subject listing based on LC subject headings; (3) a title listing; and (4) a series listing.[35] The Washington list was a prototype for the *Monthly Catalog of United States Government Publications* issued by the Government Printing Office using the MARC format, an instance that runs counter to the general trend of federal leadership in the documents field.

The State of State Documents: Past, Present, Future, was prepared as a handout for the Pre-Conference on State Documents held in Albuquerque, New Mexico, November 10, 1976.[36] It emphasizes the southwestern and mountain plains states but includes information on nationwide programs, the S&LDTF guidelines, and other tabulations.

THE 1980s

In 1980 a workshop was held for the documents librarians of the state libraries west of the Mississippi who deal with state documents issues. Twenty-seven librarians attended. It was the first meeting of document librarians responsible for administering statewide programs. Because it was limited to librarians with this narrow interest, the discussions were detailed and practical. Most participants administered depository library programs, and all agreed that acquisition was a major challenge. One of the meetings was devoted to making update reports on the S&LDTF publication, *State Publications: Depository Distribution and Bibliographical Pro-*

33. David W. Parish, *State Government Reference Publications: An Annotated Bibliography* 2d ed. (Littleton, Colo.: Libraries Unlimited, 1981), 355 p.

34. Washington State Publications, 1973/74, 1975.

35. "Washington State Produces Annual Checklist in MARC Format," *Government Publications Review* 3 (Spring 1976): 89.

36. Brenda F. Shelton Olds, ed., *The State of State Documents: Past, Present, Future*, (Austin, Tex.: Legislative Reference Library, November 1976). ERIC ED 142 174.

grams, a survey of state documents distribution centers.[37] This western state library documents librarians group has had one more meeting, in Portland, Oregon, in 1983, to review state documents activities in the states, discuss the maintenance of service during a period of reduced financial support, and hear presentations on automation and public awareness.

The year 1982 saw the culmination of the work of the State and Local Documents Task Force on guidelines for state documents activities in the adoption of four new guidelines by ALA Council.[38] (See Appendix A.) The guidelines summarize the minimum requirements for state checklists and for depository legislation. For putting documents into cataloging databases and for distribution center activities, the guidelines provide general suggestions and proposed service functions. Detailed discussions of the guidelines are found in the chapters on checklists, cataloging, and libraries.

Another Task Force project, the maintenance of the Documents on Documents Collection, is a continuing activity between meetings of the Task Force. The Documents on Documents Collection is a collection of materials produced in the administration of state documents depository programs. A Documents on Documents committee, consisting of a chairperson and seven regional members, each responsible for about seven states, was established to collect the documents from all the states. Materials collected included laws, regulations, manuals, brochures, forms, and publicity items.

In 1984 users' guides were published, listing the materials in the *Documents on Documents Collection.*[39] The 1973–79 collection, consisting of twenty-eight fiche, is in ERIC (ED 247 940); the guide for this part is one ERIC fiche (ED 247 939). The 1980–83 collection is twelve fiche in ERIC (ED 263 923) and the guide is one fiche (ED 263 922). The current collection, which includes items received in 1984 and later, is still circulated in the original formats and is available on interlibrary loan from Lauri Sebo, University Research Library, University of California, Los Angeles, CA 90024.

The final milestone in this chronology is the announcement that beginning with the January 1987 issue of the *Monthly Checklist of State Publications,* a companion subject index will appear at the end of each issue. The announcement concludes:

37. Margaret T. Lane, comp., *State Publications: Depository Distribution and Bibliographical Programs,* compiled for the State and Local Documents Task Force, Government Documents Round Table, American Library Association, Texas State Publications Clearinghouse Documents Monograph Series, nos. 2 and 2A ([Austin, Tex.]: Texas State Library, 1980–81), 2 v.

38. American Library Association, Council, *Minutes, 1982;* Council Document #12 (Exhibit 9).

39. Margaret T. Lane, comp., *A Guide to the Documents on Documents Collection, 1973–1979 [1980–1983],* compiled for State and Local Documents Task Force, Government Documents Round Table, American Library Association (Chicago: GODORT, 1984), 2 v.

The Library will continue to produce the annual index.

Other minor changes will be noticed in the bibliographic listing, aside from a more attractive publication. Titles within monographic series will not be listed under series titles as in the past, but rather each title will be analyzed in full with the series recorded in a note position, more closely resembling LC cataloging practice. Monographs in multiple parts which covered many geographical areas in a state, which produced long lists in past issues, will appear in a note describing what type of area each volume or sheet covers.[40]

Any failure to recognize the importance of this new feature of the *Monthly Checklist* in other chapters of this text is attributable to the last minute nature of this important information.

Other milestones have occurred in individual states or in the lives of individual state documents librarians. New legislation, newly focused attention on the state documents program (Utah and North Carolina are 1985 and 1986 examples), and important regional meetings (the second Western Council of State Librarians meeting in 1983 and the formation of the Southeastern Library Association GODORT in 1982) have all been factors in the continuing interest in state documents sparked in 1887 by state librarians.

The awarding of the James B. Childs Award to the present author, whose library career was primarily in state documents, is an instance of the effect of state documents on the life of an individual. The award, for "contributions to the growth and development of government documents librarianship," was based in part on the Louisiana state documents program. The successes of the Louisiana program include the indexed, cumulative checklists (including one for the period before the depository legislation), continued publication of the state agency names and histories, regular distribution with shipping lists, adoption and maintenance of a classification scheme, and two short-lived projects, cards with documents and annual microfilming.

Such localized and individual milestones have increased over the years and, it is hoped, have had a beneficial effect on access to state publications.

40. Informal memorandum seen at ALA Midwinter meeting, Chicago, January 1987.

3
STATE
AGENCIES

In this chapter the relationship of state agencies to state publications will be examined. Definitions of the term *state agencies* will be discussed, some of the various forms of state agency names will be listed, and finally, how these variant forms affect the work of librarians will be explained.

Any librarian and any user of state publications must begin, whether consciously or not, with state agencies. By definition, it is the *publications of state agencies* with which we are concerned. A study of state documents begins with an understanding of the structure of state government. For matters of acquisitions, cataloging, and reference, the state agency is pivotal.

James Bennett Childs, the premier figure in the documents world, whose entire career at the Library of Congress was devoted to documents, emphasized over and over that one must become familiar with government agencies in order to use their publications effectively. His last major work, the article on documents in the *Encyclopedia of Library and Information Science*, stressed his conviction that government agencies are central to the acquisition and use of government publications.[1] Childs believed that if one knew the place of an agency within the government, one could predict the publications the agency might produce. This theory applies to state agencies also. In addition some agencies act as distributors of their own publications or, less frequently, issue checklists of their own publications.

David Parish in *State Government Reference Publications* illustrates the application of this idea by citing typical state agencies and typical titles in a list arranged by subject. For example, for the subject "highways," he lists transportation departments and highways divisions as issuing state highway maps and drivers manuals.[2]

Another reason to begin with state agencies is that the state agency is the place of origin for state publications; that is, a publication is not a

1. James B. Childs, "Government Publications (Documents)" in *Encyclopedia of Library and Information Science*, vol. 10 (New York: M. Dekker, 1968+).

2. David Parish, *State Government Reference Publications: An Annotated Bibliography*, 2d ed. (Littleton, Colo.: Libraries Unlimited, 1981), 264.

state publication unless it is issued by a state agency. This generalized statement has some exceptions that arise from recent efforts of librarians to expand the parameters of state publications by including those items produced under contract with state agencies and those partially supported by state funds, such as the highway studies, environmental impact statements, and water management studies in Iowa, Hawaii, and Wyoming, respectively. Examples of publications issued under contracts with state agencies can be identified in the *Monthly Checklist of State Publications* with "prepared by" statements that give the names of companies. For example:

> IOWA. DEPT. OF TRANSPORTATION.
> Interstate bridges of Iowa: a descriptive list of bridges over the Mississippi, Missouri, Des Moines, and Big Sioux Rivers, prepared by Dennett, Muessig & Associates, Ltd. for Dept. of Transportation. (Ames) 1982. 51.+

Publications that are issued in cooperation with federal or other agencies are probably only partially supported by state funds. For example, the Maryland State Highway Administration issued a publication on the Ritchie Parkway in cooperation with the city of Rockville.[3]

Definition of State Agency

Having stressed the role of state agencies vis-a-vis their publications, it is appropriate to define the term *state agency*. The definitions from state depository legislation resemble one another closely. One of the broadest is the Colorado definition:

> "State agency" means every state office, whether legislative, executive, or judicial, and all of its respective officers, departments, divisions, bureaus, boards, commissions, and committees, all state-supported colleges and universities which are defined as state institutions of higher education, and other agencies which expend state-appropriated funds.[4]

Note that the three branches of government are named, state-supported educational institutions are specifically included, and miscellaneous agencies are picked up by a catch-all phrase referring to agencies that receive state funds. The Virginia law refers simply to "any branch of the State government," and the Nevada law reads, "the legislature, constitutional officers or any department . . . ." Educational institutions are frequently mentioned specifically. Oklahoma lists them as "state-supported colleges, universities, junior colleges and vocational-technical schools."

3. *Monthly Checklist of State Publications* 76 (April 1985): 300.
4. The Colorado definition and definitions from other states are found in Margaret T. Lane, *State Publications and Depository Libraries* (Westport, Conn.: Greenwood Press, 1981), 94–97.

Other interesting variations in the definitions are the phrase "permanent or temporary in nature" in the Connecticut definition and the express mention of institutions and hospitals in the Utah definition.

For depository legislation, a definition of the term *state agency* is essential. State agencies are naturally concerned about the applicability of the legislation to their individual agencies and give close scrutiny to the language that determines whether the legislation affects their particular agency. Because the participation of state agencies is an indispensable prerequisite in such legislation, the definition must recognize the political exigencies that exist. Depository legislation does not always encompass all branches of government or all types of institutions, and the definitions of state agency reflect this. A reference librarian must also be aware that a state may have more than one definition of state agency. For example, civil service acts and administrative procedure acts must deal with the problem of a definition. For a state documents librarian, a simple, broad definition, such as the one adopted by the ALA Government Documents Round Table of the State and Local Documents Task Force is the most practical:

> *State Agency*—A corporate body created by the state legislature, or governor, or another state agency under the authority of the legislature, acting as the state's agent, and/or being funded partially or wholly by state funds or operating at the direction of the state.[5]

The Fifty States

Each state is unique, particularly in the eyes of its own citizens. Alaska is the biggest; California, the most populous—each state has its claim to fame. The states differ in such factors as area, population, natural resources, industrialization, agriculture, and per capita income. Because of these differences, the functions of state government differ from state to state. Florida has a Department of Citrus; Alaska, a Seafood Marketing Institute; New Mexico, an Office of Indian Affairs; and New York, a Metropolitan Transportation Authority.

However, since all states must have agencies to perform necessary governmental functions for their citizens, there are certain agencies common to all states. Under the federal Constitution, the states are all considered equal, and there are many parallels in state agencies from state to state. The *Manual on the Use of State Publications* has tables for sixteen areas of state government indicating the exact name of the agency in each state that functions in each area. Listed are state agencies for agriculture, banking, budgets, conservation—fish and game, conservation—forestry, education, health, highways, insurance, labor, mines, motor vehicles, public

5. See Appendix A, "Guidelines for State Documents," Introduction.

utilities, state tax commissions and boards of equalization, welfare, and workers' compensation. Only in the field of mines and minerals are there a substantial number of states (nine states, mostly in New England) without a department or agency functioning in the area.[6]

The tables in the *Manual* were each checked by an appropriate agency, in many instances a federal agency. Librarians in the U.S. Department of Agriculture, U.S. Public Health Service, U.S. Bureau of Public Roads, U.S. Department of Labor, (U.S.) Bureau of Mines, and other federal agencies cooperated in supplying additional information and verifying the listings. This way of looking at state agencies might be described as a horizontal, subject approach to state agencies to distinguish it from an alphabetical, state-by-state, Alabama to Wyoming, approach. Libraries that acquire state documents only in special subject fields would do well to remember that in many instances there are federal agencies that function in the same subject areas as state agencies. As the tables in the *Manual* show, there are also national, nongovernmental agencies that are concerned with topics within the province of state agencies.

All states follow the federal pattern of a constitution and three branches of government. Agencies of the state exist in all three branches of government. Some generalizations about the kinds of agencies within the different branches of state government will provide an understanding of the types of publications they issue.

Judicial Branch

The judicial branch of state government has fewer and smaller agencies than the executive or the legislative branches. The primary agencies of the judicial branch are the courts. The courts are organized on a hierarchical basis, with the highest court in the state usually being called the supreme court. A notable exception is the highest court in New York, which is called the New York Court of Appeals. The lowest level in the state court system does not usually issue publications. Opinions of the lower courts may be oral or, if written, a part of the court record rather than a publication. An exception is the possible publication of court rules for the use of the local bar.

The principal publications of the higher courts are the decisions or opinions rendered in the cases brought before the courts. These are commonly referred to as "reports" or "law reports" and are published both in an official edition and by private publishers. In about twenty states the privately published edition is the only one available and is part of a geographically oriented series. Other publications include court rules, memorials, and occasional publications, such as descriptions of court buildings.

---

6. Jerome K. Wilcox, ed., *Manual on the Use of State Publications* (Chicago: American Library Association, 1940), 10.

In addition to the courts, the judicial branch may have an agency that performs administrative or research functions for the court system, typically called a judicial council. Such an agency tends to issue statistical reports. In some states a separate retirement system operates for judges and court employees, and publications consist of rules and regulations and annual financial statements. For example, Illinois has a Judges Retirement System, and its Board of Trustees issues an annual report. A judicial ethics board is another example of a state agency within the judicial branch. In New York, for example, this agency is called the State Commission on Judicial Conduct.

Legislative Branch

The legislative branch, usually known as the Legislature or the General Assembly, has two houses (Nebraska is the lone unicameral exception). Publications include session laws, calendars, rules, and rosters.

Session laws, or acts, are the laws enacted by the legislature. The final step in the legislative process, submission to the governor for his or her signature, is followed by the numbering and promulgation of the laws. The laws for each session of the legislature (usually a one- or two-year period) are arranged in numerical order, which is also chronological order, and published with titles such as session laws, public laws, or acts. The resulting volume may also include private acts (that is, legislation relating to a single individual or a local area) and resolutions of various kinds (plain, joint, or concurrent). Each volume of the session laws has a subject index and often includes tables arranged by bill numbers or authors or sponsors of the acts. The subject index is of limited use because it guides one to the enactments of only the one or two years covered in the volume.

The publication that collects all the laws of a state and arranges them by subject is referred to as a code or compiled or revised statutes. In general, these works are commercial publications and are not considered state publications. However, the *Monthly Checklist* lists them if they are published by the state or have been officially adopted by the state. The *Minnesota Statutes, 1984* were published by the Revisor of Statutes, State of Minnesota, and are for sale by the State Register and Public Documents Division. In South Carolina, on the other hand, a commercially published code was adopted as the official code by the General Assembly.

In order to conduct its business, the legislature may publish calendars giving the status of bills as they proceed through the legislative process, rules similar to or supplementary to Roberts' *Rules of Order,* and rosters of the membership of each house or each committee. In some states, committee reports are published. Seventeen committee reports are listed for California in the April 1985 issue of the *Monthly Checklist.*

In addition to the legislature or general assembly, the legislative branch may include other agencies. At the federal level the Library of Congress and the Government Printing Office are within the legislative branch. At the state level, Minnesota, for example, has a Legislative Reference Library. The drafting of bills prior to introduction may be the province of a separate agency known as the Legislative Council (Nebraska) or Legislative Service Commission (Ohio). The publications of such agencies may include background studies of problems of concern to the legislature. Digests of bills and summaries of legislation may also be published by such agencies. If the legislative branch has a separate budget office or a legislative auditor—Iowa has a Legislative Fiscal Bureau and Montana has an Office of the Legislative Fiscal Analyst—the publications of those agencies, are, of course, budgets, audits, and other financial reports.

The legislative bodies may create committees or commissions that remain part of the legislative branch—a practice often followed when a special study is needed. For example, the New York Legislature created a Commission on Rural Resources that issued preliminary reports on two topics (one on government and management and the other on human relations and community life).

The entities within the legislative and judicial branches of government seldom issue publications for publicity or public relations purposes. The publications are largely reportorial and are usually serial in nature. Court reports and session laws are chronological and are kept current on a regular basis as the codes and revised statutes are. Private publishers are the most up-to-date in issuing these publications. They do not include illustrations and do not use colored inks or exotic typefaces. Such how-to booklets as the rules of court (prepared for the use of attorneys), or leaflets on how a bill becomes law are common exceptions. In most states, the courts and the legislatures do not prepare descriptive annual reports, but only statistical reports or summaries of legislation. The entities within the legislative and judicial branches of government tend to be few in number and traditional in their publishing patterns.

Executive Branch

The executive branch is the most structurally complex of the three branches of government, and, perhaps not incidentally, it issues the most publications in every state. Except for the administration of justice and the enactment of laws, most other activities within the scope of state activity are performed by the executive branch. These activities include keeping the peace, providing education, promoting health and welfare, helping unfortunates, regulating the economy, providing public services, regulating persons with relation to each other and with relation to the state, and managing natural resources.

Executive agencies are voluminous in number, varied in form, and prolific in publishing. In recent years, many states have reorganized the structure of the executive branch following the federal example, sometimes calling the reorganization agency a "little Hoover commission." After a lapse of time, a state may have another reorganization of its executive agencies. Speaking with the voice of experience, the author cautions librarians working with state agency names not to put off a project because of the imminence of reorganization or even the prospect of a new constitution. It can take years for state action in these areas—almost twenty-five years for the new Louisiana constitution! If there is a need for a list of state agency names, do not postpone its compilation because of possible future changes.

The names by which the different entities in the executive department of state government are known vary from state to state and within a state. Whether a body is called a bureau, a commission, or a committee does not give a clue to the method of its creation, its membership, or its functions and activities. For example, for the subject "Energy," Parish lists these types of agencies: board, department, office, program, authority and division.[7] The casual approach adopted by the states in naming new state agencies justifies the use of the general term *state agency* for any state-created entity.

Intergovernmental and Regional Agencies

Closely related to state agencies established within the three branches of government are other agencies that function at the state level but also involve another level of government or another state. Because such agencies publish significant amounts of information relating to the state, the state documents librarian should be aware of these agencies and their publications. State documents librarians should learn about these intergovernmental agencies and monitor the bibliographic control of their publications because they tend to "fall through the cracks." These hybrid agencies are neither state, federal, nor local. They are sometimes called quasi-state agencies. They are, according to one writer, "often overlooked."[8] States do pay attention to each others' activities as illustrated by the number of interstate associations. The 1984 *National Organizations of State Government Officials* lists one hundred such organizations.[9]

Prominent among the agencies that have a state and federal orientation are the state agencies that administer unemployment laws and those that provide marketing information for farmers. The similarity of labor and marketing reports from state to state is directly attributable to federal

7. Parish, *State Government Reference Publications*, 261–62.

8. Milton G. Ternberg, "Regional Government Organizations and Their Publications," *Government Publications Review* 9 (September–October 1982): 493.

9. *National Organizations of State Government Officials; Directory* (Lexington, Ky.: Council of State Governments and National Conference of State Legislatures, 1984).

reporting requirements. For the librarian who is cataloging or who is preparing checklist entries for publications of these agencies, examples are available from other states. Labor area trends, because they are issued for so many different areas, can have consolidated entries in the checklist, a practice adopted in some states.

Agricultural experiment stations and cooperative extension services also have strong federal links. Some states do not include these publications in their state checklists, and the Center for Research Libraries, which collects state documents comprehensively, collects only selectively for agricultural experiment stations. Bibliographic control is not lacking in this area. The National Agricultural Library is the federal agency that collects and indexes the publications of experiment stations and cooperative extension services. The *Monthly Checklist of State Publications* includes both these agriculturally related agencies in the checklist under the states; regional cooperative extension services are in the section for associations of state officials and regional organizations at the end of the listing for monographs. The regional cooperative extension agencies are multistate agencies that cooperate with the U.S. Department of Agriculture.

Many other multistate and multijurisdictional agencies have been created to deal with a variety of problems. The Council of State Governments in the 1983 edition of *Interstate Compacts and Agencies* lists sixty-six agencies formed pursuant to interstate compacts. Such compacts are established when each participating state adopts identical legislation. The purposes for which these compacts are formed fall into the following general areas:

> Bridges, Navigation and Port Authorities
> Conservation and Environment
> Corrections and Crime Control
> Education
> Nuclear Energy
> Parks and Recreation
> Pest Control
> Planning and Development
> Taxation
> Transportation
> Water Apportionment
> Water Pollution Control
> Water Resources and Flood Control[10]

A definition designed to identify publications of such agencies was drafted by the State and Local Documents Task Force:

10. Council of State Governments, *Interstate Compacts and Agencies* (Lexington, Ky.: the Council, 1983).

An intergovernmental document [is] one which emanates from more than one entity, one of which is a state agency.[11]

The Task Force has published *Guide to the Publications of Interstate Agencies and Authorities* to help identify these publications. The list is limited to agencies appointed pursuant to statutory compacts and is based on the agencies found in *Interstate Compacts and Agencies.*[12]

Copyright

Contrary to popular belief, state agencies do have the right to copyright their publications. The prohibition against copyrighting of publications of the U.S. Government found in Title 17, U.S. Code, section 105, is often rephrased as "government publications cannot be copyrighted," leading to the assumption that state publications cannot be copyrighted.[13]

Here we first consider which state publications can be copyrighted and then look at some examples of state publications that have received copyright protection.

Not every state publication can be copyrighted. Some of the most significant state publications are in the public domain. Public domain documents include acts of the state legislature and opinions of the state courts and of the attorneys general. The parts of the compilations of these documents that are provided by private enterprise can be copyrighted. Headnotes, annotations, and indexing sections are all eligible for copyright protection. Under the 1976 copyright legislation the copyright notice must indicate which parts of a compilation are in the public domain and which are protected. The notice in the Texas Administrative Code is an example of the way such a copyright notice is stated:

> All information appearing in this title (which information includes, but is not limited to, cross references, tables of cases, notes of decisions, tables of contents, indices, source notes, authority notes, numerical lists, and codification guides) other than the actual text of rules may be reproduced only with the written consent of both the State of Texas (through the Office of the Secretary of State) and Shepard's/McGraw-Hill. Any such information that appears on the same page with the text of any rule, however, may be incidentally reproduced in connection with the reproduction of such rule, provided such reproduction is for the private use

11. "State and Local Documents Task Force—Minutes; Annual Meeting, July, 1982," *Documents to the People* 11, nos. 1 and 2 (March 1983): 32.

12. Jack Sulzer and Roberta Palen, *Guide to the Publications of Interstate Agencies and Authorities* (Chicago: American Library Association, 1986); Council of State Governments, *Interstate Compacts and Agencies* (Lexington, Ky.: the Council, 1983).

13. The federal law reads, "Copyright protection under this title is not available for any work of the United States Government . . . ." *U.S. Code*, Title 17, section 105.

of a subscriber and not for resale. There shall be no other restrictions on the reproduction of information published in this title, and the State of Texas and Shepard's/McGraw-Hill hereby consent to any such reproduction.[14]

Some states have enacted statutes permitting or requiring copyright of state publications. The Michigan statute, for example, is permissive. It reads, "The state administrative board may copyright literary, educational, artistic, or intellectual works in the name of this state and license the production or sale of those works."[15] Oregon has a copyright provision limited to a single work, "The Secretary of State may cause the Oregon Blue Book to be copyrighted."[16]

The Pennsylvania statute, on the other hand, is mandatory:

> The Department of Property and Supplies [now the Department of General Services] shall have the power, and its duty shall be: . . .
> (i)To copyright, in the name of the Commonwealth, all publications of the Commonwealth, or of any department, board, or commission or officer thereof, including the State Reports, which under existing or future laws it shall be necessary to have copyrighted, and such other publications as the Secretary of Property and Supplies, with the approval of the Governor, shall deem it advisable to copyright;[17]

Reasons for copyrighting include (1) securing any potential revenue to the government, (2) ensuring faithful reproduction of text, and (3) providing a measure of control so that the works will be used in the best interests of the government.

The public domain concept and the lack of commercial value have been cited as reasons for not copyrighting government publications.[18] The American Library Association took a strong stand against the copyrighting of National Technical Information Service (NTIS) publications, resolving "that the American Library Association strongly endorse the principle that publications produced with public monies remain free of copyright constraints."[19] The NTIS position, that U.S. interests would be best served by having NTIS publications protected by copyright, was based in part on

14. *Texas Administrative Code, Annotated,* Title 16, Economic Regulation (Colorado Springs, Colo.: Shepard's/McGraw-Hill, 1982), A-2.

15. *Michigan Compiled Laws Annotated* (St. Paul, Minn.: West Publishing, 1981), Title 17, section 401.

16. *Oregon Revised Statutes* ([Salem]: Oregon Legislative Counsel Committee, 1981), section 177.120, 1981 replacement part.

17. *Purdon's Pennsylvania Statutes Annotated* (St. Paul, Minn.: West Publishing, 1962), Title 71, section 636.

18. Phyllis I. Dalton, Constance E. Lee, and Beulah Mumm, "Government and Foundation Publishing," *Library Trends* 7 (July 1958): 117.

19. "Resolution on Copyright of Government Funded Publications," *Documents to the People* 4, no. 5 (September 1976): 13–14.

the perceived need to restrain publication in foreign countries. The United Nations policy is similar in spirit to that of the American Library Association:

> to facilitate the dissemination of the content of its publications as widely as possible by all reasonable means. General retention of copyright would give an impression of restriction and of setting up a procedural barrier—namely, the need to request permission to use material.[20]

In Texas, "Documents are copyrighted by authors, by divisions, and by departments, including everything from annual reports and serials to monographs and agency manuals."[21]

State documents librarians have a particular interest in noticing whether state publications are copyrighted if they are responsible for preparing microfilm or microfiche copies for distribution or for sale. The Texas State Library has a release form, "Release Form to Permit Microfilming of Copyrighted Publications," with a simple statement:

> The _____ (agency name) _____
>
> agrees to permit the Texas State Publications Clearinghouse of the Texas State Library to prepare microform copies (both microfilm and microfiche) of the following copyrighted publications issued by the agency and to allow the Clearinghouse to sell these microform copies to libraries and individuals at a nominal charge.[22]

Examples of copyrighted state publications collected in 1982 in response to a query in *Documents to the People* include New Mexico Calendar of Events, Historical Report of the Secretary of State [of] Arkansas, Diseases of Arkansas Forests, The California Water Atlas, and the Texas Administrative Code.

Status of State Agencies

Chronologically, there must be a state agency before there can be state publications. If an agency is not a state agency, its publications are not state publications. Publications become state publications either because they are issued by state agencies or because they have some association with a state agency. Examples of the latter are grant reports and research studies commissioned by state agencies.

20. United Nations, Department of Conference Services, *United Nations Editorial Manual* (New York: United Nations, 1983): 495.
21. Brenda Olds, "State Copyrighting" in "Documented by the Legislative Reference Library," *Public Documents Highlights for Texas* 1 (Fall 1978): 6.
22. "Form Letter with Release Form for Copyrighted Publications," in *Docs on Docs,* 1973–1979, item TX:D3.

One guideline for determining state agency status is the method by which the agency was created. State agencies are created by the state constitution, by laws, by executive orders, by legislative resolutions, by rules of court, or even informally by a governor's press announcement. The duration of a state agency is governed by the means by which it is created; constitutional agencies have a life concurrent with the constitution, but informally created agencies may pass out of existence with a change in the political atmosphere. Sunset laws, a new type of legislation that dissolves an agency unless affirmative action is taken to continue it, have been enacted in a number of states.

Typical state agencies and also typical publications issued by those agencies are listed by Parish. His arrangement is by subject; an example is:

Consumers (See also Agriculture)	Consumer's Council, Division	Annual Report
	Attorney General	Consumer Finance Reports
	Financial Fraud Division	General Warning Pamphlets
	Business Regulation Department	Laws on Consumerism in (State)[23]

In addition to the creation and demise of state agencies, librarians and their patrons are interested in changes of agency names and changes in status. The tracing of name changes is necessary for locating the publications of an agency in a bibliography or catalog. Usually these changes are recorded by cross-references or by a history note. An example of a history note is that for the California Commission on School Governance and Management, which reads, "Commission created as a part of the Hughes-Hart educational reform act of 1983 (SB813), signed in July of 1983."[24] Another example can be seen in the page from the Nebraska list (Figure 1) at the entry for "Gasohol Com."

Changes in status, that is, transfer of a subagency from one major agency to another, are also important in the discovery of publications on both a retrospective and a current basis. Retrospectively, the problems created by a transferred agency are no different from those of an agency with a name change. On a current basis, however, it is important to know the latest status of an agency in order to find it in the telephone book or other directories. Many such entries can be seen in the Louisiana listing, "Louisiana State Agency Names," because of the reorganization acts in that state.[25]

23. Parish, *State Government Reference Publications*, 260.

24. *Monthly Checklist of State Publications* 76 (April 1985): 260.

25. Margaret T. Lane, comp., "Louisiana State Agency Names," *Public Documents* no. 67 (January–December 1982).

A2600   COMMUNICATIONS, DIV. OF
         1800 N. 33RD. 68501. 471-2761

A2700   MATERIEL DIV. (Purchasing)
         5TH FLOOR, STATE OFFICE BLDG. 471-2401

A2800   OFFICE OF PLANNING & PROGRAMMING (see P2500 after June 30, 1976)

A2900   BUILDING DIV.
         10TH FLOOR, STATE CAPITOL. 471-3191

         Administrative Services, Div. of (Education), see E2200
         Admissions (UNL), see U0812
         Admissions, Office of (UNO), see U6333
         Adult & Continuing Education, Dept. of (UNL), see U3810
         Adult Restorative Dentistry, Dept. of, see U4305, U2805
         Advanced Emergency Medical Care, Bd. of Examiners in, see H2300
         Advisory Com. for Older Nebraskans, see A4550
         Advisory Council for Vocational Education (UNL), see U3992

A4000 AERONAUTICS, DEPT. OF
         P.O. BOX 82088. 68501. GENERAL AVIATION BLDG.,
         LINCOLN MUNICIPAL AIRPORT. 471-2371

         Aerospace Studies, Dept. of (Air Force ROTC) (UNL), see U3730
         Affirmative Action Office, see P2100
         Affirmative Action Office (UNL), see U0590
         Afghanistan Studies, Center for (UNO), see U6855
         Aging, Center on (UNO), see U8262

A4500 AGING, DEPT. ON   (Comm. on Aging until July 17, 1982)
         5TH FLOOR, STATE OFFICE BLDG. 68509. 471-2306

A4550   ADVISORY COM. FOR OLDER NEBRASKANS

         Agricultural Communications, Dept. of (UNL), see U2015
         Agricultural Economics, Dept. of (UNL), see U2030
         Agricultural Education, Dept. of (UNL), see U2045
         Agricultural Engineering (Mechanized Agriculture), Dept. of (UNL), see U2060
         Agricultural Experiment Station (Lincoln), see U2300
         Agricultural Extension, see U2250

A4800 GASOHOL COM.   (Agricultural Products Industrial Utilization Com. prior to September 1981)
         1ST FLOOR, STATE OFFICE BLDG. 68509. 471-2941

A4800 AGRICULTURAL PRODUCTS INDUSTRIAL UTILIZATION COM.
         (GASOHOL COM. after August 1981)

         Agricultural Statistics, Div. of, see A5100
         Agriculture & Environment Com., see L3715
         Agriculture & Natural Resources, Institute of (UNL), see U1500
         Agriculture Pollution Control Div., see E6600
         Agriculture, College of (UNL), see U2000

Figure 1. Classified list of agencies

State Agency Histories

Each state needs a list that records the authority by which each state agency came into being and, if no longer current, the reason for its demise. In some states this information is recorded in the state checklist rather than as a separate list. The sources for data on the creation and expiration of state agencies are both formal and informal. The formal sources include the constitution, the acts, executive orders, rules and regulations, legislative resolutions, and court rules. These sources are all state publications. In other words, state publications are used to establish that an agency is a state agency. Telephone books, city directories and other nonofficial sources can be used as supplementary sources of information.

Informal creation of state agencies is more difficult to document. Occasionally, creation or name changes of minor bureaus and offices or of governors' commissions can be documented only by a verbal confirmation from individuals associated with the agency. An example is the Louisiana agency which the governor's secretary reported as created in a press release. Interagency cooperative groups likewise can come into being without traceable origins. A Louisiana example is the Interdepartmental Committee on Health, Education and Services; nothing more definite is known about its establishment than that the year was 1942.

If an agency is considered a state agency because it receives state funds, the appropriation acts must be searched. The Illinois law, for example, includes in its definition of state agency the statement "and which agencies expend appropriations of State funds," and the Virgin Islands statute says, "receiving governmental funds for its operation in whole or in part, or any entity having bonding authority . . . ."[26]

To keep a list of state agency names and changes up to date, the customary practice is to read the acts after each session of the legislature. This practice is time consuming and tedious. An alternative procedure is possible if one has a list of state agencies with citations to the code or revised statutes of the state, and if the state statutes are in a computer database. After each legislative session the citations can be compared with the sections of the code that have been added, amended, or repealed. This checking pinpoints any changes in name, any abolitions, and probably any changes in status. The "sections added" table can be scanned for sections added in blocks, inasmuch as the creation of a new agency undoubtedly involves the addition of more than one section to the code. States are beginning to put legislation into databases on a current basis and can produce lists of code sections affected by each legislative session, but no example of using such a database to check the code sections creating state agencies, as proposed here, is known.

26. Margaret T. Lane, *State Publications and Depository Libraries* (Westport, Conn.: Greenwood Press, 1981), 354 (Ill.) and 538 (V.I.).

Lists of State Agencies

A list of state agencies can serve as both an acquisitions and a reference tool. For example, the Nebraska list, "Guide to State Agencies," is an annual publication designed for ordering state agency publications. It provides three basic types of information for each agency: "(1) address or telephone number; (2) the agency classification number, used in classifying its publications; and (3) information concerning recent name or structural changes."

The explanation in the preliminary pages of the Nebraska list continues:

> Agencies are arranged by the key word of their name; subdivisions are arranged under their parent agency in such a way as to reflect their structural relationship to the parent agency. Cross references are provided for all agency subdivisions and for variant agency names. "Nebraska" and "State" have been deleted from most agency names when they are the initial words to facilitate indexing.[27]

In addition to the deletion of the name of the state and the word *State* tighter typesetting and space economies are achieved by omitting *Lincoln* (the state capital) and the telephone area code common to most of the state agencies.

The form of the name and the arrangement of the list of state agency names need not necessarily follow cataloging rules. The Nebraska list, for example, has inverted names and is arranged by a classification scheme. Figure 1 shows the use of cross-references (Aerospace Studies), information on a name change (Gasohol Com.), and the bringing together of related agencies (Department on Aging and the Advisory Commission for Older Nebraskans).

In Chapter 10, state agency names as used in cataloging and authority files are discussed. The state agency lists designed for ordering publications from state agencies, such as the Nebraska one, include nonpublishing as well as publishing agencies. The Nebraska *Guide to State Agencies* is more complete than the telephone directory, according to the state library commission staff.

In some other states (Massachusetts, New Mexico, and Oklahoma are examples) the addresses for state agencies are included in the checklist. The 1977 Florida workshop handout had a directory of state agencies with addresses and telephone numbers.[28]

27. Nebraska Library Commission, *Guide to Nebraska State Agencies*, 1982 (Lincoln, Neb.: The Library, 1982), Foreword.

28. "Florida Public Documents Workshop, October 28, 1977," 13–15, in *Docs on Docs*, 1980–1983, item FL:M.

Listings of state agency names should include as cross-references any popular names by which state agencies are known. Commissions are often known by the name of the commission chairperson. The New Jersey popular name list, although prepared as an index to state documents, includes some agencies known by popular names (Booher Commission, Drug Study Commission, Little Hoover Commission, and Lord Committee).[29] Likewise, the Louisiana author headings lists include some popular names, such as the Dock Board and the Forgotten Man's Committee.[30] Sources for popular names are patron requests (the basis for the New Jersey list) and newspaper headlines (used in Louisiana). Shepard's popular name tables should be remembered as a reference source for popular names.[31] Popular names in Shepard's are derived from those used in court reports. However, because of the national scope of the Shepard's publication and because supplements are issued only annually, a locally compiled list of popular names is useful.

Studies by Legislative Commissions

As the activities of state agencies come under legislative scrutiny, especially during the budgetary process, the need to eliminate unnecessary costs and possible waste may be revealed. From time to time legislative interim committees or special study commissions are appointed to address such vexing problems. Such commissions focus on the single subject under study and are temporary in nature. Some states have created agencies to study the problems of access to and dissemination of state information. The 1984 Mississippi report by the legislative Joint Committee on Performance Evaluation and Expenditure Review (PEER) was particularly thorough.[32] The report uses a broad definition of the term publication: "any medium by which state agencies dispense information to the general public or to specialized agency clientele, whether through paper, film or electronic means." Among the recommendations of the report are (1) written policies for all phases of the production program, (2) designation of one person to be responsible for all aspects of agency publications, and (3) use of the most efficient and economical modes of distribution. The PEER committee endorsed the Mississippi depository library law as an efficient method of distribution.

29. New Jersey, State Library, Reference Section, "Popular Names Index to New Jersey State Documents" (Trenton, N.J.: The Library, 1977), in *Docs on Docs*, 1973–1979, item NJ:H.

30. Lane, "Louisiana State Agency Names."

31. *Shepard's Acts and Cases by Popular Names, Federal and State*, 3d ed. (Colorado Springs, Colo.: Shepard's, 1986).

32. Mississippi, State Legislature, Joint Committee on Performance Evaluation and Expenditure Review, *An Overview of Publications of Mississippi State Agencies* (Jackson, Miss.: 1984).

The committee found a problem of noncompliance with depository regulations and observed that those agencies that were in compliance had a designated person responsible for agency publications (as suggested in the committee's overall recommendations). The committee recommended that the legislature (1) should revise the law to provide for semiannual lists of publications from the state agencies, (2) should hold the executive head of each agency personally responsible for compliance, and (3) should create a civil penalty for noncompliance. Furthermore, the recommendation suggested that the state auditor include in audit procedures a test for compliance with the depository library regulations. The committee cited the *Handbook for State Agencies and Depository Libraries* prepared by Gerald Buchanan as the source for all information needed by state agencies.[33] The recognition by the committee of the availability of the manual and its endorsement of the depository library program are noteworthy. Not all such special studies consider the state's depository program or the role of libraries as distribution outlets.

The 1981 Virginia report that dealt primarily with annual reports used the Virginia checklist as a source for determining the number of annual reports issued and concluded, "The list appears incomplete."[34] If this assessment is true, the deficiency reflects as much on the state agencies (which should appreciate the value of the collections at the state library) as on the state library itself (which undoubtedly makes every effort to ensure inclusion of all annual reports). The only mention of libraries in the section on distribution procedures is a suggestion that letters offering annual reports to libraries may be preferable to automatic shipment of such reports, a suggestion unpopular with librarians. A regular response to such letters on an annual basis would be a burden on libraries that maintain a file of all the annual reports of an agency. The distribution to a number of libraries throughout the state that the Virginia State Library has been handling is not mentioned. Virginia does not have legislation providing for a system of depositories.

In conclusion, the advice of James B. Childs must be remembered. Although it is state publications and the information they contain that are of interest to the user, it is the state agencies that are the key to this information.

---

33. Gerald Buchanan, *State Depository for Public Documents: Handbook for State Agencies and Depository Libraries* (Jackson, Miss.: Mississippi Library Commission, 1978), in *Docs on Docs*, 1973–1979, item MS:H.

34. Virginia, State Information Committee, "Report, State Publications, Part I" (July 21, 1981).

4 DISTRIBUTION

Continuing the previous chapter's emphasis on state agencies, this chapter considers the distribution of state publications by state agencies. State agencies publish in order to distribute; distribution is the final step in publishing. The primary goal of state agencies in publishing a state document is to make the information therein available to the appropriate audience. Distribution embodies the idea of "making available" and is almost synonymous with publishing, which means "making generally known."

The emphasis in this chapter is on distribution of publications, particularly publications in paper copy. Paper, for many years the predominate form of distribution, continues to be the principal medium through which distribution is made to libraries and to out-of-state individuals, although an increasing number of publications are being distributed in microform, particularly microfiche.

An understanding by librarians of the methods of distribution provides the basis for identifying and acquiring state publications. Some distribution is mandated by statutes of various kinds. Different kinds of statutes apply to the three branches of government, to in-state and out-of-state distribution, and to libraries and individuals. The discussion of these various kinds of statutory distribution is followed by a section on other distribution procedures, such as mailing lists, state bookstores, and direct requests. The distribution of state information, as distinguished from state publications, is the final section of this chapter.

Statutory Distribution

Statutory distribution may be provided for in several separate statutes for such areas as legal publications, exchanges, executive department publications, depository systems, and even individual titles, or may be similar to the general distribution statute in Wisconsin that encompasses all types of distribution. The different types of statutory distribution statutes merit individual discussion.

LEGAL PUBLICATIONS

Legal publications, that is, publications of the legislative and judicial branches of government, are the oldest type of publications, and their distribution is regulated by statute in many states. Because most legal publications are published at regular intervals, statutory provisions can specify particular recipients for specific titles. Typically, major state agencies, members of the legislature, judges or clerks of court, and certain libraries are designated by statute as recipients of session laws, court reports, or legislative journals. Sheriffs, district attorneys and other officials may also receive publications if mentioned in the statutes as recipients of specific publications. This statutory distribution may be automatic or may require that a formal request be made. Automatic distribution is usually limited to a single copy, although the distribution requirement for the state library or the university library may provide for multiple copies to be used for internal library use as well as exchange.

An interesting observation on the distribution of legal materials was made by William Robinson:

> Nevertheless, if a state has an obligation to provide legal materials to convicted felons, one wonders if it is not also obligated to provide at least minimal information about judicial decisions to its citizens through publicly supported academic and public libraries.[1]

EXCHANGES

Statutes are also the basis for the extensive exchange arrangements among the states for out-of-state publications. Under an exchange statute, state agencies supply multiple copies of a publication to a library, usually the state library, for redistribution. Exchange legislation, promoted by libraries for libraries, was designed to enrich the collection of the library administering the exchange as well as to promote prudent distribution through reciprocity. Because legal publications are issued on a regular basis as serial publications, it is possible to exchange on a volume-by-volume or year-by-year basis. Exchanges, however, are much less adaptable to the variety and diversity of the publications emanating from the executive branch of government. Today both the number of libraries participating in exchanges and the number of titles in exchange programs are drastically reduced. The mere fact that only one library in a state benefits from an exchange is the principal disadvantage, and the possibilities of changes in the needs and interests of that library require adjustments in the exchange arrangements. Terry Weech in his discussion of exchanges said that exchanges "have always had serious limitations."[2]

1. William C. Robinson, "Tennessee State Government Publications in Tennessee Academic and Public Libraries," *Tennessee Librarian* 32 (Spring 1980): 16.

2. Terry L. Weech, "Collection Development and State Publications," *Government Publications Review* 8A, nos. 1 and 2 (1981): 54.

EXECUTIVE BRANCH PUBLICATIONS

Executive branch publications are more numerous and more diverse than legal publications. The subject matter is more general; the format is more varied. In a general public library, executive publications are more useful than are the laws and reports that come from the legislative and judicial branches of government. Executive branch publications include statistical compendiums, directories, and scientific research studies as well as consumer-oriented publications on products and procedures. Although many are serials, important monographs are also published by executive agencies. Some of these are listed in the "New State Publications" column in *Documents to the People*.[3] Other sources are the lists by David Parish in *Government Publications Review*, which began in 1976, and the state documents section of the "Notable Documents List" compiled by the Notable Documents Committee of the American Library Association's Government Documents Round Table.[4]

Statutory provisions for wide distribution of serial titles issued by executive agencies are not common, although there may be specific distribution requirements for the annual report of the agency. Ex officio distribution of department reports to certain officers, such as the clerks of court or sheriffs, is necessarily specified by statute.

Legislation governing the preparation of executive branch publications may provide a distribution pattern for specific titles. An example is the Louisiana statute providing for the printing and distribution of the constitution in 1954.[5] Certain libraries, often designated by name, are sometimes included in these statutes. Less frequently, distribution is mandated for "public libraries." The Maryland law says "each public, circulating library," and Minnesota has a provision for "the public library of any city of the first class."[6] The Maryland statute provides for distribution on request whereas the Minnesota statute makes distribution mandatory. The legislation on distribution can be located in *American Library Laws* under the index heading, "Distribution of Public Documents."[7]

3. The column started in January 1982 and has appeared irregularly.

4. The Parish column appeared in several issues of each volume from 1976 to 1981. Since 1982 it has appeared annually in the November–December issue. The "Notable Documents List" appeared in *RQ* 23 (Spring 1984): 283–90; *RQ* 24 (Spring 1985): 265–74; and *Library Journal* 111 (May 15, 1986): 38–43.

5. *Acts of the Legislature of the State of Louisiana, Regular Session 1954* (Baton Rouge, La.: Thos. J. Moran's Sons, 1954), Act No. 380. "The Secretary of State shall forward a copy of the Constitution to each sheriff and clerk of court and justice of the peace for the use of their respective courts, and to each member of the legislature. The Secretary of State shall . . . be authorized to dispose of the remainder at a price . . . ."

6. *The Annotated Code of the Public General Laws of Maryland, State Government* (Charlottesville, Va.: Michie, 1984), section 2-1310; *Minnesota Statutes Annotated* (St. Paul, Minn.: West Publishing, 1987), title 15, section 18 in 1987 supplementary pamphlet.

7. *American Library Laws*, 5th ed., ed. Alex Ladenson (Chicago: American Library Association, 1983).

In the states, the individual governmental agencies do not usually have the library distribution or depository systems that some federal agencies have, such as the Census Bureau or the Geological Survey. Paul Pross, a Canadian political scientist, found that the agencies that publish the greater number of items tend to exhibit the most sophisticated handling procedures; those agencies that publish only rarely, he says, possess virtually no techniques for distributing the few items they produce.[8]

DEPOSITORY SYSTEMS

A comprehensive depository system is the method of distribution that provides the greatest access to published items for the most people at the lowest cost. Legislation establishing depository systems is usually instigated by the library community within a state to make state publications accessible and available. Because of the importance of having publications easily available to the general public, the depository legislation in many states emphasizes the inclusion of public libraries in the depository system.

Depository systems provide for the forwarding of publications to a library distribution center and redistribution to the individual depository libraries. The library distribution center serves as a link between the state agencies and the libraries of the state. The centralization of acquisition efforts reduces costs and staff time for both the state agencies and the libraries. The activities of the library distribution center benefit the state agencies, the libraries, and by extension, the public.

State agencies benefit from a depository system through the reduction of individual requests and through the use of bulk postage rates. A real, but less tangible, benefit to state agencies is that a publication placed in a library becomes known to a wider audience through listing and cataloging. In a library, additional publications can be called to the attention of the prospective user by the librarian, who can also supplement the research with nongovernmental sources.

For libraries the principal benefit of a depository distribution system is the timely and automatic receipt of publications. A substantial reduction in acquisition work and records for these somewhat elusive publications results from depository distribution. Because many state publications are available without cost, a savings of the purchase price is not usually a factor; the elimination of the ordering process is more significant. The many features of depository systems will be discussed in Chapter 9.

Out-of-State Distribution

Distribution within the state has been the focus of much of the preceding discussion. Statutory provisions for distribution usually provide for

8. A. Paul Pross and Catherine A. Pross, *Government Publishing in the Canadian Provinces* (Toronto: University of Toronto Press, 1972), 34.

in-state distribution only, most voluntary distribution is in-state, and state depository systems are composed almost exclusively of libraries located in the state.

Exchange arrangements have already been mentioned as a method of out-of-state distribution. Another type of out-of-state distribution involving a greater breadth of materials is the sending of publications to the Library of Congress, the Center for Research Libraries, and, in some states, the British Library, formerly the library of the British Museum. Most distribution to these libraries is handled by a library center in the cooperating state. All three libraries have agreements with the various states for the forwarding of state documents. There is, however, some direct mailing from state agencies to the Library of Congress. The appearance of titles in the *Monthly Checklist of State Publications* that are not in the local checklist provides evidence of this practice. Twenty-two states have statutory provisions requiring distribution of at least one copy of each state publication to the Library of Congress. Occasionally there is a statutory requirement that a particular publication be sent to the Library of Congress.

The statutes providing for exchanges and those naming specific libraries are the primary types of statutes to which out-of-state libraries look. Out-of-state libraries sometimes receive less favorable treatment than in-state libraries, on the theory that they can borrow the documents through interlibrary loan.

Other Distribution Methods

State agencies often maintain mailing lists for their publications. These mailing lists may change with a new administration, if not more frequently. An annual purge of mailing lists is one measure adopted in several states as a method of controlling expenses. Another measure that has found acceptance in Maryland and Minnesota is a prohibition against distribution to legislators. In those states, legislators are made aware of state agency publications by bibliographical listings and are sent copies of publications only in response to specific requests.

Some states have bookstores or other sales outlets. Catalogs and lists of publications for sale are available. The Pennsylvania General Services Administration and the Minnesota Department of Administration sell documents and compile such lists. Less formal lists of state publications for sale are the California list of codes from the Department of Finance and the Iowa "Notice of Legal Publications and Price List," issued by the State Printing Board. The Virginia State Library publishes (pursuant to a statutory requirement) an annual list, *Virginia Publications in Print*, which includes both free publications and those which are for sale. These state sales agency catalogs and lists, similar to the one published in Virginia, are partial answers to the continuing complaint that the public does not know where and how to obtain state documents.

VOLUNTARY DISTRIBUTION TO INDIVIDUALS AND LIBRARIES

Distribution to individuals differs from distribution to libraries. Individuals receive publications in response to direct requests for specific titles (the weekly market bulletin, for example), in answer to a query ("What are the licensing rules for day care centers?"), or, in some instances, because of a departmental policy (board of health publications distributed to new mothers). Especially in agencies where the top official is elected, distribution of publications to individuals is a political asset and may be more extravagant than in more conservative agencies. State officials value the prerogative of controlling distribution, even though it may waste state money and may fail to place the publications in permanent locations.

On the other hand, libraries always try, and sometimes succeed, in being placed on a mailing list. If libraries make a specific request for a particular title, they are careful to add "and all future issues" for all serial titles. They ask to be placed on the mailing list "for all regulations on nuclear waste disposal" or, more generally, "for all publications of your commission (or board, or department)."

Some strategies adopted by state agencies to control wasteful distribution of publications may be encountered by both individuals and libraries. As listed in a recent Mississippi study, these include requirements for nominal subscription fees; stamped, self-addressed envelopes; written requests; response to reader satisfaction questionnaires; and sale, either at cost or at a profit.[9] Requirements such as these illustrate the difficulties faced by those seeking to acquire state publications. Although many state publications are distributed without charge, special conditions must be met for others. The user should always remember that state publications go out of print quickly and are often not available after the initial distribution.

Distribution Status of State Information

While state *publications* are always distributed (if Pross's definition is followed),[10] this is not true for state *information*. Information, according to the thinking of the NCLIS Public Sector/Private Sector Task Force report, is an intangible that can be made available regardless of the medium

---

9. Mississippi, State Legislature, Joint Committee on Performance Evaluation and Expenditure Review, *An Overview of Publications of Mississippi State Agencies* (Jackson, Miss.: 1984), 11–12.

10. Pross, *Government Publishing*, 17.

through which it is transmitted.[11] The information available through a toll-free 800 telephone number is not distributed in the same sense that a printed guide for taxpayers distributes information, but is individualized and personalized for the particular inquirer.

There is no state where *all* state information is distributed from a single source; such a circumstance is inappropriate in a democracy. The spoken word and the public addresses of state government officials, for example, are not centrally controlled in this country; they issue from many different sources. As more information is being stored in databases, it is necessarily decentralized. Even the distribution of paper copies of publications, the predominate method of distribution until recent times, has never been totally centralized in any state. Exceptions always exist for distribution by a state agency that can secure a legislative exemption permitting special distribution. Microform publications, radio, television, electronic databases and other means of disseminating state information naturally have diversified distribution methods.

STATE RECORDS DISTINGUISHED

According to Pross, the extent or range of distribution is the key that distinguishes state publications and state records. The definition created by Pross for official publications reads, in part, "reproduced and circulated to groups and individuals other than those advising or negotiating with the government concerning the subject matter of the documents."[12] Records that are part of the working files of an office or are in an archives collection are outside the scope of this discussion. Such records are available to the public through Freedom of Information Act procedures.

Nevertheless, librarians should inform themselves of available information, regardless of whether or not it is distributed. Librarians in all types of libraries should be aware of the existence of unpublished official information (public records, databases, or the personal knowledge of an expert) and the need for referral to the appropriate sources. Particularly in special libraries, librarians often go beyond mere referral and acquire unpublished information in response to specific requests.

MICROFORM PUBLICATIONS

Microfilm and microfiche publications resemble paper most closely and may be distributed in the same manner. A microform publication may be either the original publication of a state agency or a republication. State

11. U.S. National Commission on Libraries and Information Science, Public Sector/Private Sector Task Force, *Public Sector/Private Sector Interaction in Providing Information Services* (Washington, D.C.: GPO, 1982), 16.

12. Pross, *Government Publishing*, 17.

agencies are only beginning to adopt microfiche as a medium of original publication. Microfiche has been found appropriate for state administrative codes, for example, because these codes are extremely bulky and must be updated frequently.

Republication in microformat, whether for distribution, preservation or saving space, is usually undertaken by a library or an archives unit, although there are some retrospective commercial projects, such as the Minnesota 1860–1924 collection and the Wisconsin 1852–1914 collection, both by Brookhaven Press.[13] Library and archives filming is usually comprehensive—all state publications distributed to the depository libraries, or all publications issued by the state—so that a historical record will be preserved for future use. The filming of the New York and the Massachusetts documents by Research Publications, Inc., is an exception to the general commercial practice of doing special subject projects.[14] Typical examples of commercial undertakings include the microfiche collections of session laws, constitutional conventions, water reports, and correction studies. Of course, for some users, the need for readers or printers limits the use of state publications in a microformat.

A major project undertaken by the Harvard Law School Library involved the filming of over 6,000 volumes of state reports. The library selected state documents because they were in the public domain and were little used. The subject areas were banking, insurance, labor, public utilities, and taxation. Serials in these areas were filmed for thirteen states. The nature of state documents and the "fascinating" information they include are commented on in an article by Naomi Ronen describing the project.[15]

AUDIOVISUALS AND RADIO AS INFORMATION

Some indication of the lack of activity in film production by state agencies can be observed in film catalogs, which list very few entries by the names of the states. Motion picture films are produced by state agencies on a limited basis, and copies are not widely distributed. Occasionally a state library may receive a copy of a state agency-produced film. Documentary films for departments of tourism, education, and health have been made in some states.

A 1981 study, "Public Service Announcements for Television and Radio by Virginia State Agencies and Institutions," found that

13. *Minnesota Public Documents, 1860–1924* (LaCrosse, Wis.: Brookhaven Press); *Wisconsin Public Documents, 1852–1914* (LaCrosse, Wis.: Brookhaven Press).

14. Massachusetts, *Commonwealth of Massachusetts Publications* (Woodbridge, Conn.: Research Publications, 1975+); New York (State), *Official Publications* (Woodbridge, Conn.: Research Publications, 1974+).

15. Naomi Ronen, "Creating a Micropublishing Project: A Non-Commercial Perspective," *Microform Review* 11 (Winter 1982): 8–13.

In Virginia's state government, comparatively few agencies and institutions produce public service announcements in the form of filmed or taped materials; fewer than a half-dozen do so on a regular basis. Those which do produce such materials, however, regard them as an important part of their overall informational activities.[16]

Posters are another form of visual presentation of information issued in some states.

TELEPHONE LINES AND DATABASES

Making state information available by means of toll-free telephone lines is limited almost entirely to the residents of the state. Almost all the states have in-state hot lines for legislative bill status. Fifteen states have toll-free numbers for tourist information for out-of-state inquiries.[17]

Databases and electronic bulletin boards are even more limited in their use than other formats for state information because communication hardware and appropriate software programs are necessary. Generally, state agencies have not established policies for making machine-readable information available outside the agency that created the database. Minnesota and Florida are exceptions. In Minnesota, a private company, Legislative Associates, has a contract to provide a system that delivers legislative information services to state agencies, such as a daily news summary, a calendar, bill detail reports, bill list reports, bill tracking, and four additional reports. Minnesota agencies using this information are the Governor's Office, the Attorney General, five state departments and the University of Minnesota. Nongovernmental users are law firms, public utilities, trade associations, labor unions, and insurance companies.[18]

In Florida the statutes were amended to give legal authority to state and local agencies to provide remote access to computerized records. A July 1984 survey of state and local government officials in Florida indicated that 75 percent of the respondents had public records stored on computers, and 54 percent had received requests for copies of large portions of their computerized databases. Large law firms, title companies and real estate agents had requested access to specific files.[19] The Act (Chapter 85-86) was effective July 1, 1985. Under the new legislation, agencies are permitted to charge a fee for "remote electronic access, granted under a

16. Virginia, State Information Committee, "Public Service Announcements for Television and Radio by Virginia State Agencies and Institutions" (Richmond: March 1981), 1.

17. *The Great 800 Toll Free Directory, 1984* (Jackson, Miss.: The Great 800 Directory Company, 1984), 329–39.

18. Keith Aleshire, "New Data Base Aids Minnesota Legislature," *Government Computer News* 7 (June 1985): 76–78.

19. "Florida Law Would Permit Remote Access to Data," *Government Computer News,* 19 (July 1985): 52.

contractual arrangement with a user." The prior Florida law distinguished between copying (for which a charge was permitted) and inspection (which was free), but this distinction is blurred when information is stored electronically and can be transmitted electronically. Because electronic images are not "copies" and electronic access is "inspection," new legislation was necessary.

A new method of access to government information is now available in Ohio. Bypassing traditional distribution of hard-copy publications under state depository laws, a new online reference service, OhioPi, has been made available to twenty Ohio libraries. This new reference service is similar to a program developed in Indiana. Information sources include current and proposed legislation, judicial calenders and opinions (full text), directories, newsletters, and a statistics system for demographic information, politics, finance, health, safety, transportation, agriculture, manufacturing, business, and education. Page Lewis, public relations writer at OCLC, in describing OhioPi, indicates that state depository laws are no longer effective because of the vulnerability of printing budgets to budget cuts and because of the lack of timeliness of printed reports. She suggests that access to Ohio state government information is now "as easy as 'Pi'."[20]

Understanding distribution of state publications involves not only knowledge of the services of the state agencies, whether exercised pursuant to statute or voluntarily, but also familiarity with the procedures applicable to libraries, particularly depository arrangements. Distribution varies in each of the three branches of government, according to the recipient, and by type of material. Distribution is the agencies' means of communicating with the public. An article by Kathleen Heim on public access to government information provides a cautionary note for the conclusion of this chapter. Heim's remarks, adapted to apply to state publications and to the general public, are:

> Heretofore, librarians have tended to concentrate on printed materials with some attention to recorded and visual items. They continue to lag in satisfying the data needs of [the library community]. Documents librarians have the opportunity to recapture this function through facilitation of primary source material in the form of machine-readable data . . . . To continue to shrug off (at the very least) bibliographic responsibility for the . . . resources of the [state] government[s] is to fail to provide access to a growing portion of government-produced information.[21]

20. Page Lewis, "OHIONET 'OhioPi' Demonstrated at OCLC," *OCLC Newsletter* (April 1986): 19.

21. Kathleen M. Heim, "Government Produced Machine-Readable Statistical Data as a Component of the Social Science Information System: An Examination of Federal Policy and Strategies for Access," in *Communicating Public Access to Government Information; Proceedings of the Second Annual Library Government Documents and Information Conference,* ed. Peter Hernon (Westport, Conn.: Meckler Publishing, 1983), 68.

5
LIBRARIES

In this chapter the discussion shifts from the state agencies that produce state publications to the libraries that facilitate their use. Although the connection between state publications and libraries is not as obvious as that between state agencies and state publications, it cannot be denied that the association with libraries is necessary if state documents are to be fully available and accessible.

Individuals can usually secure their own copies of items in print but must turn to libraries for out-of-print items. Archives collections may include printed materials as well as manuscript records for state agencies, but they do not encourage circulation. Public information centers may give help with consumer problems and answer short factual questions, but they provide no guidance for the historian.

The usefulness of state documents is tied to libraries. For books in general, films, recordings, and other materials often used in libraries, the library is a convenience rather than a necessity. For current information, libraries may be only one of several sources. For historians who may be searching for source documents, legal researchers, or environmental advocates, however, libraries may be the only answer for items not of archival quality. Because state publications have many characteristics not shared by ordinary library materials, availability in libraries is essential. State publications can be made truly available to users only through libraries for many reasons.

The Role of Libraries

State publications are not uniform in format or content, they are issued in small quantities, they go out of print rapidly, and they are not easily identified. When state publications are deposited or acquired in the libraries of the state, they become available to the general public at a convenient place, during many hours of the day and evening, with trained and competent guidance in their use. This availability is the theory underlying depository library programs.

The opposite scenario—availability at the office of the state agencies issuing the publications—is a dismal picture. The place, a state agency office at the capital, is convenient only for those living nearby; the hours during which the publications can be examined are limited to a traditional Monday-through-Friday, nine-to-five pattern; and although personnel familiar with the publications may be at hand, they usually are not trained in the interviewing techniques used by the reference librarian, do not have secondary sources at hand to supplement the information in the publications, and may give access to publications and information as a secondary function rather than, as in libraries, as a primary service.

Library Attitudes

The cardinal rule for handling documents in a library is: *treat documents the same as other materials.* There are exceptions, of course, but these should be kept to a minimum. The tendency to relegate documents to the basement and to consider documents librarians as different from the rest of the staff is unfortunate. The warning by Albert Halcli that documents must be brought "out of the ghetto" has been reiterated by McClure and Hernon, who declare, "organizationally, the documents collection needs to be aligned with, or part of, a department in the library that is both powerful and involved in decision making."[1]

The location of state documents in a library should be determined by the criteria used for other library materials. Some state documents, for example, the state blue book and the statistical abstract, are necessary for ready reference and should be shelved at the reference desk. Some are frequently used (for example the state wildlife magazine in a public library) and should be kept in a location convenient for the casual reader. Other state documents fall into the rare books category and must be housed with other rare materials.

Documents librarians must take every opportunity to ensure that documents are recommended, available, and used whenever appropriate. Librarians should review library procedure manuals and be certain that state documents receive special consideration. Including references to documents in library statistics, the publications program, and publicity activities help assure the absorption of documents into the total library outreach program.

In the library procedure manual, which every library should have, practices unique to state documents should be inserted in appropriate places. The copy of the manual used by the state documents librarians might have the state documents provisions specially marked or highlighted.

1. Albert Halcli, "How to Escape from the Documents Ghetto," *Illinois Libraries* 54 (June 1972): 412–15; Charles R. McClure and Peter Hernon, *Improving the Quality of Reference Service for Government Publications* (Chicago: American Library Association, 1983), 141.

"Where are the state documents?" is a state documents question that the library procedure manual should answer, because very often documents are an exception to the general arrangement of library materials by Dewey or Library of Congress classification schemes. If documents from the home state and from out of state are incorporated into the collection without differentiation, then no special mention is required, although such a mention serves as a reminder for those librarians accustomed to a separate documents collection.

Separate documents collections may or may not include state documents. For example, at Duke University, Durham, North Carolina, out-of-state documents are in the documents collection along with federal, foreign, and international documents, but North Carolina documents are in the North Carolina collection; at Louisiana State University, out-of-state documents are integrated into the general collection under the appropriate Library of Congress classifications, and Louisiana documents are in the Louisiana collection; and at Louisiana Tech University, all documents are located in the separate documents collection.

The inclusion of the home state documents in a special state collection, that is, a collection that separates materials by jurisdiction and includes both primary and secondary sources as well as works by local authors, is unique to state documents. Users of state documents are often users of complementary state materials, such as histories of the state, publications of state associations, and other secondary sources. For documents of the home state, the advantage of keeping the primary source material, which includes most state documents, in the same area as the secondary materials that amplify and supplement it is an additional reason for maintaining a separate state collection.

Some librarians present strong arguments against locating the state documents in the state collection. They cite the shorter hours, limitations on circulation, and closed shelves that may apply to special state collections, all incompatible with the maximum use of the documents. Other librarians take the position that state documents belong in the collection with federal documents because the patron may not know whether the information needed is state or federal, as in the case of highway or welfare regulations. Also, documents from different levels of government may complement each other in certain subjects, such as federal and state obscenity reports.

In the library procedure manual, immediately following the statement giving the location of the state documents, a statement should indicate that the documents are available to the general public. Everyone on the library staff, including student and temporary workers, should be alerted to the special obligations that a depository library assumes to give service to those beyond the customary clientele of the library. In libraries that have federal depository as well as state depository status, the responsibility to make government materials easily available to all potential users has become common knowledge as a result of the adoption of the federal standards and guidelines, visits by federal inspectors, and increased communications from the Government Printing Office in recent years.

In many states, however, there are state depository libraries that do not have federal depository status, as shown in Table 3. In these cases, there is no federal model to set the pattern for public use. In most states the law or the state regulations alert librarians to the duty to make state publications received on deposit fully available to the general public. Each individual in charge of a state depository collection must make certain that all the library staff know that the state documents collection is maintained and serviced for the use of the public.

The library procedure manual should also record definitions for *state publication, state agency,* and other necessary terms, such as *quasistate publications,* if the library places these materials in a separate collection.

Statements on how state documents are handled (classified, cataloged, or shelved), if handled differently from the general collection, and any circulation policies that differ from those of the general collection, are also appropriate for the library procedure manual. The handling of individual state documents in a library that incorporates the documents into the general collection, a practice followed in small libraries that receive few documents, is not an issue here. However, a separate classification scheme for state documents, adopted perhaps because it can be copied from the state checklist by library clerks, requires explanation. Likewise, if the cataloging of state documents has a low priority or is dispensed with, this must be stated in the manual as a reminder. If special shelving areas are allocated for state documents, or if state documents are part of a noncirculating collection, this must be stated in the manual as well.

Handling of documents in a depository library usually has special constraints and restrictions. In a depository library, the interlibrary loan responsibilities may be more extensive for state publications than those generally in effect in the library, and this difference should be clearly stated. For example, the Wisconsin rules and regulations for depository libraries require that depository libraries "provide access to all Wisconsin public documents, not merely those held in the individual depository collection. Document interloan is thus an integral depository function."[2]

A final statement in the library procedure manual should specify the ownership of depository materials if ownership is retained by the state or the state library, and duties of the library with respect to discarded material. For example, in Illinois ownership of documents sent to depository and exchange libraries is retained by the Illinois State Library.[3]

2. Wisconsin Division for Library Services, Reference and Loan Library, *Manual for Wisconsin Document Depositories* (Madison, Wis.: Wisconsin Department of Public Instruction, January 1975), 4. In *Docs on Docs,* 1973–1979, item WI:H.

3. *Illinois Register,* Title 23, Education and Cultural Resources, section 3020.210. In *Docs on Docs,* item IL84:F.

Table 3. *Number of State and Federal Depositories in Rank Order by State*

	STATE DEPOSITORIES	FEDERAL DEPOSITORIES
California	149	110
New York	98	92
Pennsylvania	60	62
Ohio	54	58
New Jersey	53	43
Michigan	50	49
Texas	48	63
Washington	46	21
Wisconsin	44	30
Iowa	41	20
Louisiana	38	26
Minnesota	38	26
Missouri	37	31
Oregon	34	20
Mississippi	32	12
Illinois	28	57
Florida	24	37
Kansas	24	18
Arkansas	20	17
Colorado	20	24
New Hampshire	19	9
Idaho	18	11
New Mexico	17	11
Oklahoma	16	21
Alaska	14	9
Montana	14	9
Connecticut	13	22

Whether documents should be singled out for special attention upon arrival at a library is an open question. Yes, documents must be identified as they come into the library if the library is a depository. Yes, documents must be channeled to the proper department if the library has created a special section for them. No, documents do not need particular notice taken of them if the library is not a depository and if all documents are merged into the general collection.

Handling documents that are absorbed into the general collection is not a topic for special consideration because all materials, including documents, are handled under the constraints of the same library policies. Although documents may present problems in libraries that merge documents into the general collection, the solutions to those problems are tailored to the general procedures of the library. Yuri Nakata in *From Press*

Table 3. (continued).

	STATE DEPOSITORIES	FEDERAL DEPOSITORIES
Maryland	13	24
Utah	13	11
Indiana	12	35
Maine	12	12
Nebraska	12	14
South Carolina	11	18
Virginia	11	35
Nevada	9	8
South Dakota	7	11
Tennessee	6	26
Massachusetts	5	34
North Dakota	5	10
Hawaii	3	11
Georgia	1	27
Rhode Island	1	11
Wyoming	1	10
Alabama	0	25
Arizona	0	13
Delaware	0	7
Kentucky	0	20
North Carolina	0	35
Vermont	0	8
West Virginia	0	15

Sources: Survey by Marilyn K. Moody, Iowa State University, April 1984 (unpublished); U.S. Congress, Joint Committee on Printing, *Government Depository Libraries*, S. Prt. 98-220 (Washington, D.C.: GPO, 1984), 12.

to People correctly points out, "Most small nondepository libraries do not acquire more government publications than can be integrated into the general library collection."[4]

Separate versus Integrated Collections

A brief review of the old question of whether a library should have a separate collection for documents is appropriate. Experienced documents librarians will say, "No, we've heard it all," or "I inherited a separate collection (or an integrated collection) and can't change now." Nevertheless, for the record, and for librarians new to the field, a brief recapitulation is in order.

4. Yuri Nakata, *From Press to People: Collecting and Using U.S. Government Publications* (Chicago: American Library Association, 1979), 33.

The mission of the library, the number and kinds of documents received, the physical facilities, the budget (even depository acquisition is not free), and the user community all have a bearing on the handling of documents in a particular library. Documents may be handled in special collections, completely integrated into the main collection, or mixed between a special collection and the general collection. Separate collections, those that are documents-oriented or those that are limited to a specific state, are shelved as a unit in a special room or area of the library. These collections use the special indexes and guides available for state documents and may have a catalog limited to the collection. In a separate collection, the library staff provides service in that area only. On the other hand, complete integration of state documents means interfiling state documents in the general classification scheme used by the library, shelving throughout the library stacks, bibliographic access through the library catalog, and reference assistance from the general reference staff. The chapter on organization and arrangement in Nakata's *From Press to People* is recommended both for an overview of the factors affecting the choices for handling documents and for a clear statement of the advantages and disadvantages of the choices.[5]

Having a separate collection is seen primarily as an economic advantage because of reduced processing and the related savings in costs. Classification and cataloging data can be copied from checklists or shipping lists and procedures for getting the publication onto shelves can be standardized for implementation by clerical staff. The opportunity for the documents staff to become experts in documents reference work is also cited as an advantage of the special collection. The special reference tools and indexes that provide access to the information in documents can be mastered and used to their full potential in the ideal separate collection. Agency publications are often kept together by the classification scheme, an asset for some library users.

An integrated collection, on the other hand, is more convenient for the user. The card catalog or online catalog is the sole key to all library materials, and there is no need to remember to check in a special department. The integrated collection provides, through the classification scheme used in the library, a subject approach to the documents. Duplication of government reference tools is minimized in an integrated collection.

Mixed collections have sometimes had a bad press. If the "important" documents are cataloged and the remainder sent to the documents collection, it becomes difficult to remember the special documents collection.

---

5. Nakata, *Press to People*, 33–36. A similar statement, directed to law librarians achieving federal depository status for the first time, is in Kathleen T. Larson, "Establishing a New GPO Depository Documents Department in an Academic Law Library," *Law Library Journal* 72 (Summer 1979): 490–93.

Who remembers the unimportant? More pertinently, who decides what is important?

In contrast to these federal documents patterns, state documents have always had a fourth type of collection — the special state collection which integrates the documents with the historical and secondary materials relating to the state. These state collections are, of course, special collections, but not special documents collections. They derive their name from the name of the state: the Louisiana collection or the Oregon collection. In these state collections, state documents librarians have been "mainstreaming" state documents without applying a label to the process. Some of the advantages cited as benefits of special documents collections are also present in special state collections, particularly the possible availability of quality reference assistance.

Whether the differences between government publications and other library materials should result in different organization and handling of the documents in a library has been a recurring concern for librarians. It has been called a "debate" by Michael Waldo, who wrote a historical account of the organization of federal documents depository collections based on the library literature.[6] The issues he listed were: the possibilities of using specialized indexes and catalogs, the expense of complete conventional cataloging, delays in processing, and assistance from librarians who have become experts. A final factor, the convenience of the library patron, is one that Waldo reports has seldom been substantiated. He points out more than once that assumptions and opinions instead of hard data formed the basis for decisions relating to most of these issues.

In a recent book Peter Hernon, a scholar with an extensive background in government publications, gives three reasons why federal documents depository libraries decide to treat documents separately: (1) the Superintendent of Documents classification scheme and the indexes that use it; (2) the volume of publications, which makes the system economically feasible; and (3) the nature of the distribution, which requires verification of receipt.[7] Attempting to transpose these factors to state documents reveals that many states do not have classification schemes or indexes using these schemes, that the volume of state publications from an individual state in no way compares with the federal output, and finally, that the verification of receipt is usually not so rigidly enforced a requirement at the state level.

While the same general arguments, advantages, and disadvantages that apply to federal documents are relevant to state documents (cost effectiveness, processing speed, and expert reference service), the following circumstances must also be taken into consideration for state documents:

6. Michael Waldo, "An Historical Look at the Debate Over How to Organize Federal Government Documents in Depository Libraries," *Government Publications Review* 4, no. 4 (1977): 319–29.

7. Peter Hernon and Gary R. Purcell, *Developing Collections of U.S. Government Publications* (Greenwich, Conn.: JAI Press, 1982), 126.

(1) the lack, in many states, of the indexes and reference tools that might serve as aids to the use of the collection; (2) the possibility of handling out-of-state documents in a different way from in-state documents; and (3) for in-state documents, the feasibility of assembling both primary and secondary material relating to the state in one collection.

Indexes and reference tools are indispensable even when a documents collection is fully classified and cataloged. Federal documents librarians know that cataloging of congressional publications is no substitute for the *Congressional Index Service.* Yet, at the state level such in-depth tools do not exist. The standard guide to state reference tools is Parish.[8] Parish's list shows incomplete or uneven coverage in most reference areas, although recent publications (and online databases) fill some of the lacunae in some states. Louisiana, Ohio, and Virginia are among the few states with comprehensive, indexed listings of their state publications. Reliance on local reference tools in lieu of cataloging is not a viable alternative in most states.

The idea of handling home-state documents in a special collection (which might be either a state collection or a documents collection) and out-of-state documents in another fashion is possible. The fact that a library receives more home-state documents than out-of-state documents might form the basis for a differentiation in handling within the library.

Finally, the inclusion of in-state documents in a special state collection is an alternative not practical for federal documents. Every state has libraries that maintain special state collections. In fact, union lists of these collections are compiled in some states, such as Louisiana and Maine. The state is a small enough jurisdiction to permit assembling materials relating to it. The convenience of having both primary sources (state publications) and secondary sources (texts and journals) in one location is important to many users.

If state documents are integrated into the general library collection, they are brought to the attention of the user by subject. Documents acquired in a subject field selection process are often handled without special "document" treatment.

A documents collection integrated with the general library collection meets one of the primary considerations in the handing of documents: ready availability. Writing about local documents, a Michigan librarian stated the rule that "documents must be available and accessible during all hours in which the library is open for service."[9]

---

8. David W. Parish, *State Government Reference Publications: An Annotated Bibliography,* 2d ed. (Littleton, Colo.: Libraries Unlimited, 1981).

9. Dianne L. Bish, "On Local Documents: Local Policy and Procedure, Part III," *Red Tape* no. 9 (August–September 1980): 4.

SURVEYS ON LIBRARY HANDLING

Two published accounts of the handling of home-state documents show that the separate document collection arrangement is the most widely used. The more comprehensive survey was made in 1973 by Paula Rosenkoetter, a student at the University of Missouri library school. She reported on responses from 122 libraries selected because of a known or presumed interest in state documents of their own state:

> 57.4%—separate documents collection
> 21.3%—in main collection
> 12.3%—divided between documents collection and main collection
> 9 %—separate historical collection.[10]

A report limited to state libraries made in 1966 by Mary Schell revealed a slightly different pattern, although separate document collections had the highest percentage, and separate state collections, the lowest.[11] Based on replies received from over three-fourths of the states and converted to percentages, Schell's findings were:

> 40 %—separate documents collection
> 17.5%—in main collection
> 22.5%—divided between documents collection and main collection
> 20 %—separate state collection.

One other report on the handling of home-state documents, limited to a single state, gives a contrary account. In Michigan only one of thirty-nine libraries responding to a survey had a separate documents collection.[12]

The debate chronicled by Waldo, at least in the mind of one library educator, should be over. Peter Hernon's book on public access does not discuss the question of separate treatment as an issue, but premises the entire text on the idea that documents should be "mainstreamed." In his concluding chapter Hernon observes:

> Mainstreaming government publications implies increased awareness, improved services, tighter bibliographic control, improved institutional status for documents, and better collections; in short, mainstreaming suggests integration—bibliographically, administratively, and service-wise. Mainstreaming has not yet received the national attention it deserves, although a number of practicing documents librarians are consciously

10. Paula Rosenkoetter, "Treatment of State Documents in Libraries," *Government Publications Review* 1 (Winter 1973): 120.

11. Mary Schell, "Acquisition, Handling and Servicing in State Libraries," *Library Trends* 15 (July 1966): 138–39.

12. "The Government Documents Survey of the Wayne Oakland Library Federation," *Red Tape* no. 7 (March–April 1980): 6.

attempting to "mainstream" government documents in their specific library setting.[13]

With the new technologies now being used in libraries, the basic issues observed by Waldo are becoming less important. Specialized catalogs and indexes can now be online, the expense of complete cataloging can be reduced by copying cataloging data already in a bibliographic utility, and delays in processing can be minimized by computerized check-in procedures. This technological progress, as it expands to the documents field, exposes more librarians to the world of documents and makes documents less of a specialized category and less of a mystery.

Standards

This section looks at statements on state documents that have been formally adopted by national organizations. Such statements may be standards, guidelines, or rules and regulations.

LIBRARY FUNCTIONS AT THE STATE LEVEL

Standards for the state documents of the state in which they originate are part of the *Standards for Library Functions at the State Level* adopted by the Association of Specialized and Cooperative Library Agencies of the American Library Association. They have been revised over the years and the 1985 edition is the third version. The statements relevant to state documents are standards 39 and 51:

> 39. The state shall maintain a complete collection of its own state government and of current documents of comparable states . . . .[14]

Standard 39 does not have an exact parallel in the earlier version of the standards. The 1970 edition referred to "a central depository" and required that "depository libraries should be designated throughout the state so that the people will have ready access to state publications."[15] The 1985 version refers to the development of regional centers within the state. Standard 39 includes in its subsection a statement that "a checklist of state documents should be published periodically by the state."

13. Peter Hernon and Charles R. McClure, *Public Access to Government Information: Issues, Trends, and Strategies* (Norwood, N.J.: Ablex Publishing, 1984), 404.

14. American Library Association, Association of Specialized and Cooperative Library Agencies, Subcommittee for Library Functions at the State Level, *Standards for Library Functions at the State Level*, 3d ed. (Chicago: ALA, 1985), 13.

15. American Library Association, American Association of State Libraries, Standards Revision Committee, *Standards for Library Functions at the State Level*, rev. ed. (Chicago: ALA, 1970), 36.

51. Every state shall make clear administrative and legal provision for each of the following library-related responsibilities at the state level . . . (7) bibliographical control and distribution of state documents and publications . . . .[16]

Bibliographical control presumably encompasses retrospective checklists. In the 1970 version, the reference was more specific: "if no checklist of earlier publications has been made, the depository library should oversee such a project." The duty to issue a current checklist is stated in Standard 39.

STATE DOCUMENTS GUIDELINES

Other ALA-approved guidelines include those drafted by the State and Local Documents Task Force of the ALA Government Documents Round Table. The most widely known of these is the first one, "Guidelines for Minimum State Servicing of State Documents," adopted in 1975.[17] These servicing guidelines were designed to set forth the state-level tasks that should be undertaken in each state. They specify the obligations that some state agency in each state should assume; they set forth the minimum requirements that each state should observe to provide access, bibliographic control, use and preservation of its state documents. The servicing guidelines provide for a definitive collection within the state; distribution within the state, outside the state, and to the Library of Congress; a checklist of documents; an authority list of state agencies; and a full-time professional administrator. Ideally, definitive collection ensures preservation; the distribution system, availability to the public; the lists, bibliographic control; and the administrative personnel, access and use. Critics note that there is no specific statement on the duty to provide access and availability and that, in a democracy, the public has an inherent right to such material. The criticism is legitimate. At the time these guidelines were drafted, the underlying principle that service to the public was the goal seemed obvious.

Four other sets of guidelines originating in the State and Local Documents Task Force received ALA approval in 1982. "Guidelines for State Documents Checklists," "Guidelines for Inputting State Documents into Data Bases," "Guidelines for State Publications Depository Legislation," and "Guidelines for State Distribution Center Activities" are discussed in other chapters.

Guidelines for the handling of documents within an individual depository library have not been adopted nationally. Individual states have made rules and regulations for the local depository libraries, which can

16. American Library Association, *Standards*, 3d ed., 20.
17. See Appendix A, "Guidelines for Minimum State Servicing of State Documents."

be examined in the text by Lane and in the *Documents on Documents Collection*.[18]

ARCHIVISTS' STANDARDS

State archivists traditionally care for the unpublished records of government agencies. The standards adopted by the Society of American Archivists extend this custodial function to include state publications as well as manuscript records. The preservation of state publications can, according to the archivists' standards, be assumed by a library. Some libraries retain permanent, noncirculating copies of all state documents. In some states the depository legislation requires that documents "shall remain on permanent deposit" (Arkansas) or that certain libraries "retain permanently at least one copy of each document distributed by the center for the purpose of historical research" (South Dakota). Library maintenance of a historical collection does not necessarily mean that the collection will be arranged by the provenance of the material and may pose an additional disadvantage for the historian if the library is not located near the archives unit. Reproduction of a complete file of state documents in a microformat is one solution to this dilemma. The observation of James B. Childs that documents constitute a borderline area between archives and libraries indicates a need for cooperation between archivists and librarians in the preservation of state documents.[19] In addition, the standards provide that in the absence of a state checklist, the archival agency of the state should prepare one.[20]

Legislation Affecting Libraries

State documents librarians have an interest in certain areas of legislation, including (1) distribution and exchange laws, (2) depository library legislation, (3) state printing laws, and (4) laws and resolutions on the issuance of state publications by state agencies.

18. Margaret T. Lane, *State Publications and Depository Libraries* (Westport, Conn.: Greenwood Press, 1981); Margaret T. Lane, comp., *Documents on Documents Collection, 1973–1979* and *1980–1983* (Chicago: American Library Association, Government Documents Round Table, State and Local Documents Task Force, 1984–1985). The 1973–1979 Collection is in ERIC microfiche (ED 247 940). The 1980–1983 Collection is in ERIC microfiche (ED 263 923). The current materials may be borrowed from Lauri Sebo, University Research Library, University of California, Los Angeles, CA 90024.

19. James B. Childs, "Government Publications (Documents)" in *Encyclopedia of Library and Information Science*, vol. 10. (New York: M. Dekker, 1968+), 42.

20. Ernest Posner, *American State Archives* (Chicago: University of Chicago Press, 1964), 358.

DISTRIBUTION AND EXCHANGE LAWS

Historically, state documents collections were based on distribution and exchange laws. Some laws provided for distribution of state publications to certain libraries. Sometimes the libraries were named specifically in the legislation. The statutes providing that multiple copies of certain titles should be sent to a designated library for use in the library and for exchange are an offshoot of the library distribution statutes. These statutes placed a duty to distribute on the secretary of state or another agency and related mostly to legal publications and serial publications. The statutes not only named the class of libraries (or the specific libraries) to which distribution was to be made but also named the publications themselves—the acts of the legislature, the journals of the house and the senate, or the reports of the supreme court. A statute authorizing a new publication may include such a section providing for special distribution.

A recent spin-off of this type of legislation provides restrictions on distribution of publications by state agencies. The restrictions recognize that agencies in the executive branch issue and distribute publications, a fact not addressed by earlier distribution statutes. The restrictions may be very broad and prohibit all distribution except in response to a specific request, or they may require annual purging of mailing lists. A special restriction provided in the legislation of Maryland prohibits distribution to members of the General Assembly except in response to special dispensation or specific requests.[21] The harshness of this prohibition is tempered by the requirement that a list of titles be given to the legislators to advise them of the availability of newly issued publications. These economy-in-distribution statutes are an outgrowth of the proliferation of publications since the advent of mimeograph and copying machines.

When depository legislation was drafted in Nebraska, a computer program made it possible to identify all the laws requiring state agencies to distribute publications. These laws were amended to include the new clearinghouse in the distribution.[22] When other states have statutes in a computer database, they, too, can make a similar statutory search.

Not all state documents librarians are affected by the distribution and exchange laws of their state. A small public library, not within one of the groups favored in the law, concerns itself with the distribution laws only to the extent of knowing where to turn for an interlibrary loan.

DEPOSITORY LEGISLATION

Depository legislation provides more fringe benefits for small libraries not designated depository libraries than exchange and distribution legis-

21. *The Annotated Code of the Public General Laws of Maryland, State Government* (Charlottesville, Va.: Michie, 1984), section 2-1312.
22. Dallas Y. Shaffer, "State Document Legislation Nebraska: A Case Study," *Government Publications Review* 1 (Fall 1973): 22.

lation. The mere existence of a dynamic depository program in a state means increased access and availability even for the smallest library: access because the program is supported by a checklist that identifies the available publications, and availability because the depository libraries often have a duty to provide interlibrary loan.

For libraries fortunate enough to enjoy depository status, the primary benefit is trouble-free, automatic receipt. In a state with a truly comprehensive system, the assurance that *all* documents are arriving is a distinct advantage. However, such a state of affairs is a utopia that is seldom, if ever, found.

The elements of depository legislation are set out in the ALA GO-DORT State and Local Documents Task Force Guidelines.[23] A commentary explains and expands the guidelines. Detailed discussion of the legislation guidelines is in Chapter 5.

STATE PRINTING LAWS

The manner in which a state handles state printing is of interest primarily to citizens of that particular state. Printing laws can encompass not only the actual procurement of the printing, but also the control of what items may be printed. State documents librarians should acquaint themselves with the method of procuring state printing in their own state and should know whether there is an agency that exercises control over the amount of state printing or that has the authority to condense or edit state publications.

A few states, California and Kansas for example, maintain their own printing plants. Other states have printing contracts for various classes of materials, and in some states the individual agencies may enter into contracts for individual publications.

Standards for state printing have been suggested in several states. The South Dakota *Guidelines for Printing and Publishing South Dakota Public Documents* gives detailed rules for state printing and includes examples of appropriate title pages.[24] The Oklahoma *Manual for Publications Officers* has a section on standard format for state publications which suggests proper title page information and format and gives examples of complete and incomplete title page information. The Oklahoma Rules and Regulations, section 204, reads:

> *204 Standard Format for State Publications*
>   To achieve bibliographic control of state government publications and to assure that the identity of a publication can be ascertained in terms of the issuing authority, author, and subject matter sufficient to distin-

23. See Appendix A, "Guidelines for State Publications Depository Legislation."
24. South Dakota Public Documents Study Commission, *Guidelines for Printing & Publishing* (Pierre, S.Dak.: 1972). In *Docs on Docs,* 1973–1979, item SD:M1.

guish it from other publications, the following information shall be included on the title page or other suitable place near the beginning of each state publication required to be deposited with the Publications Clearinghouse:

(1) full name of the issuing agency, including the division or subdivision responsible for publication, and the parent body;

(2) name of any personal author to whom credit is intended to be given;

(3) title of the publication; and

(4) date and place of publication.

For Periodicals and Serials also include:

(5) frequency of issue;

(6) volume and number of issue; and

(7) date of issue.[25]

LAWS AND RESOLUTIONS AFFECTING STATE AGENCIES

Laws and resolutions that affect state agencies have been discussed earlier in the chapters on state agencies and distribution. They are repeated here so that the different, various kinds of legislation that state documents librarians should monitor and be aware of can be looked at as a group. The laws that require a state agency to issue a report, to include a printing statement, and to forego issuing a report are included in this group.

A simple statement that an agency should publish a report, if it is found in general legislation pertaining to an agency, is not only difficult to spot as it proceeds through the legislature but also hard to locate after the legislation is passed. Such legislation may include a mention of distribution requirements for the report. The general index to the statutes may not index these clauses under the word *distribution*, and the publication may not even be called a report.

Sometimes issuance of a state report or publication is dictated by a federal agency or by federal legislation. State legislation must take such circumstances into account. A printing budget for the state youth commission, for example, must provide for the printing of a quarterly news report if the federal government requires such a report.

Laws providing for the inclusion of a printing statement on each publication are of fairly recent origin. Florida was probably one of the first states to require this. These laws have particular relevance for editors of state checklists. Citation to the section of the law authorizing the issuance of the publication is an important part of the statement and if issuance is based on a waiver or exception, the printing statement highlights this

25. Oklahoma Department of Libraries, Oklahoma Publications Clearinghouse, *Manual for Publications Officers* (Oklahoma City: the Department, November 1984), Appendix F, p.3. In *Docs on Docs*, item OK85:H.

irregularity. Printing statements may also include a statement of the cost of the publication. The Louisiana statement used when the 1948 law was in effect was: "This public document was published at a cost . . . to provide Louisiana citizens with an up to date bibliography listing of state documents, under the authority of special exception by the Division of Administration." The Oklahoma cost statement reads, "This publication is printed and issued by the Oklahoma Department of Libraries as authorized by 65 O.S.1981, sec. 3-110."

Another special type of legislation relates to the distribution of publications. In Chapter 4 this legislation was cited as a cost-controlling device. Such legislation provides that no distribution shall be made to legislators, or that no distribution shall be made without a specific request. Annual purging of mailing lists, another cost-cutting measure found in some state statutes, is also discussed in Chapter 4.

Finally, the state documents librarian should be on the lookout for legislation that permits the nonissuance of reports. For example, in 1972, Louisiana passed a resolution which suspended the laws requiring state agencies to prepare, print or publish, and distribute annual or biennial reports.[26] More recently, in 1986, Louisiana passed a package of individual acts repealing the requirement that annual reports be published. It was considered politically inexpedient to oppose this legislation, which had the purported intent of cutting costs, particularly distribution costs, in a time of economic austerity. Librarians in the state are monitoring the effect of this legislation and are studying ways of ensuring that the information formerly in the discontinued reports continues to be available.[27]

Types of Library Collections

A state documents collection may encompass, at a minimum, the contiguous states, or at the other extreme, all the states. On the other hand, the collection of documents of the home-state is often thought of by the name of the state (the Louisiana collection or the Texas collection). Much in the preceding chapters has concerned home-state collections, mainly because more libraries have such collections. Collections of out-of-state documents, described first in this section, are found principally in state libraries and large research libraries. Depository collections, which are usually in-state collections, are the other major type of collection discussed.

COMPREHENSIVE COLLECTIONS

Today the two major fifty-state collections of current state documents in the United States are those at the Library of Congress in Washington

26. Louisiana, Legislature, Senate Concurrent Resolution, no. 99, 1972 Regular Session.
27. The twenty-four acts are indexed under the term *reports* in West's *Louisiana Session Law Service.*

and at the Center for Research Libraries in Chicago. The collection at the Research Libraries of the New York Public Library can also be considered a comprehensive collection, particularly for older state documents.

The Library of Congress collects state documents for the use of the Congress because it is the library for the Congress. In 1910, the Library of Congress began a listing of its state document acquisitions, primarily to acknowledge receipt of the publications. Although this listing, the *Monthly Checklist of State Publications,* is always cited with a deprecating remark that the listing is not a complete one, the *Monthly Checklist* is, nevertheless, a remarkable publication. For 1985, 28,168 titles were listed.[28] In an effort to achieve coverage comprehensiveness, the *Monthly Checklist* lists any publications not previously listed which are five years old or less. Thus publications which for one reason or another were not listed at the time of their publication can still be included within a later *Monthly Checklist* issue. The Library of Congress has encouraged the enactment of state legislation requiring the forwarding of state publications to the Library and has published a model act for this purpose.[29]

Acquisition for inclusion in the *Monthly Checklist* is comprehensive in scope and excludes only legislative bills, blank forms, press releases, announcements of meetings and programs, and minor educational materials. The Library of Congress card number within an entry indicates that an item has been added to the permanent collections of the Library of Congress.

The Library of Congress does not keep all the documents sent for listing in the *Monthly Checklist.* The Library of Congress acquires *and retains* administrative reports, statutory reports, planning and policy statements, and other substantive reports. The Library also retains individual publications that contain important information on current events or that provide a state perspective on issues which are of national importance.

In order to permit a second selection opportunity, the new Government Publications Section established a special state documents shelving area for monographs that were not initially selected for the general collection. This special collection begins with the January 1980 issue of the *Monthly Checklist* and uses the *Monthly Checklist* item numbers to label and identify the publications. The librarians in the Government Publications Section record the date of each use on each piece as an aid to the reevaluation that is to take place after five years.[30]

The Center for Research Libraries has an active acquisitions program for all publications of the fifty states. According to a 1981 report:

28. The number of publications listed is recorded cumulatively for the year on the last page of each issue.

29. "Model Law," *Monthly Checklist of State Publications* 60 (December 1969): iv.

30. "Introduction," *Monthly Checklist of State Publications* 77 (August 1986).

The Center receives depository shipments from 24 states: Alaska, California, Connecticut, Illinois, Indiana, Iowa, Kansas, Louisiana, Massachusetts, Michigan, Mississippi, Missouri, Montana, Nebraska, New Mexico, New Jersey, New York, Oklahoma, Oregon, South Dakota, Texas, Utah, Virginia, and Washington. In addition, documents are received directly from issuing agencies, ordered from state checklists and the *Monthly Checklist of State Publications*, and accepted as gifts from member libraries.[31]

The state documents collection at the Center was first established in 1952 and is, perhaps, for recent years, more comprehensive than that at the Library of Congress. Publications are not screened by a selecting officer, with the result that all items sent pursuant to depository programs are retained. In addition, any publication required by a member library is secured if at all possible. The statement in the Center's research guide is:

> Since January 1952 the Center has collected on a continuing basis and as comprehensively as possible all documents of all 50 U.S. states and territories, and of their various departments and agencies, except session laws and compiled statutes. In addition, well over 100,000 volumes of pre-1952 state documents have been deposited by member libraries.[32]

Other exclusions recognized by the Center are publications of colleges and universities, and publications of state historical societies, horticultural societies and similar agencies which receive little or no state support.

The Center retains the agricultural experiment station publications it receives, but does not claim or solicit them. Of the exceptions listed, only the session laws and compiled statutes are clearly within a rigorous definition of state publications, and even these are an exception in some libraries. Publications of colleges and universities, such as catalogs, university press, and newsletters, are a relatively common exclusion from the broad definition, as are publications of historical societies and the like.

In contrast to the practice at the Library of Congress, which catalogs items added to its collections, the Center for Research Libraries checks in the publications and then shelves them by the name of the issuing agency.

The Research Libraries of the New York Public Library (NYPL) have an outstanding collection of state documents. In 1935 this collection was

---

31. Ann Germany, "Center for Research Libraries," in Margaret T. Lane, comp., *State Publications: Depository Distribution and Bibliographical Programs*, State and Local Documents Task Force, Government Documents Round Table, American Library Association. Texas State Publications Clearinghouse, Documents Monograph Series no.2A ([Austin]: Texas State Library, August 1981), 46–47. Telephone interview with Ann Germany, Documents Librarian, Center for Research Libraries, November 6, 1986, updated the number of states making depository shipments to twenty-six.

32. "Research Materials Available from the Center for Research Libraries" (Chicago: Center for Research Libraries, 1980), 4–5.

described as "undoubtedly the most complete collection [of American state documents] available in the United States."[33] The NYPL collection serves as a supplement to the Library of Congress collections for retrospective items that the Library of Congress has not added to its collections. The collection at the Center for Research Libraries, because it was started as a current collection in 1952, is not consistently strong for earlier years.

It may be worthwhile to search the documents catalog of NYPL for titles previously unknown in a given state, unless, as is true in Louisiana, the NYPL holdings are already recorded in the state bibliography. It is an expensive, forty-volume set, which can be brought up to date through RLIN, the cataloging utility into which the NYPL enters its bibliographic records.[34]

OTHER COLLECTIONS OF NOTE

Few other libraries maintain comprehensive state collections today. In 1966, Robert B. Downs listed six state libraries (Connecticut, Massachusetts, Nebraska, Pennsylvania, Rhode Island, and Tennessee), the University of Illinois library, the New York Public Library, and the University of North Carolina library as collecting state documents from all the states. Libraries that collected on a regional basis included:

Northeast—New Hampshire State Library
New England—University of Maine and Harvard
Appalachian region—West Virginia University
Southeast—University of Georgia
West—California State Library, University of California at Berkeley, University of Colorado, Oregon (13 states), and Washington State (11 states)
Northwest—University of Colorado.

Downs also reported that Texas State, Virginia State, and Indiana University libraries collected documents from surrounding states.

Special mention must also be made, according to Downs, of the comprehensive collection at the University of Chicago library in the area of social sciences, legislative materials at Harvard, legislative and legal materials at the University of North Carolina, and the collection at the American Antiquarian Society in Massachusetts, which is comprehensive through 1876.[35]

33. A. F. Kuhlman, "The Need for a Comprehensive Check-list Bibliography of American State Publications," *Library Quarterly* 5 (January 1935): 37.
34. New York Public Library, Economics Division, *Catalog of Government Publications in the Research Libraries* (Boston: G. K. Hall, 1972). 40 v. Reviewed by Philip Van De Voorde in *Government Publications Review* 5, no. 3 (1978): 376–77.
35. Robert B. Downs, "Government Publications in American Libraries," *Library Trends* 15 (July 1966): 189–91.

Listed consistently over the last fifty years as having strong collections of documents within their state of origin are:

Alabama State Department of Archives and History
Georgia State Library
Massachusetts State Library
New Jersey State Library
Pennsylvania State Library
Vermont State Library
State Historical Society of Wisconsin.

These eight libraries were listed by Downs, White, Casey, and the ALA GODORT State and Local Documents Task Force survey.[36] No other libraries appeared in all four compilations. Of these eight libraries, the Massachusetts State Library and the State Historical Society of Wisconsin also have strong out-of-state collections.

DECLINE OF MULTISTATE COLLECTIONS

Historically many states had multistate collections. Reasons for the decline of these include the increase in quantity of these publications, the difficulties in acquiring them, the increase in size of the individual items and a reputation for being lesser used publications.

It is particularly in the executive branch that the increase in the quantity of publications is noticed. Individual agencies are producing more titles, and the number of agencies within the executive branch has grown. Independent agencies, which are also producing many publications, have also been established in various states.

With an increase in the number of agencies, difficulties in acquiring the publications increase. Formerly, when publications were largely legislative and judicial, exchanges could be arranged on a volume-by-volume basis. Acquiring publications of the executive branch is more difficult not only because exchanges are less likely, but also because the multitude of executive agencies makes establishing contact with issuing agencies arduous.

In sets of session laws the volumes get fatter and fatter toward the end of the shelf with recent volumes, indicating the increased amount of

---

36. Ibid., 178–94; L. D. White, "State Document Centers," *ALA Bulletin* 26 (August 1932): 553–55; Genevieve M. Casey and Edith Phillips, *Management and Use of State Documents in Indiana*, Research Report no. 2 (Detroit: Office of Urban Library Research, Wayne State University, 1969). ERIC microfiche ED 046 473; Margaret T. Lane, comp., *State Publications: Depository Distribution and Bibliographical Programs*, State and Local Documents Task Force, Government Documents Round Table, American Library Association, Texas State Publications Clearinghouse, Documents Monograph Series, nos. 2 and 2A ([Austin]: Texas State Library, 1981). No. 2 is also in ERIC microfiche ED 195 283.

material. For instance, the Louisiana session laws doubled in size between 1950 and 1985.

The reputation that state publications have for being little used usually is more a justification for a decision to limit collecting than one based on an increase in titles, the difficulty in acquisition, or the greater amount of shelf space required. Ray O. Hummel, Jr., writing in 1968 about state library collections, said,

> Most state libraries which formerly had acquired nearly all documents of other states found that many were not really needed. Acquisition policies became much more selective . . . . Part of this change in policy was due to regional storage plans, such as the Center for Research Libraries in Chicago, but in most cases the libraries simply had found that the material was not being used.[37]

The survey by Weech of studies on documents use indicates that most such studies are limited to federal documents and that document use at all levels of government should be studied. Weech found that the studies surveyed suggested a difference in state and federal use patterns.[38]

The 1980 study by Gary Purcell, "The Use of Tennessee State Government Publications," surveyed users in ten Tennessee libraries, drawn from public, academic and special library fields.[39] Purcell found limited public awareness of the nature and value of Tennessee state publications and a tendency of the users to use recent publications.

Three 1983 studies in the special state information issue of *Government Publications Review* are surveys based on responses by librarians.[40] Because they include findings on the relative use of specific kinds of reference access, they are discussed in Chapter 8.

Libraries that acquire state publications in particular subject areas choose to do so because they recognize that state documents can expand a subject collection with current, authoritative information.

Another criterion used in building out-of-state collections is type of publication. Parish's book is based on this principle. The nine types of publications distinguished by Parish are guides:

37. Ray O. Hummel, Jr., "State Library Collections—Past, Present, Future," *Southeastern Librarian* 18 (Spring 1968): 26.

38. Terry L. Weech, "The Use of Government Publications: A Selected Review of the Literature," *Government Publications Review* 5, no. 2 (1978): 183.

39. Gary Purcell, "The Use of Tennessee State Government Publications," *Tennessee Librarian* 32 (Spring 1980): 20–31.

40. Barbara J. Ford and Yuri Nakata, "Reference Use of State Government Information in Academic Libraries," *Government Publications Review* 10 (March–April 1983): 189–99; Nancy P. Johnson, "Reference Use of State Government Information in Law Libraries," *Government Publications Review* 10 (March–April 1983): 201–11; Gary R. Purcell, "Reference Use of State Government Information in Public Libraries," *Government Publications Review* 10 (March–April 1983): 173–87.

1. Official state bibliography
2. Blue books
3. Legislative manuals and related references
4. State government finances
5. Statistical abstracts and other data sources
6. Directories
7. Tourist guides
8. Audiovisual guides, atlases, and maps
9. Bibliographies and general references.[41]

DEPOSITORY LIBRARIES

In texts on federal documents, it is customary to include a chapter on the Government Printing Office as the agency that administers the depository library program, followed by chapters on the depository libraries and the handling of documents in those libraries. Here, in a text on state documents, the fifty agencies that administer state documents and the programs they administer are so diverse that a detailed description is not possible. Moreover, the administering agencies in the state programs are themselves depository libraries which adds to the confusion. Furthermore, in most states, publications are of the kind that federal documents librarians call "non-GPO"; that is, they must be acquired for distribution from the individual agencies.

For those who issue state publications, depository systems provide a convenient, economical distribution system. For the distribution center, the depository legislation forms the structure of its operations. For the general public, depository legislation provides prompt, convenient, easy access to the publications of the government, assuming, of course, that the system operates at the optimum level and has the active and concerned support of state agencies, the distribution center, and the depository libraries.

Depository library programs are a special way of providing access to state publications. These programs not only provide for geographical distribution throughout the state, but also ensure that representative, basic collections of state documents are available to all. This section of this text covers depository legislation, creation and administration of depository library systems, characteristics of depository libraries, amount and kinds of publications distributed, responsibilities of depository libraries and impact of a depository library system on participants and others. The advantages of a depository program to state agencies, depository libraries, other libraries, and the public can be noticed throughout the discussion. Handling in the individual libraries and the costs and procedures to organize the documents for use are discussed in Chapter 9 on processing.

41. Parish, *State Government Reference Publications*, 2d ed., 7.

History

Depository legislation for state documents dates back at least to 1905 when the Wisconsin law provided for distribution of state publications to libraries that could "suitably care for and advantageously use copies of the public documents printed at the expense of this state."[42] A change in emphasis came about in 1945 with the adoption of the California legislation. The California law began with a statement: "It is the policy of the State of California to make freely available to its inhabitants all state publications by distribution to libraries."[43] The idea that people have a right to know what their government is doing is basic to recent depository legislation. Washington legislation states this succinctly: "Utilize the depository system to permit citizens economical and convenient access to state publications."[44]

Designation

The way depository libraries are designated and the criteria governing the designation may be prescribed by statute or may be determined by a library agency. In contrast to the federal law, which provides for congressional designation, the state laws, with the exception of Tennessee, provide for designation either by statute or by a library agency. Nakata and Kopec identify this as a "potential for quality control" inasmuch as the designating agency, usually the state library, knows the qualifications of the libraries in the state.[45] In Tennessee, the governor may name depository libraries under a 1917 law, and, in fact, two Tennessee libraries were designated in 1974 (Memphis State University) and in 1979 (East Tennessee State University).[46] Washington and Florida have appeal procedures if a designation is denied.

Types

Types of libraries that may become depositories vary from state to state.[47] Public libraries and public academic libraries are candidates in all

42. *West's Wisconsin Statutes Annotated* (St. Paul, Minn.: West Publishing, 1979), section 43.05.

43. *West's Annotated California Codes, Government Code* (St. Paul, Minn.: West Publishing, 1980), section 14900.

44. *West's Revised Code of Washington Annotated* (St. Paul, Minn.: West Publishing, 1987), section 40.06.020 in 1987 pocket part.

45. Yuri Nakata and Karen Kopec, "State and Local Government Publications," *Drexel Library Quarterly* 16 (October 1980): 42.

46. "Letter from Winfield Dunn, Governor, to Dr. Billy M. Jones, President, Memphis State University, May 8, 1974, designating the University as a depository for state documents," in *Docs on Docs*, 1980–1983, item TN:Bl; "Letter from Ray Blanton, Governor, to Dr. Arthur H. DeRosier, Jr., President, East Tennessee State University, designating the Sherrod Library of the University as a depository for state documents, January 8, 1979," in *Docs on Docs*, 1980–1983, item TN:B2.

47. Lane, *State Publications and Depository Libraries*, 172–73.

states. Private academic libraries are within the program in most states. Special libraries may become depositories in some states; Idaho special libraries are within the distribution program in Idaho. California, Florida, and Oregon have special provisions permitting law libraries to become depositories. These states brought law libraries into their depository systems earlier than the federal government did: Florida in 1941, California in 1965, Oregon in 1971, and the federal government in 1978. A list of sections from legislation specifying types of libraries which may be depositories is found in Lane.[48] The types of libraries that may become depositories is sometimes left to the discretion of the agency that administers the depository program; this is true in Connecticut.

Table 4. *Number of Depository Libraries in Rank Order*

STATE DEPOSITORIES IN RANK ORDER	NUMBER OF STATE DEPOSITORIES[a]	POPULATION IN RANK ORDER[b]	TOTAL AREA IN RANK ORDER[c]	EDUCATIONAL INSTITUTIONS IN RANK ORDER[d]
California	149	1	3	2
New York	98	2	30	1
Pennsylvania	60	4	33	3
Ohio	54	6	35	6
New Jersey	53	9	46	20
Michigan	50	8	23	10
Texas	48	3	2	5
Washington	46	20	20	24
Wisconsin	44	16	26	19
Iowa	41	27	25	21
Louisiana	38	19	31	33
Minnesota	38	21	12	17
Missouri	37	15	19	9
Oregon	34	30	10	27
Mississippi	32	31	32	30
Illinois	28	5	24	4
Florida	24	7	22	11
Kansas	24	32	14	23
Arkansas	20	33	27	31
Colorado	20	28	8	26
New Hampshire	19	42	44	37
Idaho	18	41	13	47
New Mexico	17	37	5	39
Oklahoma	16	26	18	28
Alaska	14	50	1	43
Montana	14	44	4	42

48. Ibid., 185–87.

Number

The number of depositories per state also varies widely, as shown in Table 4. A 1984 survey by Marilyn Moody counted 1097 in-state depository libraries and 175 out-of-state.[49] The numbers range from 149 in California and 98 in New York to none in Alabama, Arizona, Kentucky, North Carolina, and Vermont. Georgia, Rhode Island, and Wyoming reported that only the state library was a depository. Over half the states send to some out-of-state libraries, usually the Library of Congress and the Center for

Table 4. (continued)

STATE DEPOSITORIES IN RANK ORDER	NUMBER OF STATE DEPOSITORIES[a]	POPULATION IN RANK ORDER[b]	TOTAL AREA IN RANK ORDER[c]	EDUCATIONAL INSTITUTIONS IN RANK ORDER[d]
Connecticut	13	25	48	25
Maryland	13	18	42	22
Utah	13	36	11	44
Indiana	12	12	38	15
Maine	12	38	39	34
Nebraska	12	35	15	36
South Carolina	11	24	40	18
Virginia	11	14	36	16
Nevada	9	43	7	49
South Dakota	7	45	16	41
Tennessee	6	17	34	13
Massachusetts	5	11	45	8
North Dakota	5	46	17	40
Hawaii	3	39	47	46
Georgia	1	13	21	12
Rhode Island	1	40	50	45
Wyoming	1	49	9	50
Alabama	0	22	29	14
Arizona	0	29	6	32
Delaware	0	47	49	48
Kentucky	0	23	37	29
North Carolina	0	10	28	7
Vermont	0	48	43	38
West Virginia	0	34	41	35

[a] Survey by Marilyn K. Moody, Iowa State University, April 1984 (unpublished).
[b] Statistical Abstract of the U.S.: 1986, 106th ed. (Washington, D.C.: GPO, 1985), 10–11.
[c] Ibid., 194.
[d] Book of the States, 1986–87 edition, v. 26 (Lexington, Ky.: The Council of State Governments, 1986), 344.

49. Marilyn K. Moody, "Survey of State Depositories," Iowa State University, April 1984.

Research Libraries. Overseas depositories include England (for Illinois, Louisiana, New York, and Ohio publications), Canada (Alaska and New York), Australia (New York), and Japan (Michigan).

Termination

The right to terminate depository status may be with the depository libraries or the distribution center or both. If a depository library exercises the right to terminate its designation, an appropriate notice may be required (in Connecticut, it is three months). In Alaska, either party may give six months' notice.

Responsibilities

The general obligations that depositories assume are usually stated in the depository library law. Specific, detailed duties are customarily outlined in rules and regulations. Duties may include an obligation to receive, provide service, circulate, give interlibrary loan service, keep, bind, publicize, make available, maintain records, claim, catalog, permit inspections, attend meetings, or supply information.

In a depository library, the handling of the documents upon receipt must conform to the depository library law of a given state. If rules and regulations have been adopted for the depository program, these also must be observed. Provisions requiring that documents be made available would, by implication at least, impose an obligation on the library to have a check-in procedure to record what had been received. Occasionally the law or the rules and regulations require cataloging. This is true in Illinois, New Hampshire, and several other states.

Special restrictions on depository libraries in Montana and Washington State require that all contacts with state agencies be made through the distribution center. This kind of restriction is at the same time a limitation of a given library's right to acquire freely and an economy device designed to make the depository library system more attractive to state agencies. Such a restriction is an impediment that results in serious inconvenience to the library if the distribution center does not acquire or handle all documents promptly. For the state agencies, such a restriction is an advantage because it reduces the number of requests by channeling them through a single source.

After state documents are received at the depository library, various additional requirements may be involved. Most of these requirements are common sense, but some are required by regulation in some states. The duty to open packages, to claim missing items, to record receipt, to catalog, and to shelve all coincide with normal library procedures. Specific statements on the duty to proceed promptly with the absorption of the depository material into the library collection are a pragmatic recognition of past delays; depository libraries have, in times of stress, been known to postpone opening the depository packages because the packages can be easily identified from the wrapping and address labels. Unlike a book dealer pressing for payment, the document distributor does not follow up after making the shipment. The derelictions of libraries in the processing of depository shipments have decreased in recent years, a change possibly attributable to the imposition of specific regulations or a general upgrading of awareness of the importance of these duties. The duty to catalog is not a common one. New Hampshire is one state that imposes this duty, presumably to emphasize the importance of processing the documents in the same manner as other books.

Reference Service

Reference service for state documents—that is, providing information and assistance as needed—is basic to their use, which in turn is the reason for their being in the library. For depository libraries, reference service is the most important function. The duty to provide assistance in the use of state publications is frequently stated in depository regulations. Even when this duty is not stated expressly, it can be inferred from the general tenor of other duties; for example, the duty to make state publications available. At least for first-time users, availability in the broad meaning of the word, is possible only with assistance.

Good reference service for state documents for one's own state requires a specialized knowledge of the history of the state, the structure of its government, its constitution, and the many supplementary, secondary sources of information. Librarians familiar with the state publications of one state give reference service for out-of-state documents on the basis of their familiarity with the documents of that state. Reference service, in its broader aspect of information service, is discussed in more detail in Chapter 8.

Interlibrary loan, as an extension of reference service, is also sometimes mentioned as a specific duty required of depository libraries. State publications, or even government publications in general, are not mentioned directly in the ALA Interlibrary Loan Code.[50]

Interlibrary loan is mentioned specifically in Title 19, *U.S. Code,* as one of the responsibilities of a federal regional depository, and this example is followed in the laws of Montana and Nebraska. In these states, the state library agency is required to provide interlibrary loan service. In Montana this service is to be provided by the state library "to those libraries without depository status," and in Nebraska interlibrary loan service is to encompass local, state, federal, and other governmental publications and be extended to citizens of the state.

It is in the rules and regulations that most states impose interlibrary loan responsibilities on the depository libraries. The statement in the Wisconsin manual is particularly explicit:

---

50. American Library Association, *Interlibrary Loan Code* (Chicago: ALA, 1981).

Depositories should provide access to all Wisconsin public documents, not merely those held in the individual depository collection. Document interloan is thus an integral depository function.[51]

Because of the interlibrary loan obligations imposed by statute and regulation, there has developed in some states a secondary network for borrowing and lending documents that operates outside the framework of a formal interlibrary code. In their book on public access Hernon and McClure mention these "informal channels of communication" and attribute them to a desire to circumvent the ordinary interlibrary loan procedures which may place undue restraints or cumbersome procedures on documents librarians.[52]

Other duties imposed in depository libraries relate to the duty to keep documents that are received through the depository library program. Some depositories collect all documents, and some select the items needed in their collections. Selection may be made by the distribution center, as in Washington State, or may be made by the individual depository libraries. Some states, Missouri for example, require depository libraries to receive at least a basic collection of documents. No state permits selection by individual title or series as the federal government does in its item number scheme. The historical collection depositories, variously designated as full or complete depositories, assume the greatest degree of responsibility for retaining copies of state documents. If permitted by regulations, this obligation may be satisfied by substitution of a microform copy.

In some states maintaining copies of state documents in a depository library means keeping copies in the library; in other states, circulation outside the library is encouraged.

An extension of the duty "to keep" is the duty "to bind" according to the policies of the library for binding other materials. Binding and other means of preservation are one of the topics in Chapter 9 on processing.

Surveys

A collection of reports on depository distribution and bibliography programs was published by the ALA GODORT State and Local Document Task Force in 1980 and 1981 and has been used by several writers.[53] The collected reports supplied information on the following topics: Name of Agency, Legal Authority, Place in State and Parent Organization, Staff, Powers and Duties, Depository Libraries, Documents Distributed, Exchanges and Out-of-State Distribution, Dissemination of Cataloging Data, Microforms, State Agencies and Their Duties under Depository Laws, Cur-

51. Wisconsin, "Manual for Wisconsin Document Depositories," 4. In *Docs on Docs*, 1973–1979, item WI:H.

52. Hernon and McClure, *Public Access to Government Information*, 303.

53. Lane, *State Publications: Depository Distribution*.

rent Checklist, Publications Other than the Checklist, Budget, Outstanding Features of Program, Major Problems of Program, Current Projects Being Emphasized, Workshops, Special Programs, Councils or Advisory Boards, and Hopes for the Future.

The reports vary in length, with some of the longer ones describing the state classification scheme or the preparation of the state checklist in great detail while others are limited to bare factual statements. The section on problems was completed by almost all the states while the "hopes for the future" was a less popular section.

In the area of problems almost half the states reported acquiring the documents as a concern. Learning of the existence of the documents; contacting the state agencies (one state mentioned hundreds of contacts; another referred to the turnover in state agency staff); receiving enough copies ("limited printing" and "limited distribution" and publications produced under special grants were cited as problem areas); and lack of agency cooperation are all parts of the acquisition problem. Lack of agency cooperation was the aspect of acquisition that was most frequently mentioned. One state referred to lack of understanding and another to failure to appoint a liaison. Two states mentioned ongoing efforts to achieve better cooperation.

Lack of staffing funds, time, and space is a problem area known to all librarians. Again, almost half the librarians mentioned problems of this kind. Libraries referring to lack of funds were mostly those in states without a depository system, although two states cited lack of funds for entering documents in a database. Three states mentioned lack of funds available to state agencies and the consequent reductions in printing.

Lack of staff, described by one librarian as "ridiculous" and another as "chronic," was cited by ten or more states. Lack of space is a problem in at least three states.

Problems of cataloging and classification are concentrated on the authority files, possibly because this was stressed in the cover letter for the survey. Inputting into databases, classification schemes, and backlogs were each mentioned by more than one librarian.

In one state the catalog backlog was given as one of the reasons for the delay in distribution of the checklist. Two states have problems relating to the shipping list. The "need for access to state documents" cited by one state could also be described as a checklist problem.

Only three states specifically mention lack of legislation as a problem.

Even miscellaneous problems have some degree of repetition from state to state. Four states have organizational problems, three mention microforms, and two feel their document librarians are not familiar enough with state documents, or as one of them stated, "the program needs to 'spread the word' concerning the information potential of state documents."

A surprising number of states did not express their hopes for the future. A number listed projects involving retrospective collections or tools. Projects requiring an ongoing commitment include microfiche, database input, and checklist changes (automating, indexing, cumulating). Three states would like to have a statistical abstract. Workshops, special programs, in-depth consultation, and publicity were mentioned by a half dozen states. Legislation is the goal of five states.

The first analysis of the data in the Task Force publication was made by Ronald Haselhuhn.[54] His study was made on the basis of the first Task Force publication, which included reports from forty states. Haselhuhn developed tables showing the frequency of publication of checklists, the number of publications required for distribution, and the depository library receiving state documents.

A second study based on the Task Force publication encompassed all the states.[55] The authors, Yuri Nakata and Karen Kopec, solicited responses from the ten states not represented in the first study. These responses subsequently became the basis for the supplementary report by the Task Force. Tables include states with depository arrangements, ways states make documents available in microformat, and states inputting bibliographic data into databases.

Terry Weech in an article on collection development analyzed the Task Force publication for data on the number of depositories and the number of titles distributed.[56]

Depository Legislation Guidelines

The legislation that undergirds the depository system ensures the stability of the system and is important for the publishers of state publications, the distribution center, and the users of state publications.

Guidelines for drafting legislation for depository programs have been adopted by ALA GODORT State and Local Documents Task Force as "Guidelines for State Publications Depository Legislation." These list the necessary provisions for such legislation. The substance of the first guideline specifying definitions for *state agency* and *state publication* has been discussed in the introductory chapter of this book.

The second guideline calls for a specific administering agency for the depository program. This agency is referred to as the distribution center or the clearinghouse. The distribution center, now located almost exclusively in the state library agency, is critical to the functioning of the system.

54. Ronald P. Haselhuhn, "Bibliographic Control and Distribution of State Documents," *RQ* 20 (Fall 1980): 19–23.

55. Nakata and Kopec, "State and Local Publications."

56. Terry L. Weech, "Collection Development and State Publications," *Government Publications Review* 8A, nos. 1 and 2 (1981): 47–58.

The location of the distribution center in the state capital gives it the advantage of quick and easy access to state agencies. In addition, personal contacts with state personnel are possible, and interoffice delivery is feasible.

The requirement that the state agencies furnish copies of their publications to the distribution center is the central feature of depository legislation. The whole program depends on state agencies supplying distribution copies. Whether or not the law should recite penalties for noncompliance is a subsidiary question. Although some states have sanctions for noncompliance (the Oklahoma mandamus provision is often mentioned in this connection), most states rely on constant monitoring of state agency publishing. A continuing relationship must be established between state agencies and the distribution center which might not be enhanced by punative measures. The "Guidelines for Distribution Center Activities" (another S&LDTF guideline) uses the words, "educate and advise state agencies on library and user needs through training sessions, manuals and brochures, and personal contacts."[57]

Another element of depository legislation is the authority to distribute in microformat. Producing microfiche copies of state publications and using these copies for distribution reduce the number of copies the state agencies must supply. Use of microfiche is particularly helpful when state agencies do not have enough copies for full distribution by the center. Microformat distribution is suggested as an element of depository legislation and a prudent measure for possible future use. Amending a law is always problematical and including possible future needs when drafting legislation is always advisable.

The guideline on systematic and automatic distribution is a statement of the duty required of the distribution center. It may also serve as a safeguard against sluggish distribution by the distribution center.

The sixth guideline enunciates the ultimate purpose of the depository library programs: " to ensure easy availability to the public." Provision for both full and partial depositories is recommended so that even libraries that cannot maintain a full depository collection can make a basic collection available to the public.

Regulations for Depository Libraries

Rules and regulations for the depository libraries are established at the state level, not nationally. Libraries serving remote areas, libraries that have frequent interlibrary messenger service, and libraries that have no selection privileges or very conservative privileges represent only a few of the special conditions affecting depository libraries that cannot be properly

57. See Appendix A, "Guidelines for State Distribution Centers."

addressed at the national level. Depository regulations may establish the relationship between the distribution center and the depository libraries if this is not specified in legislation.

In addition, regulations may define the duties and obligations of the depositories. Depository libraries may be required to meet certain standards with respect to hours, staff, reference service, and provisions for publicizing the documents. A recent requirement in some states is that the depository library have a microform reader. The most elementary requirement, that packages be opened promptly, is a recognition of past transgressions in some libraries. The standards are designed to provide access and availability. The number of documents to which this access and availability is provided depends on the state. Some states, such as New Hampshire, require depository libraries to accept all documents distributed. Others designate a core collection of items that depository libraries must receive.

Guidelines for All Libraries

In addition to guidelines for the governance of depository libraries, guidelines for handling in-state documents in the other libraries in the state are likewise important. The author recommends ten such guidelines. These guidelines are written for all libraries in the state, large or small, depository or not, public or private. They are minimum requirements and are less onerous than state-level guidelines such as the ALA GODORT S&LDTF guidelines in Appendix A, which are all addressed to state documents librarians who have state-level responsibilities. The guidelines proposed here are for all state documents librarians. They are internal to the library and do not depend on the cooperation of other libraries or agencies. Compilation of a checklist, for example, is a much more arduous undertaking than merely having a copy of the checklist in the library.

All libraries in the state should:

1. *Receive the state checklist.* State checklists are serial publications, which means that the library should be on the mailing list, if the checklist is not received through the depository system. The checklist is almost always free to libraries within the state. It serves as an announcement tool and, if the checklist meets standards, provides addresses for ordering. As a reference tool, it is indispensable.

Almost all libraries in the state should have all the bibliographical listings that constitute the record of state publications. This is not always possible because for some states this record is not complete; in other states, the early bibliographical tools are Bowker or Hasse, which are out of print, or the *Monthly Checklist of State Publications,* which is a noncumulative source that requires year by year searching.[58] If a library is specialized, or does not purport to provide for historical research, a complete file for the bibliographical record is unnecessary. The general rule, however, remains: have a copy of the state documents checklist in the library.

2. *Provide assistance in the use of documents access tools.* Although indexing terms used in state checklists are sometimes Library of Congress subject headings and may be familiar to library patrons, often they are keywords or are limited to state agency names. Likewise, if a local classification scheme is used, interpretation is required.

3. *Know what documents the library has and where to borrow those it does not have.* If the library keeps state documents together, either in the documents department or in the special state collection, the shelflist will show the library holdings. Some libraries mark holdings in a copy of the checklist, a practice that should be limited to nondepository libraries.

If the state has depository libraries, "knowing where to borrow" is an easy requirement to meet because the libraries with complete collections are usually indicated in the checklist. Occasionally some of the retrospective bibliographical tools (for example, Foote's 1803–1934 bibliography or the Swanson Ohio list) include holdings.[59] In states with regional networks, the holdings of the library that serves as the resource center for the network are known. A state depository system that includes partial depositories might publish the item selections for those libraries, although there is no example of this type of publication in the *Documents on Documents Collection.* Any libraries in the state should be prepared to secure any state document on interlibrary loan.

4. *Have documents available whenever the library is open.* Keeping documents in a storage area or in the rare book room, areas which are open only a limited number of hours, is an unacceptable practice. One of the advantages of housing documents in a library as opposed to housing them at the state agency is that libraries are usually open longer hours than state agencies. Other advantages of library servicing of state documents—availability outside the capital city, neutral access, supplementation by secondary materials, and concentration of publications of many state agencies in one place—are lessened or diminished if hours of library access are limited.

5. *Publicize the documents.* Even if documents are integrated into the general collection of the library, an occasional exhibit or display might

58. Richard R. Bowker, *State Publications; A Provisional List of the Official Publications of the Several States of the United States from Their Organization.* (New York: Publishers' Weekly, 1908). 1 v. in 4; Adelaide R. Hasse, *Index of Economic Material in Documents of the States of the United States,* pub. no. 85 (Washington, D.C.: Carnegie Institution of Washington, 1907–22); *Monthly Checklist of State Publications,* v. 1+. (Washington, D.C.: GPO, 1910+).

59. Lucy B. Foote, *Bibliography of the Official Publications of the State of Louisiana 1803–1942,* (Historical Records Survey) American Imprints Inventory, no. 19, (Baton Rouge, La.: Louisiana State University, 1942); Ohio Historical Society, *Union Bibliography of Ohio Printed Documents, 1803–1970,* comp. Patricia Swanson (Columbus, Ohio: 1973).

feature state documents. Catharine Reynolds wrote the classic article on publicity for documents.[60] Many of her suggestions are applicable to state documents.

6. *Include statistics and text on state documents in the annual report for the library.* If the library is a depository for state documents, that fact should be mentioned in the librarian's reports. Libraries are proud of their federal depository status, but sometimes fail to mention their designation as state depositories. Very special acquisitions, for example, the proceedings of a constitutional convention, can be cited in the library's annual report, even though they were received without charge as a depository item.

7. *Compile a manual on the handling of state documents in the library,* or at least have a paragraph in the general library procedure manual. Whether a separate manual, a few instruction sheets, or a paragraph in the general library manual is appropriate depends on the size of the local state documents collection. In some states, California and Louisiana for example, manuals on state documents have been prepared by state library associations committees. These manuals can be annotated and individualized to serve as tools within the local library.

8. *Provide staff training for those working directly with state documents as well as the entire library staff.* The training for workers in the state document section involves becoming familiar with the history of the state and the structure of the state government and may necessitate learning a special classification scheme and the quirks (if any) of the state checklist. In depository libraries, studying the depository library law and rules and regulations and, in some states, learning that documents are received in trust rather than as library property are essential steps in learning to be a state documents librarian.

9. *Cooperate with the state distribution center by reporting documents that should be distributed.* Through letters of encouragement and positive criticism, libraries can support the distribution center in its activities. Even libraries that are not depository libraries can strive to meet this guideline and contribute to the strengthening of the depository system in the state. The benefits of a depository system accrue to nondepository libraries as well as to depository libraries.

10. *Consider the need for a basic or core collection.* Such a collection would include, in addition to the documents checklist already cited, the state blue book; a guide to state government agencies; the state statistical abstract; official maps of the state; the revised statutes or code; directories for schools, manufacturers, and licensed occupations; and major annual reports. Check Hernon's article for the section on a given state and consider acquiring all the titles he lists for that state.[61] Also use the new edition of

60. Catharine Reynolds, "Discovering the Government Documents Collection in Libraries," *RQ* 14 (Spring 1975): 228–31.

61. Peter Hernon, "State Reference Sources," *Government Publications Review* 7A, no. 1 (1980): 47–83.

Parish, which gives a state-by-state list in each of nine categories: official state bibliographies; blue books; legislative manuals; state government finances; statistical abstracts; directories; tourist guides; audiovisual guides, atlases and maps; and bibliographies.[62]

Although this last guideline is worded in permissive form, recommending merely that the librarian consider the need for a core collection, it is reasonable to recommend that every library have at least a minimal number of state publications. The state blue book or its equivalent collects the basic information about the state that *any* library should have available. The state statistical abstract, if one has been compiled, is equally useful. In small libraries, state documents can be limited to a few titles that can be shelved on the ready reference shelf along with the *World Almanac*.

Core Collections

The idea of core collections, or basic collections, probably originated in California, stimulated by the depository library program in that state. The first basic California list was a suggested list; the second, a depository requirement. Weech lists California, Connecticut, Iowa, Missouri, and Pennsylvania as having core collections.[63]

A core collection is one that should be available in any depository library. It includes those publications necessary for minimal state reference service. In some states the core collection is very limited: the Louisiana list has only ten titles. In others, although the number of items may be small, one of the items may be annual and biennial reports, which increases the number of volumes received substantially.

Michael Cotter, an active state documents librarian in North Carolina, prepared a core collection of North Carolina state documents in 1985.[64] His list includes fourteen titles which all North Carolina libraries should have (he called this level 1), seventeen titles for intermediate collections in metropolitan libraries (level 2), and six titles for comprehensive collections in research libraries. He suggests that the intermediate collections should have all publications from levels 1 and 2, a total of thirty-one titles, and the comprehensive collections should have all titles on the list, a total of thirty-seven titles.

Conclusion

The role of libraries as providers of the information in state publications has been described in this chapter. Library efforts to preserve in

62. David W. Parish, *State Government Reference Publications*, 2d ed.

63. Terry Weech, "Collection Development and State Publications," *Government Publications Review* 8A, nos. 1 and 2 (1981): 49.

64. Michael Cotter, "Core Collection of North Carolina State Documents," *The Docket* 12 (October 1985): 3–6.

each state this unique source of information by building large collections through exchanges, later efforts to provide access to these library collections through checklists, and recently the development of depository systems for state publications to provide access regardless of geographical proximity to the capital city have been mentioned. The attention given by the ALA GODORT State and Local Documents Task Force to guidelines for state publications focused on state-level services by libraries and librarians. The depository legislation guidelines of the ALA GODORT S&LDTF have been discussed in some detail because they provide a framework for measuring and analyzing this special kind of legislation. Other library legislation in the state documents field is touched on briefly. Collections of out-of-state documents are described. Core collections, which are lists prepared by librarians to standardize acquisitions, point to the next chapter.

6
ACQUISITION

The channels of distribution for state documents described in Chapter 4 influence the way publications are acquired. Distribution in response to a direct request is the most frequently used method of acquiring a state document. It is common knowledge that many state publications are "free for the asking." Some states have depository distribution programs that make acquisition automatic for those libraries that are members of the program. A few states have bookstores, thus making acquisition of state publications almost like that of commercial publications. Exchange programs, although a somewhat outmoded practice, are still in effect in some states. Finally, purchase, either directly from the issuing agency or from a dealer, is a possible acquisition procedure. All these different distribution practices affect the acquisition process.

The purposes for which state documents are acquired also affect acquisition practices. If a library maintains a comprehensive historical collection of state documents, it practices an active and aggressive acquisition procedure. A depository library that is required to accept everything forwarded to it adopts a more passive attitude.

This chapter will discuss the methods of acquisition, the purposes for which state documents are acquired, and the customary routines and forms that facilitate acquisition of state publications.

Acquisition Methods

The methods of acquisition, whether by request, depository program, exchange arrangement, or purchase, differ according to who is acquiring and what is being acquired. Request or purchase are possibilities open to both libraries and individuals, and are available for both home-state and out-of-state publications. Depository programs and exchange plans are limited to libraries. Depository programs handle home-state publications; exchange programs serve as a means of acquisition for out-of-state publications.

BY REQUEST

A request addressed to the issuing agency is the most widely used procedure to obtain a state publication of one's own state. All libraries in a state, large or small, depository or nondepository, occasionally require a state document. Many individuals need a state publication or, more likely, particular data from a state publication from time to time. The public often seeks information without knowing that it may be found in a state publication; librarians who know the functions and responsibilities of state agencies can identify appropriate state document sources. Because most state publications are available without charge, a request addressed to the state agency responsible for preparing the publication is usually the first step. The general form used by the library for requesting free material (often this is a postcard) should suffice. Individuals making requests might consider giving a reason for the request if the material is not the kind that is customarily published for wide distribution and to distinguish the request from those made by schoolchildren for general information about the state or its products to which the state agency might not attach great importance.

In order to request a specific publication one must know first, the name and address of the issuing agency and second, the title. Guides for locating this information are discussed later in this chapter. The acquisitions tools listed here include directories of state agencies as well as checklists of state publications. Some state publications checklists give state agency addresses in addition to bibliographic information, a practice that is recommended in the S&LDTF checklist guidelines.[1] If a particular publication is needed, it is important to make the request promptly because state publications are frequently issued in small quantities, usually go out of print quickly, and are not often reprinted. If a specific publication is not needed, a general request can be made. A general address, such as "Tourist Bureau, State Capitol (or State House)," with city, state and zip code, can be used rather than the exact address of the issuing agency.

DEPOSITORY PROGRAMS

Another frequently used method of acquiring state documents is through a state documents depository program. Such programs make state documents readily available throughout the home state. Many states have depository programs, some of which include a few out-of-state libraries. The number of libraries permitted to participate and the quantity of items received vary widely from state to state. The number of in-state depositories is not related to either the area or the population of the state. The closest correlation seems to be with the number of educational institutions in a

---

1. See Appendix A, "Guidelines for State Documents Checklists."

state.[2] The number of documents received in the depository libraries is dependent, first, on the number of documents published and, second, on the proportion of known documents distributed. The distribution rate is greater in states having recent legislation that have specific definitions which encompass a broad scope of publications and also in states having a diligent administrator who seeks out fugitive documents.

Depository programs, although an acquisition method for libraries, make state publications readily available to individuals as well. Libraries provide access not only to the specific publication needed, even though out-of-print, but also to related nongovernmental publications. Advice about the arrangement and indexes of publications and guidance in the use of these publications is also available in libraries that are part of a depository program. The copy in the library can be reproduced for home use, because state publications are not usually copyrighted. Another feature of depository programs is that interlibrary loan is often an integral part of the program. The Wisconsin library manual has an especially strong statement on service through depository libraries which requires depository libraries to provide access to all state documents, regardless of whether they are in the individual depository collection.[3] While depository programs are not a means by which individuals acquire personal copies of publications, these programs provide access to state publications to everyone.

EXCHANGE PROGRAMS

Exchange, a third method of acquiring state documents, was very popular in the 1930s. Because the exchanges were becoming burdensome at some state libraries, A. F. Kuhlman, chairman of the ALA Documents Committee in the 1930s, recommended that the state university library should be designated as the exchange library. His proposal, which was adopted by the Documents Committee, was careful to specify that such distribution should not compete in any way with distribution that could be effectively carried on by the state law library or historical library.[4]

At present, exchanges are used primarily by law libraries. Exchanges, by their nature, are designed for libraries collecting the documents of other states. As a practical matter, they are usually limited to legal pub-

2. Margaret T. Lane, *State Publications and Depository Libraries* (Westport, Conn.: Greenwood Press, 1981), 177.

3. Wisconsin Division for Library Services, Reference and Loan Library, *Manual for Wisconsin Documents Depositories* (Madison, Wis.: Wisconsin Department of Public Instruction, January 1975), 6. In *Docs on Docs*, 1973–1979, item WI:H.

4. A. F. Kuhlman, "A Proposal to Modify the System of Exchange and Distribution of State Publications in Certain States," in American Library Association, Committee on Public Documents, *Public Documents; Their Selection, Distribution, Cataloging, Reproduction and Preservation, 1934*, ed. A. F. Kuhlman (Chicago: the Committee, 1935), 67.

lications which can be exchanged on a volume-by-volume or year-by-year basis. Since session laws have become available on microfiche, the exchanges of hard-copy volumes of these laws have decreased. Currently these legal exchanges are often handled by a dealer who accepts the copies received for exchange purposes, gives a credit to be applied to similar material from other states, and handles all the details of shipping and record keeping.

An exchange program conducted by the Council of State Governments library for legislative research studies operated in the states for a time but is no longer functioning. It is more practical to request information or publications by telephone when they are needed than to incorporate them in a library for possible use. The Council of State Governments library makes its collection available to all the member states.

An exchange arrangement is limited to only one or two libraries in a state, most often the state library. Exchanges are based on legislation allocating multiple copies to a library in the state for "distribution and exchange when consistent with the best interest of the state."[5]

PURCHASE

Purchase of state documents, in most states, means contacting the individual state agencies. Some of the tools listed later in this chapter give ordering information for various types of publications from each of the states. Fisher's guide to legislative material is an example.[6] Ordering requires the same investigation into the name and address of issuing agency and title of publication as when requesting a publication. Payment in advance is a common requirement. For libraries that make frequent purchases, whether for copies in addition to the depository copies, for copies in nondepository libraries, or for out-of-state documents, a record of state agency names and addresses with notes on payment requirements is helpful. The Documents Department at Duke University, Durham, N.C., maintains such a list in a loose-leaf format. Because of the continual changes in the information, the library does not publish the list.

Sometimes it is possible to purchase documents from a book dealer. Some dealers who handle book orders for libraries will supply state documents but they require the specific addresses of state agencies when ordering state publications. One such dealer is the Book House in Corvallis, Oregon, which advertises "since 1962 jobbers serving libraries with any book in print."[7] Standard handling charges are added. Because purchasing state documents is complicated and outside the usual commercial

5. *The Compiled General Laws of Florida, 1927* (Atlanta: Harrison, 1929), section 1691.
6. Mary L. Fisher, ed., *Guide to State Legislative Materials*, 3d ed., American Association of Law Libraries Publications Series, no. 15 (Littleton, Colo.: Rothman, 1985).
7. The toll-free number is (800) 248-1146.

channels, dealers prefer that orders for state publications be placed by libraries that are customers for other services as well.

Buying a microfiche copy of a state document is also an acquisition method that is possible in some states. Original publication in a microformat by state agencies is a procedure that is in its infancy. Microfiche is fairly widely used in bills and bill indexes and in several states the state documents checklist is produced in microfiche. Some state administrative codes, such as the North Carolina code, are published in microfiche. Republication in a microformat is a more frequent occurrence than original publication in that format. Usually a library or an archives unit has taken on this responsibility. Republication enables other libraries to purchase items that have been issued in limited quantities and also permits distribution in a depository program. Texas has an extensive republication program. The monthly list of Texas documents indicates the number of fiche for each item filmed so that the cost can be determined easily. The Minnesota program makes microfiche available for distribution to the depository libraries and also for sale in either fiche format or hard copy reproduced from fiche.

The microfiche program inaugurated by Information Handling Services (IHS) attempted to offer a broad range of state documents and a fully indexed checklist. The now defunct IHS *State Publications Index,* which had originally been called the *Checklist of State Publications,* was based on the various state checklists and the collection at the Center for Research Libraries.[8] For some of the publications in the checklist, microfiche of the full text was produced. The publications for which this fiche was made were selected from several broad topics: criminal justice, health and safety, and environment. A complete set of the microfiche is available at the Center for Research Libraries, where the filming was done. The publications were listed for a brief period in a database in Bibliographic Retrieval Services (BRS). Several factors may have contributed to the demise of this enterprise: the poor quality of the first issues of the checklist, the start of the marketing effort for the fiche at a time when federal funds were decreasing and budget cuts were prevalent, and perhaps a cost-versus-benefit factor.[9]

8. *State Publications Index* (Englewood, Colo.: Information Handling Services, 1977–1981). Quarterly.

9. Herb Cohen, "An Immodest Proposal—State Publications When and Where You Want Them (Almost)," *Illinois Libraries* 58 (March 1976): 200–4; "IHS Announces State Publication Program," *Government Publications Review* 3 (Fall 1976): 249–50; "Information Handling Service's Checklist of State Publications and State Publications Microfiche Program: Two Viewpoints," *Documents to the People* 6 (November 1978): 234–35, 239; Ruth D. Hartman, review of *Checklist of State Publications, Government Publications Review* 7A, no. 5 (1980): 432–33; Carol M. Tobin, review of *State Publications Index, RQ* 20 (Summer 1981): 412; Joe Morehead, "The Challenges of Teaching State and Local Government Publications" in David W. Parish, "State and Local Byways," *Government Publications Review* 13 (July–August 1986): 543. Morehead's statement chronicles the rise and fall of the IHS project.

Purposes of Acquisition

Acquiring for a comprehensive collection, a current depository collection, an out-of-state collection, the subject fields in which a library specializes, or redistribution to depositories within the state are all reasons for acquiring state documents. Although not mutually exclusive, they require different acquisitions procedures.

Some parallels can be drawn between state acquisition activities and the federal area. For example, for federal documents, fifty-one regional libraries are complete depositories; at the state level only one or two libraries in each state should attempt to acquire complete, historical collections. In the federal depository program, there are over 1300 depositories; in the state depository programs, the number of depositories varies from none in a few states to 181 in New York.

Another comparison can be drawn for foreign collections and out-of-state collections. Foreign collections are completely outside the scope of the federal depository program except insofar as the federal documents are handled in the Smithsonian exchange programs.[10] Large research libraries which are members of the Research Libraries Group, Inc. use the new collection development tool, the RLG Conspectus. The Conspectus is a subject-arranged tool useful as a location device and as an indication of collection strengths. Geographical areas and forms of materials are among its components making it analogous to the earlier Farmington plan, which relied on designated libraries to specialize in the publications of selected countries.[11] As far as the states are concerned, there are several areas of state documents acquisition beyond the boundaries of the home state: (1) all documents from all states (only the Library of Congress and the Center for Research Libraries approach this goal), (2) selected documents for all states (large research libraries such as Duke, the Philadelphia Free Library, and Stanford), (3) all documents from neighboring states (many libraries attempt this as shown in the article by Robert Downs in *Library Trends*),[12] and (4) selected documents from selected states, which is a wide open category.

A comparison between depository clearinghouse acquisition and federal acquisition is not easily made. The Government Printing Office does not need to acquire the publications it distributes, except for the non-GPO items, because GPO is a printer. State clearinghouses do face an acquisitions problem because in almost all cases the state printer is not

10. "Smithsonian Institution Libraries," in *Encyclopedia of Library and Information Science*, Vol. 28 (New York: M. Dekker, 1980): 42.

11. Nancy E. Gwinn and Paul H. Mosher, "Coordinating Collection Development: The RLG Conspectus," *College & Research Libraries* 44 (March 1983): 193.

12. Robert B. Downs, "Government Publications in American Libraries," *Library Trends* 15 (July 1966): 189–91.

the distributor. The distribution made by the State Printing Office in California is a well-known exception to this generalization.

COMPREHENSIVE COLLECTIONS

Establishing a comprehensive, historical collection of state publications that can be relied upon as a record of state publishing should be the responsibility of at least one library in each state. The major collection of state publications within the state should be preserved as a cultural asset of the state for future generations. This is not, and cannot be, a national responsibility. The Library of Congress selects only certain documents for permanent retention, and the Center for Research Libraries, although it retains all documents received, is a private institution governed by its members. Although only one or two libraries in each state will attempt to acquire and maintain full sets of home-state documents, it is important that this be a goal of the library community of the state.

The standards adopted by the Society of American Archivists provide that "Responsibility for assembling and preserving a complete record set of published state documents normally rests with the state archivist . . . . This responsibility may be discharged by arrangement with the state library or other appropriate state institution."[13] The differences between library collections and archival collections should be considered and addressed appropriately in each state. Both libraries and archival facilities are organized for service, but libraries tend to have long hours for service, a wide range of users, interlibrary loan arrangements, and organization of materials according to expected use, whereas archival agencies often have nine-to-five hours for accredited users and organize materials strictly by provenance. Arrangement by provenance, which for state documents is the issuing agency, is a convenient approach for historical research and for any use that focuses on state agencies.

HOME STATE COLLECTIONS

In nondepository libraries, acquiring documents in order to establish a documents collection for the home state should be based on the official checklist issued by the state. Depending on the thoroughness of the checklist, additional sources must also be consulted. Under ideal conditions, the state checklist will include all items in the *Monthly Checklist of State Publications* and the *State Government Research Checklist*.[14] In cases of doubt,

13. Ernest Posner, *American State Archives* (Chicago: University of Chicago Press, 1964), 358.

14. *Monthly Checklist of State Publications* (Washington, D.C.: GPO, 1910+). Monthly; *State Government Research Checklist* (Lexington, Ky.: Council of State Governments, 1947+). Bimonthly.

one must use these major tools as well as the state library's acquisitions list; the newspaper issued at the capital city; the publications of state agencies (particularly newsletters and annual reports); the statistical abstract for the state; and any library association newsletters issued in the state.

DEPOSITORY COLLECTIONS

A depository collection consists of documents of the home state distributed by the state document distribution center. For those libraries in the program, depository status means automatic receipt of documents. The extent of the collection received varies from state to state. This variation occurs because the distribution may not attempt to include all known state documents. A 1980 survey estimated that for all known documents of a state the distribution ranged from 100 percent (in Louisiana and Mississippi) to 13 percent (in New York).[15] Also, an individual library may elect not to receive everything available for distribution. Most states permit libraries to be selective or partial depositories. In some states the distribution center makes the decision on what a depository receives and no selection is permitted; all libraries are complete depositories. In other states a basic or core collection is sent to all depositories and additional selections are permitted. In still other states, the selective depositories have complete freedom of choice within established categories.[16]

OUT-OF-STATE COLLECTIONS

Acquiring documents from states other than the home state is another type of collecting. Again comprehensive collecting is limited; only two libraries, the Library of Congress and the Center for Research Libraries, acquire all documents of all the states, and even these libraries have limitations in their collection policies. Collecting significant documents from all other states and collecting from a limited number of states are more usual. Certain types of documents—such as blue books, directories of manufacturers, statistical abstracts, school directories, legislative handbooks, and tourist booklets from all states—are often collected in large research libraries. If documents from a limited number of states are collected, then the states selected are usually the neighboring states and the states of California, Illinois, and New York. The addition of these three states is probably due to their large populations and their large industrial bases. The number and quality of the publications issued by those states also

15. Margaret T. Lane, comp., *State Publications: Depository Distribution and Bibliographical Programs,* State and Local Documents Task Force, Government Documents Round Table, American Library Association; Texas State Publications Clearinghouse, Documents Monograph Series, no. 2 ([Austin]: Texas State Library, 1980). Also in ERIC microfiche ED 195 283.

16. Lane, *State Publications and Depository Libraries,* 174–76.

influence their selection. California oversees a distribution program for its legislative publications for out-of-state libraries that is not as regimented as the old exchange programs, but is based on whatever degree of reciprocity is possible in the individual receiving state.

SUBJECT COLLECTIONS

Still another purpose for acquiring state publications is to support the subject areas in which the library specializes. For instance, an oil industry research center might require all the mineral reports from every state but collect few documents in other categories. An environmental collection specialist might require all documentation on this topic. An academic library collects particular subjects to support its curriculum or faculty research interests. Legislative libraries collect topics of current interest, such as lotteries or recycling, in order to make state-by-state comparisons. If the library is collecting state documents to enhance its subject collections and to meet the subject interests of its clientele, then the selection tools will also include *Public Affairs Information Service* and other subject bibliographies not limited to documents, such as *Bibliography of Agriculture* and *Resources in Education,* in addition to checklists of state documents.[17]

REDISTRIBUTION BY A DEPOSITORY CLEARINGHOUSE

Acquisition by a library distribution center or clearinghouse for redistribution is an entirely different transaction. The unique problem that a clearinghouse or distribution center administrator faces is the need to solicit multiple copies. An inquiry about a publication that is met with the response, "I'll be happy to send you a copy," requires the answer, "Thank you, but may I have twenty (or forty) copies?" This reply invariably astounds the state agency representative and calls for an explanation of the depository program by the distribution center administrator. One way around this dilemma is distribution in microfiche, which means that the distribution center can request fewer copies. In Nebraska, where all distribution is in microfiche, the clearinghouse requires only four copies of each publication.

Because acquisition is a primary duty of the clearinghouse administrator and because so many libraries in the state are depending on the clearinghouse, the administrator devotes more time to acquisition and has more established routines than a librarian acquiring documents for an individual library. Experience has shown that efforts devoted to discovery of publications and to claiming are directly related to the quantity of

17. *Public Affairs Information Service Bulletin* (New York: PAIS, 1915+). Weekly; *Bibliography of Agriculture* (Washington, D.C.: GPO, 1942+); *Resources in Education* (RIE) (Washington, D.C.: National Institute of Education, 1966+).

material received. Reading newspapers, perusing state agency newsletters and reports, visiting with state agency personnel in the elevator, and enlisting the help of library colleagues are all awareness techniques that bring documents into the distribution center. Acquisition efforts may be characterized as gentle persuasion or as nagging, but either way, constant vigilance is the key to a successful acquisition plan.

Acquisition for redistribution to depository libraries is also acquisition for the comprehensive collection in the distribution center. In most states the distribution center or clearinghouse is located in a library, usually the state library. The distribution center acquires for the library collection as well as for distribution. In the interest of making the library collection complete, the distribution center customarily gives the library the first copy or copies of any item received for distribution. California is an exception to this practice because the state library does not acquire and redistribute but relies on distribution by the state printer and the issuing agencies. Likewise, when the depository programs were established in Louisiana and Mississippi, the acquisition and redistribution were handled in the secretary of state's office in those states, and collection building at the distribution center was not one of the goals of the programs.

The clearinghouse—with its most important function being the acquisition of publications—uses all the standard acquisition procedures. In addition, because acquisition of publications is one of its primary functions, the clearinghouse typically has developed forms, established routines, and inaugurated practices particularly geared to working with state agencies.

Routines and Forms

State publications are issued in limited quantities and go out of print quickly. Only by regular, prompt contacts with the state agencies can a library be assured of getting a copy of a particular publication. Some agencies, even vitally important ones like constitutional conventions, are temporary and disappear when their functions have been achieved. Still another reason for promptness in acquiring publications stems from the nature of the publications—they are timely. The public wants a publication when it is in the news, when the topic is "hot," and when there is still time for reaction and input. Indiana's health plan which includes policy statements, priorities and goals; small business conferences, such as Minnesota's which includes priority recommendations; or a report to the governor by a special commission, such as Montana's on construction laws, are all timely items for the individuals affected.[18] Documents which set

18. Indiana Statewide Health Coordinating Council, *Indiana Plan for Health, 1982–1987*, 4th ed. (Indianapolis: 1984); Minnesota Small Business Conference Commission, *Minnesota Conference on Small Business* (St. Paul: n.d.); Montana Governor's State Building Construction Advisory Council, *Report to the Governor* (Helena: 1984).

policies and outline goals often generate great interest with the press and the public.

The acquisition of state agency publications differs in several ways from the acquisition of other library materials. State agencies in most states are located at the state capital. Libraries located in the capital city have an advantage in acquiring state publications because telephone calls and office visits are possible, while letters may be the only practical and economical means of communication for other libraries. An office visit to an agency, if timed to avoid budget preparation time and legislative sessions, can be quite productive. When the legislative session is over, or when the administration is changing, publications about to be discarded can be acquired.[19]

A characteristic of state agencies affecting acquisition of publications is that, although most state publications are free, some may require payment. Ordering state publications is often made onerous by requirements for payment in advance, by having to address the request to a particular office, or by the lack of a mailing list. State agency mailing lists are attractive to libraries because of the serial nature of state publications. The next issue of a title is received automatically when state agencies use mailing lists. Libraries should be aware that from the state agency viewpoint, such lists are often expendable. Libraries must always be ready to renew the request when receipt ceases.

Whether routines followed for state documents parallel those for federal documents depends on the original reasons for acquiring the state documents (acquisition for current use, for a comprehensive research collection or for subject enhancement of the collection); on the relationship of the state documents to the general collections in the library (whether incorporated or segregated); and on the depository status of the library and the rules of the depository system.

REQUESTS FOR SPECIFIC TITLES

An excellent collection of forms used by state distribution centers in acquiring documents for state depository programs can be found in the *Documents on Documents Collection*.[20] Some of those forms can be adapted for use by individual libraries.

Of the various forms used by a clearinghouse, the request form for individual titles can be used by librarians who are acquiring for their own

19. K. G. Eaton, "The Missing 70%: The Availability of Oregon State Documents to Libraries," *Pacific Northwest Library Association Quarterly* 33 (October 1968): 10–14.

20. Margaret T. Lane, comp., *Documents on Documents Collection,* 1973–1979 and 1980–1983 (Chicago: American Library Association, Government Documents Round Table, State and Local Documents Task Force, 1984 and 1985). The 1973–1979 collection is in ERIC microfiche (ED 247 940) and the 1980–1983 collection is in ERIC microfiche (ED 263 923). The current materials may be borrowed from Lauri Sebo, University Research Library, University of California, Los Angeles, CA 90024.

individual library. In an individual library, the state documents librarian in all probability does not have a claim form designed solely for claiming state documents. At best, the claim form is one created for federal documents, and most likely it is a general one used for requesting all types of free materials.

Request forms for querying state agencies about particular individual titles have been prepared in Connecticut, Louisiana, Mississippi and Nebraska. These forms ask for multiple copies of the publications because they were prepared for use by distribution centers, but they can be adapted for single copy requests. The forms provide for reporting various reasons for not filling the request: out of print, not yet issued, and ceased publication. The Connecticut and Nebraska forms are reproduced as Figures 2 and 3.

The legal requirements for collecting publications from state agencies impose obligations on the clearinghouse, such as notifying the agencies of the number of copies required. In addition, self-imposed routines are necessary for the efficient and effective management of an acquisitions program. Anticipated dates of publication can be calendared; follow-up on missing issues stressed in check-in procedures; new agencies contacted before the issuance of publications; and changes in state agency personnel monitored.

A calendar of "expected due" dates is not difficult to create in a library where the date of receipt is already recorded in the check-in file. It is difficult to maintain, however, because of the irregularities in publishing that afflict state agencies, and for that reason is not recommended except for the most generously staffed libraries. Follow-up on missing issues is a customary library procedure that assures the quality of acquisition decisions. With the advent of computerized serials control systems, both calendars of anticipated dates of publication and follow-up on gaps in receipt can provide lists of publications to be claimed.

NEW STATE AGENCIES

Searching out and contacting new state agencies is not part of a general library acquisitions program, but is nevertheless an important adjunct to a state documents acquisitions program, particularly for a distribution center.

Distribution centers must exercise a high degree of responsibility for discovering publications. New state agencies have no established distribution lists, may underestimate the number of copies of a publication needed to meet the demand, and may have a limited period of existence. For all these reasons, it is incumbent upon an aggressive acquisitions librarian to check the session laws after every session of the legislature or general assembly to identify newly created state agencies.

We would appreciate your sending us ———— copies of
the following publications(s) for the depository libraries
in accordance with P.A. 77-561.   Thank You.

———— We are sending a full supply of the items
listed above.

———— We cannot send a full supply, but are sending
———— copies.   (Please try to send at least
10 copies).

———— We cannot send the material you need because:

———— Supply exhausted.   ————Never printed.

———— Not yet issued   ————Ceased publication
with v.————
no.————
date ————

Other reasons: ————————————————————————

————————————————————————————————

Date———————————————— Name ————————————————

Please send publications to: Joanne Duzik
Acquisitions Unit
Conn. State Library
Hartford   06115
566-7763

Figure 2. Sample claim form. Source: *Documents on Documents Collection,* 1973–
1979, item CT:D1.

NEBRASKA PUBLICATIONS CLEARINGHOUSE
Nebraska Library Commission
State Capitol
Lincoln, Nebraska 68509
471-2045

CLAIM REPORT   Date _____

To:

Item:

Remarks:

Please report

____ Sent
____ Sending
____ Ceased publication with (vol. / no / date): _____
____ Out of print
____ New edition pending. Due _____
____ Not yet published
____ Out of stock. Due _____
____ Not our publication
____ Other:

Thank You.

Figure 3. Sample claim form. Source: *Documents on Documents Collection* 1973–1979, item NE:D.

STATE AGENCY PERSONNEL

Another routine that should be incorporated into acquisitions department procedures is monitoring changes in state agency personnel. Responding to requests for publications and honoring mailing lists is not a high priority task in state agencies, and when a person with whom one has established a working relationship leaves or retires a new connection must be established. A new person may not understand the need for a library to remain on the mailing list or to receive free copies. The lapse of such special services may go unnoticed unless an active interest in personnel changes is maintained.

The form used in clearinghouse operations often asks for names of contact persons within the state agency who can supply information about the publications of that particular agency. Name, title, department, address, and telephone number are items on this type of form. The Missouri state agency handbook lists the contact persons and requests notification of changes. The manual makes the statement, "The State Library relies on the designated 'Publications Contact' for each agency to supply us with documents for the depository program."[21]

In California when state agencies were queried in connection with a study of the depository program, it was noted that the number of contact persons was increased as a result.[22]

STATE AGENCY REPORTS ON PUBLICATIONS

If the law requires periodic reporting by state agencies to the distribution center, a special form may be created for this purpose (see Figure 4). Such a form asks for information on titles, frequency, date of publication, and in the case of Nebraska, an abstract of the document. This type of form, used semiannually in Louisiana and Mississippi and monthly in Texas, serves as a tool for checking on items received by the clearinghouse for distribution to the depository libraries. In these three states the forwarding of this information to the clearinghouse is required by statute. These forms give notice of new publications and supplement acquisitions efforts in distribution centers.

A variation of this form requests lists of items in print. The data supplied on this form, which is sent out annually in Virginia, are the basis for *Virginia State Publications in Print*.[23] An innovative approach adopted in Alaska requires an annual listing of publications as part of the state

21. Maggie Johnson and Barbara Klemke, *State Agency Handbook* (Jefferson City: Missouri State Library, 1980), 19. *In Docs on Docs*, 1980–1983, item MO:H4.

22. California Department of General Services, *Report on the Library Distribution Act, MP-698* (Sacramento: 1973), Exhibit H.

23. *Virginia State Publications in Print . . .* , 1965+ (Richmond, Va.: Virginia State Library).

MONTHLY PUBLICATIONS LIST

TEXAS STATE LIBRARY
Texas State Publications Clearinghouse

Form for reporting to the Texas State Library state documents issued during the preceding month.   Please return to the Clearinghouse by the 15th of each month.   [This satisfies the agency reporting requirements of V.A.T.S. 5442a.]

MONTH: May 1980   19   AGENCY: Texas Adult Probation Commission

TITLE:	Total Number Printed	Copies Supplied to TSL	Waiver ** Granted
Telephone Directory of Adult Probation Officers	1800	65	
Texas Adult Probation Commission Brochure (4-1-80	2500	65	
version)			

**   Check this box if amount deposited with the Texas State Library is reduced due to a waiver.

◯ Please forward additional copies of the 'Monthly List' form.

13

FORM B
11/79

Figure 4. Monthly state agency report form. Source: Texas State Publications Clearinghouse, *Texas State Documents Depository Program* (July 1980), 13.

agencies budget request (see Figure 5). The reluctance of agencies to question budget office procedures was expected to make this report effective.

Acquisition Tools

Bibliographies far exceed other contributions to the field of state documents librarianship. The reason for the many lists arises from the nature of state documents: they are not national in scope, and they are not trade books. These bibliographic listings, or guides, are needed both for discovering and acquiring state documents and also for using them. Many lists serve both as acquisitions tools and as reference tools. In this chapter those lists that include acquisition sources and that indicate frequency and price (if any) are stressed. The chapter on reference work emphasizes the information to be found in the individual state documents.

First in this chapter are the lists that serve as guides to other lists; that is, the bibliographies of bibliographies. These vary from major listings covering all the states (Palic and Parish noted below are examples) to short lists of the bibliographic tools for an individual state. The individual state listings are found in the preliminary pages of state checklists, in the reference section of state manuals, and in workshop handouts. The guides to the *Documents on Documents Collection* have a section on bibliographies that lists some of these state bibliographies.[24]

Second are the bibliographies that include the state documents themselves, which likewise may be multistate or single state. These, also, vary from major lists covering all the states (the *Monthly Checklist of State Publications* is the primary example) to the checklists issued by the individual states. A state-by-state list of a particular type of publication, such as statistical abstracts or state manuals, is a variation of this type of list.

Both these kinds of lists may be for current or retrospective publications, or both, and if the listing is for a single state, it may also include multistate tools. Here the arrangement begins with the six most recent bibliographical lists that are multistate and are intended for current acquisitions and reference work. Then follows the listing of tools that deal with the individual documents.

ALL-STATE LISTS OF TOOLS

Several writers have compiled bibliographic listings of state documents tools. Some such listings are specifically intended as selection guides and some as reference guides.

24. Margaret T. Lane, comp., *A Guide to the Documents on Document Collection, 1973–1979* and *1980–1983.* 2 vols. (Chicago: American Library Association, Government Documents Round Table, State and Local Documents Task Force, 1984); (ERIC microfiche ED 247 939 and ED 263 922). Hard copy available from: Margaret T. Lane, P.O. Box 3335, Baton Rouge, LA 70821; $3.00 prepaid, checks payable to ALA GODORT.

FY 81 ALASKA STATE PUBLICATIONS (FORM 24)
Form and Instructions

Respondent's Name	Position Title	Telephone	Mail Stop
1			

Author	Title	Date	Number of Pages
2	3	4	5

AGENCY ___6_____   PROGRAM _____

7   BRU _____   FY 83

24	FY 81 ALASKA STATE PUBLICATIONS

COMPONENT _____

9

Page _____ of _____   REVISED DATE _____
                          8

FY 81 ALASKA STATE PUBLICATIONS (FORM 24)

Purpose: The listing of an agency's publications can be an important indication of its performance and accessibility. The purpose of this form is to
provide the reader with an all-inclusive list of publications compiled by or
for a State agency with public funds from July 1, 1980 through June 30, 1981.

General Instructions: (SUBMIT WITH FY 83 DETAIL BUDGET.)

This form should be completed at the component level, and should include a
complete listing of all publications produced by or for that component
during FY 81. AS 14.56.180 defines a State publication to include "any
official document compilation, journal, bill, law, resolution, bluebook,
statute, code, register, pamphlet, list, book, report, consultant report,
study, hearing transcript, leaflet, order, regulation, directory,
periodical, or magazine issued or contracted for by a State agency."

Step by Step Instructions:
1. Enter the name, position title, phone and mail stop of the person
    responsible for completing this form.
2. Enter the author's name, last name first (if the publication was a
    "departmental" effort, the name of the agency will suffice).
3. Enter the title of the publication.
4. Enter the date of the publication.
5. Indicate the number of pages.
6. Enter the name of the department.
7. Enter the name of the program, BRU (Budget Review Unit) and component.
8. Leave blank unless this is a revision of your original submission, in
    which case enter the current date.
9. Leave blank.

Figure 5. Annual state agency publications report form. Source: *Documents to
the People* 10 (January 1982): 40.

The most recent list is the selection list by Marilyn K. Moody.[25] This list includes complete acquisition information including price. It is a brief list, only ten titles. State checklists are mentioned as a "necessary" selection tool. Each title has a full annotation. Directories of state agency addresses are not included.

A similar selection list was prepared by Mohini Mundker in 1978 based on responses to a questionnaire she circulated to about eighty librarians throughout the United States.[26] This longer list, seventeen titles, included directories.

Three other recent guides list general reference tools. Nancy Johnson lists eighteen titles, David Parish, twenty-five, and Peter Hernon, twelve.[27] Johnson's list is alphabetical and has a few titles not found on the other lists but familiar to law librarians. Parish has some specialized, earlier titles (a guide to reprints and a guide to photocopied historical materials, for example) because state documents can be located under the name of the state in these lists. Both Parish and Hernon are primarily lists of state documents tools published by the individual states; they include the general tools as a secondary service, Parish in an appendix and Hernon in introductory remarks.

The major historical compilation is the bibliography from the Library of Congress prepared by Vladimir M. Palic.[28] Palic lists three current titles: the *Monthly Checklist of State Publications*, GPO *Price List 87*, and *PAIS*.[29] The *Price List*, entitled *States and Territories of the United States and Their Resources, Including Beautification, Public Buildings and Lands, Recreational Resources*, was issued in 1967 and is today only of historical interest. Palic's retrospective list has six titles, and the list of bibliographies on special kinds of publications has twenty-three titles, of which only nine are 1950 or later.

Because these lists were issued at different times, the titles are not comparable. For example, the *State Publications Index* was included in lists

25. Marilyn Moody, "State Documents: Basic Selection Sources," *Collection Building* 7 (Spring 1985): 41–44.

26. Mohini Mundkur, "Some Selection and Acquisition Aids for Current State Documents," *Documents to the People* 6 (March 1978): 107–9.

27. Nancy P. Johnson, "Providing Reference Service Using State Documents," *Reference Services Review* 9 (January–March 1981): 89–91; David W. Parish, *State Government Reference Publications: An Annotated Bibliography*, 2d ed. (Littleton, Colo.: Libraries Unlimited, 1981); Peter Hernon, "State Reference Sources," *Government Publications Review* 7A, no. 1.(1980): 47–83.

28. Vladimir M. Palic, *Government Publications: A Guide to Bibliographic Tools*, 4th ed. (Washington, D.C.: Library of Congress, 1975).

29. *Monthly Checklist of State Publications*, v. 1+ (Washington, D.C.: GPO, 1910+); U.S. Superintendent of Documents, *States and Territories of the United States and Their Resources, Including Beautification, Public Buildings and Lands, Recreational Resources* (Washington, D.C.: GPO, 1967+). Price list 87; *Public Affairs Information Service Bulletins* v. 1+ (New York: PAIS, 1915+).

published during the time it was current, 1977–1981. Both that Index and the *State Government Research Checklist* have had title changes. The *Statistical Reference Index* is included only in lists published after it began in 1980.[30]

The characteristics of these lists are displayed in Table 5. Palic has the only comprehensive retrospective listing for both multistate and individual state tools, although Hernon and Parish have a few references to retrospective, multistate tools. All the lists except Palic's and Moody's include directories that give names and addresses of state agencies. Palic, Hernon, and Parish have both a general section that gives multistate tools and then a state-by-state section for tools in the individual states.

The only general, current, comprehensive bibliography listed in the six guides is the *Monthly Checklist of State Publications*. This comprehensive tool is one of the most popular selections for U.S. depository libraries. Eighty-five percent of the depository libraries select it.[31] This Library of Congress publication, because it has been published regularly since 1910, because of its standards of careful preparation, and because of its reasonable price, is widely used. It is scanned carefully every month by many librarians. Its deficiencies, stemming principally from the failure of the Library of Congress to receive copies of the publications for listing, are often cited; nevertheless it is the only tool of its kind.

Both Parish and Hernon list reference tools for the individual states. Hernon's list is arranged by state. It lists blue books, checklists, state statistical abstracts, industrial and manufacturing directories, Federal Writer's Project guides, and other pertinent sources. For some publishers the address is given, but for others, the user is referred to various directories. An indication of which states have depository systems makes the list useful to interlibrary loan librarians.

Parish's work is a more extensive list, 1765 titles with annotations, arranged by topics and thereunder by state. The broad scope of this publication and the useful annotations are the strong points of this list. The subject index is an indication of the diversity of publications included which begin with adolescents and barrier free schools and continue on to youth and zoology. The annotations include such remarks as "data not available in any other source" (item 646) and "useful for studying trends in educational planning" (item 738).

CURRENT INFORMATION

There are several sources for current information. The best known is the *Monthly Checklist of State Publications*.

30. *Statistical Reference Index* (Washington, D.C.: Congressional Information Service, 1980+).
31. Peter Hernon and Gary R. Purcell, *Developing Collections of U.S. Government Publications* (Greenwich, Conn.: JAI Press, 1982), 46.

Table 5. Guides to Acquisition and Reference Tools

	PALIC[a]	MUNDKUR[b]	HERNON[c]	PARISH[d]	JOHNSON[e]	MOODY[f]
Publication date	1975	1978	1980	1981	1981	1985
Acquisition tools (directories)	No	Yes	Yes	Yes	Yes	No
References tools	Yes	No	No	No	Yes	Yes
Number of current titles	3	16	8	3	19	13
Number of older titles	23+	No	4[g]	13	No	No
Publications of individual states	Yes	No	Yes	Yes	No	No

Sources:

[a]Palic, Vladimir M. *Government Publications: A Guide to Bibliographic Tools.* 4th ed. Washington, D.C.: Library of Congress, 1975.

[b]Mundkur, Mohini. "Some Selection and Acquisition Aids for Current State Documents." *Documents to the People* 6 (March 1978): 107–9.

[c]Hernon, Peter. "State Reference Sources." *Government Publications Review* 7A, no. 1 (1980): 47–83.

[d]Parish, David W. *State Government Reference Publications: An Annotated Bibliography.* 2d ed. Littleton, Colo.: Libraries Unlimited, 1981.

[e]Johnson, Nancy P. "Providing Reference Service Using State Documents." *Reference Services Review* 9 (January–March 1981): 89–91.

[f]Moody, Marilyn. "State Documents: Basic Selection Sources." *Collection Building* 7 (Spring 1985): 41–44.

[g]Hernon gives retrospective titles in a footnote.

The *State Government Research Checklist*, from the Council of State Governments, is bimonthly and arranged first by subject and then by state.[32] It stresses legislative publications. More frequently issued are two library accessions lists. One is from the Institute of Governmental Studies Library at the University of California at Berkeley and is published monthly.[33] The other is from the Merriam Center Library in Chicago and is semimonthly.[34]

These are all arranged by subject, except for the *Monthly Checklist*, which has a state-by-state arrangement. All are intended for scanning rather than identification of individual titles.

Other current sources that can profitably be checked for new state documents are the *PAIS Bulletin, Resources in Education* (RIE), and the National Technical Information Service (NTIS).[35] All of these are available online. *PAIS* has the oldest database, dating back to 1915.

The *State Publications Index,* cited by both Mundkur and Johnson, was a quarterly publication issued for several years in the late 1970s.[36] It was issued more currently than the *Monthly Checklist* and attempted to include more documents. It ceased publication in 1981, because it did not provide significantly better information than the *Monthly Checklist* from the Library of Congress, and it cost substantially more.

Lists of new documents and notable documents are published periodically in *Documents to the People, Government Publications Review,* state documents newsletters, and other local sources.[37]

Current specialized lists may be limited by subject (for example, *PAIS*), by type of publication (Tseng's list of administrative registers and codes), or by type of use (for example, the reference works by Parish and Hernon).[38] Some of these specialized bibliographies are not limited to state documents but are traditionally listed as state documents bibliographies because of the large proportion of state documents included.

The usefulness of general bibliographies that include state documents, such as *PAIS*, is governed by the purpose for which they are used. For

32. *State Government Research Checklist* (Lexington, Ky: Council of State Governments, 1947+).

33. *Accession List of the University of California (Berkeley), Institute of Governmental Studies Library* (Berkeley: the Library, 1963+).

34. *Recent Publications on Governmental Problems* (Chicago: Merriam Center Library, 1932+).

35. *Resources in Education* (RIE)(Washington, D.C.: National Institute of Education, 1966+); National Technical Information Service (NTIS) (Springfield, Va.: NTIS, 1970+).

36. *State Publications Index* (Englewood, Colo.: Information Handling Services, 1977–1981).

37. *Documents to the People* (University Park, Pa.: American Library Association, Government Documents Round Table, 1972+); *Government Publications Review,* (Elmsford, N.Y.: Pergamon Press, Fall 1973+).

38. Henry P. Tseng and Donald Pedersen, "Acquisition of State Administrative Rules and Regulations—Update, 1983." *Administrative Law Review* 35 (1983): 349–89; Parish, *State Government Reference Publications;* Hernon, "State Reference Sources."

example, to identify a known title, the *PAIS* is fine. However, if a survey of the publications of health-related organizations for a particular state is being made, *PAIS* is not the proper tool. The current state checklist is the answer. A brief look at the history of the *PAIS Bulletin* indicates one reason why it is cited so frequently as a source for state documents. The *Bulletin* was started by the Special Libraries Association to supply a subject index to materials on economic and social topics including bibliographies, reports, and state documents.[39]

COUNCIL OF STATE GOVERNMENTS

An important sponsor of publications related to state government is the Council of State Governments. The CSG, located at Ironworks Pike, Lexington, Kentucky, with membership from all the states, has a long list of publications on state government. Many are useful in acquiring state publications as well as using them. A free price list is available.

Probably the best known of the CSG publications is the *Book of the States*.[40] This biennial publication includes bibliographies on state government problems as well as numerous statistical tabulations. Publication began in 1935, and in recent years three supplementary directories have been issued in the years that the *Book of the States* is not published. These are directories that list state administrative officials classified by function, state elective officials and the legislatures, and state legislative leadership, committees, and staff.[41] Mundkur's list notes that the elective officials volume is more extensive and more economical than the *National Directory of State Agencies*.[42]

Two other CSG publications that should be consulted by all serious state documents librarians are *State Blue Books and Reference Publications* and *State Government Research Checklist*.[43]

AMERICAN ASSOCIATION OF LAW LIBRARIES

The American Association of Law Libraries (AALL) has published several titles in loose-leaf format in its Publications Series. These, because

39. R. A. Sawyer, "The Public Affairs Information Service," in National Association of State Libraries, *Proceedings* 1932 (Nashville: Brandon Co.), p. 15.

40. *Book of the States* (Lexington, Ky.: Council of State Governments, 1935+).

41. *State Administrative Officials Classified by Function* (Lexington, Ky.: Council of State Governments, 1979); *State Elective Officials and the Legislatures* (Lexington, Ky.: Council of State Governments, 1979); *State Legislative Leadership, Committees, and Staff* (Lexington, Ky.: Council of State Governments, 1979).

42. *National Directory of State Agencies, 1984–85* (Arlington, Va.: Information Resources Press, 1978).

43. *State Blue Books and Reference Publications: A Selected Bibliography*, rev. and annotated ed. (Lexington, Ky.: Council of State Governments, 1983).

they are regularly supplemented, are up-to-date, and because they are meticulously prepared, supersede earlier titles on the same topics. The *Guide to State Legislative Materials*, by Mary L. Fisher, is in its third edition. This work is number 15 in the AALL Publications Series. Another work in the same series is by Meira G. Pimsleur, who prepared checklists for statutes, session laws, attorneys general opinions and reports, judicial councils reports, and restatements. All of these are state documents except restatements, which are secondary materials.

Another series of publications by the Documents Interest Section of AALL is available from headquarters (see Appendix D). These guides, prepared by law librarians for their home states, all deal generally with state documents, usually primarily legislative documents. The first one was published in 1979 for California. The individual titles give an indication of the varied approaches taken by the authors.

DIRECTORIES OF STATE AGENCIES

Directories of state agency names and addresses are found in *State Administrative Officials Classified by Function* (cited above under Council of State Governments) and in two, more expensive commercial publications. The *National Directory of State Agencies* is issued biennially by Information Resources Press. *Taylor's Encyclopedia of Government Officials* provides information on political party functionaries as well as on elected officials.[44] Taylor's provides a toll-free telephone number for up-to-the-minute information.

STATISTICAL ABSTRACTS

Librarians know that statistical publications have a high reference value.[45] Many states have a publication that is comparable to the U.S. *Statistical Abstract*.[46] This federal publication is a convenient source for a listing of the statistical abstracts of the states.

The abstract is a relatively recent type of state publication. The Utah statistical abstract, which began publication in 1947, was the first, according to Parish. California, Montana, Oklahoma, and Pennsylvania followed in the late 1950s. Many other states began publication of statistical abstracts in the sixties and seventies.

State statistical abstracts are compilations of statistical tables assembled from various sources (some federal and some state) and arranged by topic.

44. *Taylor's Encyclopedia of Government Officials, 1985–86*, vol. 10 (Dallas: Political Research, 1985).

45. Barbara J. Ford and Yuri Nakata, "State Government Information in Academic Libraries," *Government Publications Review* 10 (March-April 1983): 189–93.

46. U.S. Bureau of the Census, *Statistical Abstract of the United States* (Washington, D.C.: GPO, 1879+).

The original source is given in a footnote or indicated in some other way. These state statistical abstracts are useful in small public libraries that do not have the publication from which the statistical tables are copied, and in large libraries that may want to be sure that they do have the source publications for the tables, because, of course, the source publications are very often serial publications and are available long before the statistical abstract compilation. The statistical abstracts are also heavily used as ready reference tools in both large and small libraries.

With the publication of *Statistical Reference Index* (*SRI*) by Congressional Information Service, the state statistical abstracts are augmented with comparable data from all the states.

SRI includes all state statistical abstracts, as well as more topically specific state publications, in its state section. The User Guide includes the following statement on the types of statistics covered:

> State-Wide Data—State statistical compendia and additional basic reports for each of the 50 States presenting data on such areas as vital statistics, health, agriculture, business conditions and economic indicators, employment, education, State taxation and finance, elections, constructions, insurance, tourism, motor vehicles and accidents, and judicial systems. (Publications containing these data are issued primarily by State agencies and university research centers. SRI coverage will include all basic State statistical compendia [available for 36 States], plus 20–40 additional reports for each State, selected to provide the best available current coverage of the above subjects.)

Because most information seekers are looking for recent data, *SRI*, which is issued on a quarterly basis, meets that need.

NONCURRENT MATERIALS

There are multistate lists and lists for individual states. Palic follows the pattern of earlier guides by listing first those lists that include the bibliographic publications of all or most of the states. The introductory essay to the state section in Palic serves as a historical account of bibliographic endeavors in this area. The introductory pages for the Wilcox list also give a historical account of early bibliographical control of state documents. Both mention the two most important early state listings: Bowker,[47] "still the best bibliographic source for the early official documents of the states,"[48] covering state publications up to 1900; and Hasse, extending the coverage to 1904 for thirteen of the states.[49] Although the title of the

47. Richard R. Bowker, *State Publications: A Provisional List of the Official Publications of the Several States of the United States from Their Organization* (New York: Publishers' Weekly, 1908).

48. Palic, *Government Publications*, 81.

49. Adelaide R. Hasse, *Index of Economic Material in Documents of the States of the United States* (Washington D.C.: Carnegie Institution of Washington, [1907–22]).

work by Hasse is *Index to Economic Materials in Documents of the States of the United States*, her interpretation of "economic" was a broad one. As Palic quotes from the Illinois volume,

> Hasse deals mainly "with the printed reports of administrative officers, legislative committees, and special commissions of the states, and with governors' messages for the period since 1809. It does not refer to constitutions, laws, legislative proceedings or court decisions."[50]

There are several states for which the Bowker and Hasse listings are the only ones available for the early years of statehood. Thus, it is important to remember the names of these two early workers in the field. On a personal note, I first heard of Bowker when Lucy Foote, my predecessor in Louisiana state documents bibliography, told me that she had included all the entries from Bowker in her Louisiana official publications list.

Another reason for remembering Bowker and Hasse is that they are multistate listings. Since the advent of the *Monthly Checklist of State Publications* in 1910, no comprehensive all-state listing has existed, with the exception of the ill-fated *State Publications Index* that appeared during the late 1970s.

The general multistate lists, except for the *Monthly Checklist of State Publications*, are noncurrent. Specialized bibliographies covering all the states are both retrospective and current in their coverage. See the listing in Palic for various retrospective publications.

Acquisition of retrospective titles is not a pressing matter in most libraries. Peter Hernon concluded that "many users draw upon recently published information, that issued primarily within the past three years."[51] He cites his recent work, *Use of Government Publications by Social Scientists*,[52] and observes further that only a few types of publications are used.

Only libraries establishing definitive and comprehensive collections of the documents in their own state have aggressive acquisition policies for noncurrent state documents. Perhaps the best source for noncurrent materials to round out a comprehensive collection is a list of items being discarded from other libraries. Depository libraries may be required to return their collections when relinquishing depository status; also, they may have permission to discard after materials are no longer current. Five years is a typical holding period. However, for the library in charge of the distribution to depository libraries, the return of materials from those libraries serves only to replace worn or lost publications because the distribution center customarily keeps the first copies for its own collections.

50. Palic, *Government Publications*, 100.

51. Hernon, "State Reference Sources," 47.

52. Peter Hernon, *Use of Government Publications by Social Scientists* (Norwood, N.J.: Ablex Publishing, 1979).

Dealers and jobbers are another possible source for state publications, particularly retrospective documents. Careful search of catalogs from secondhand dealers is a profitable source both for the state library and for any library in which the collection pre-dates the depository library law of the state. Ed Herman, state documents librarian at the State University of New York at Buffalo, has published a list of documents dealers and jobbers in *Documents to the People*.[53] The Herman compilation also includes, for each of the dealers, information on telephone number, availability of a catalog, special services, average time for service, and fees. In his list the dealers mentioning specifically that they handle state documents are:

> G. H. Arrow Company, 1133-39 North 4th Street, P.O. Box 16588, Philadelphia, PA 19123—state mining.
>
> Blackwell North America, Inc., 10300 Southwest Allen Blvd., Beaverton, OR 97005—state.
>
> James G. Leishman, Bookseller, P.O. Box A, Menlo Park, CA 94025— earth science-related materials issued by state.
>
> Moore-Cottrell Subscription Agencies, North Cohocton, NY 14868—all serials published by state governments.
>
> Julian J. Nadolny, Natural History Booksellers, 1212 Hickory Hill Road, Kensington, CT 06037—state materials relating to geology and biology.
>
> Ostby's Americana, 8758 Park Avenue, P.O. Box 89, Bellflower, CA 90706—state military references.
>
> Fred B. Rothman and Company, 10368 West Centennial Road, Littleton, CO 80127—many state statutes and session laws.

Another source where older documents are available is the Early State Records filmed by W. S. Jenkins in cooperation with the Library of Congress. A guide to this collection is available.[54]

Conclusion

Acquisition of state documents is a specialized acquisition skill. A skilled state documents acquisition librarian is aware that state documents are available from the issuing agency for a relatively short time, that most state agencies are located at the state capital, that most state documents are serial publications, and, most important, that one must be continuously alert to capture these elusive publications. One must be vigilant in scanning

53. Ed Herman, "Directory of Government Document Dealers and Jobbers, 1981," *Documents to the People* 9 (September 1981): 229–34. The original list, for 1975, appeared in *Documents to the People* 3, no. [7] (September 1975): 40–43; updated versions appeared in *DttP* 5, no. 5 (September 1977): 209–12 and *DttP* 7 (July 1979): 159.

54. U.S. Library of Congress, *A Guide to the Microfilm Collection of Early State Records,* comp. William S. Jenkins (Washington, D.C.: Library of Congress, Photoduplication Service, 1950) and Supplement, (1951).

newspapers and newsletters for new publications and new agencies. For state documents, acquisition involves not only discovering the publications (as with trade books), but also monitoring the creation and demise of state agencies.

For collecting the documents of states other than one's home state, or for looking for information available from other states that might be useful at home, the tools listed in this chapter may be useful. The Palic list is the comprehensive, definitive one; the Mundkur list was compiled from a survey of "major selection tools"; Johnson includes some legal publications; Hernon and Parish both verified their listings with librarians in each of the states; and the list compiled by Moody is the most recent. The individual titles from these six listings have been grouped here so that state documents librarians can keep up-to-date by watching for new publications from the Council of State Governments, the American Association of Law Libraries, other libraries, directories, the United States government, and statistical sources.

In many states the only obvious acquisition/reference tool is the state checklist. Almost all states have such a list, although the frequency and the content vary from state to state. The ingenious librarian will tap such additional sources as: organization manuals or "blue books"; statistical manuals; telephone directories for the capital city and state government, as well as a locally compiled list; budgets and financial reports; lists of corporate authors; state union lists of holdings; popular name indexes (this may be an unpublished source); and checklists of imprints (for retrospective materials).

Acquisition tools for state documents, current and retrospective, identify particular publications and usually include addresses for requesting or ordering. Directories are an additional source for addresses. All these tools are also reference tools. Some provide a subject approach which makes the publications available as supplementary material to that in the general library collection. Directories often provide the answer to the many reference queries for names and addresses. In a library both acquisitions and reference librarians must share these tools. One must remember that state documents tools in an individual state are not designed to be limited to a single type of use. Chapter 7 on checklists emphasizes the many uses of that kind of acquisition or reference tool.

7
STATE CHECKLISTS
AND BIBLIOGRAPHIES

For the librarian who acquires and makes state documents available, and often for the user of state documents as well, the state documents checklist is the most important access tool. It is an indispensable aid that is the key to the rich resources of state government publishing, particularly for one's own state.

Background

The major comprehensive bibliographic source for the documents of all the states is the *Monthly Checklist of State Publications,* described in the previous chapter. If there is no state list, the *Monthly Checklist* fills the gap. In Alaska, for example, the distribution of the monthly checklist is restricted, and use of the *Monthly Checklist* is recommended.

The present chapter describes checklists limited to the publications of a single state. It begins with the history of the checklists as recorded in the literature, followed by a section on the guides to the checklists. The characteristics and purposes of the checklists, the guidelines that govern checklist preparation and content, and the recent changes and trends in checklists complete the chapter.

The term *checklist* is a generic designation often used by state documents librarians, irrespective of the actual title of the publication. Perhaps the term is used because the *Monthly Checklist of State Publications* is the outstanding example, or perhaps because many of the current lists are indeed titled "checklist." The term includes bibliographies, registers, indexes, and catalogs, and its use has a sound historical basis. Wilcox, in the *Manual on the Use of State Publications,* used it in referring to the early lists by Bowker and Hasse.[1] A. F. Kuhlman, a giant in the documents field during the 1930s, also used the term.[2]

1. Jerome K. Wilcox, ed., *Manual on the Use of State Publications* (Chicago: American Library Association, 1940), 75.
2. A. F. Kuhlman, "The Need for a Comprehensive Check-List Bibliography of American State Publications," *Library Quarterly* 5 (January 1935): 52.

The state checklists that are the subject of this chapter are as varied as the fifty states that issue them. The number fifty is used advisedly and charitably because there are a few states that, strictly speaking, have no checklist. Montana, for example, discontinued its checklist in 1975 and has only a weekly list of documents received, which is sent to the depository libraries.

State checklists vary from shipping lists, which may have only minimal data in the individual entries, as in the Texas list, to lists like the Virginia annual checklists, prepared by catalogers who provide full bibliographical data including contents notes, notes on holdings at the state library, and other relevant notes. The Texas shipping list gives an example of a minimal entry:

79197 Active News El 400.6 88 10/1

The Virginia annual checklist provides an example of a full entry, as shown in Figure 6.

Some lists are reproduced from typewritten copy (Texas); some are typeset (Kentucky); some are in microfiche (Colorado); some are computer output microfiche (California); and some are online in a database (Nebraska). Because the format in a particular state is affected by frequency of cumulation, extent of distribution, and other factors, these few examples indicate format only, not quality.

The lists vary in scope; some include only items received, and others are limited to items distributed. Some omit publications of the legislative or the judicial branch, or of the state universities. Each state that prepares a checklist sets its own standards for types of information included and for the format. In some states, the issuance of a checklist is required by statute, which may vary from a mere statement of a duty to publish a list of publications received (Illinois) to a duty to publish "an official list" with certain specific data in the individual entries (Kansas). Even in the absence of a legal mandate, librarians have recognized the value of a state checklist and have prepared a list for distribution. For example, the University of Iowa produced the Iowa list for many years.

Regardless of the scope and quality of a state checklist, it is usually the most timely, most thorough, and least expensive source for bibliographical data on state documents within their state of origin. Timeliness results from compilation in the locality in which the documents are issued. In at least two-thirds of the states the checklist is compiled at the state library. Thoroughness results from the creation of a rather complete bibliographic record with information available only at the local level, and perhaps from a sense of local pride. Economy results from preparation at a single institution in the state and also from the free or minimal-charge distribution, which has been the practice of checklist publishers.

Just as periodic checklists vary from state to state, the retrospective bibliographies are also all different. Some are cumulations of the periodic

——— Virginia State publications in print July 1, 1978. [Richmond, 1978]
134 p. 23 × 11 cm.   **7898**

STATE LIBRARY, *RICHMOND*. ADMINISTRATIVE
SERVICES DIVISION
Virginia cavalcade. v. 28, no. 1-2. [Richmond] 1978. 2 nos. illus. (part col.),
maps, ports. (part col.). 28 cm. Quarterly.   **7899**

STATE LIBRARY, *RICHMOND*. ARCHIVES DIVISION
Virginia cavalcade. v. 27, no. 3-4. [Richmond] 1978. 2 nos. illus. (part col.),
maps, ports. (part col.). 28 cm. Quarterly.   **7900**

STATE LIBRARY, *RICHMOND*. GENERAL LIBRARY BRANCH
[Genealogical books.] [Richmond, 1978] 15 p. 28 cm.   **7901**

——— Some recent acquisitions of general interest available for loan.
no. 118 (April). [Richmond] 1978. 28 p. 28 cm.   **7902**

STATE LIBRARY, *RICHMOND*. INFORMATION OFFICE
News. [Richmond] 1978. 7 nos. illus. 28 cm.   **7903**

STATE LIBRARY, *RICHMOND*. LIBRARY DEVELOPMENT BRANCH
Statistics of Virginia public libraries and institutional libraries, 1976-1977.
Richmond, 1978. 39 p. maps, tables. 28 cm.   **7904**
Colored map on covers.
Includes "Colleges and university libraries in Virginia, 1976-1977," "Special libraries in Virginia,
1976-1977," "Institutional libraries, 1976-1977" and "Directory of Virginia public libraries."

STATE OFFICE OF MINORITY BUSINESS ENTERPRISE
Annual report ending, June 30, 1978. Petersburg, Virginia State College
[1978] 146 l. tables. 28 cm.   **7905**

——— Quarterly report, 1978. Petersburg, Virginia State College [1978]
3 nos. forms, tables. 28 cm.   **7906**
Of issues for 1978, the State Library has: October 1 through December 31, 1977; ending
March 31, 1978; ending September 30, 1978.

——— Virginia directory of minority-owned businesses, 1978. Petersburg,
Virginia State College [1978] iv, 162, [15] p. illus. 28 cm.   **7907**

STATE OFFICE ON VOLUNTEERISM
Annual report [1977-78] Richmond, 1978. [19] p. diagrs. 28 cm.   **7908**

——— Volunteer Virginia. v. 4. Richmond, 1978. 4 nos. illus., ports.
28 cm. Quarterly.   **7909**

Figure 6. Checklist entry showing complete bibliographic data. Source: Virginia State Library, *Check-List of Virginia State Publications, 1978*. Richmond: The Library, 1979, 104.

checklists (New York is an example); some are union lists (Ohio); some, library school theses (Florida); some, expansions of theses (Louisiana); and some are publications of the archives and records service of the state (Kentucky).

History

Brief commentaries on the development and current status of state checklists are found in the introductory sections of most of the checklist bibliographies. Particularly recommended are the historical statements by Tanselle and Palic.[3]

Tanselle gives a chronological account of the development of bibliographies of state documents, emphasizing scholarly and retrospective works. Two of the earliest efforts in the general field of documents bibliography were in the area of state documents: a Rhode Island list published in 1875 and a Maryland list in 1878. The National Association of State Librarians (later National Association of State Libraries), organized in 1889, focused attention on state documents and their importance from the historical point of view. The work of Bowker, which appeared in his *American Catalogue* and then in his comprehensive *State Publications,* followed by the start of the *Monthly Checklist of State Publications* in 1910, brings the account into the twentieth century. A number of scholarly works for individual states appeared in the first two decades of the century as well as the more general works by Hasse (13 states), Morrison (Confederate States, 1908), and Shearer (constitutional convention publications, 1917). A period of relative inactivity in the 1920s was followed in the 1930s by publications that resulted from the emphasis placed on state documents bibliography by the University of Illinois Library School, the establishment of the Public Document Clearing House, and activities of the American Library Association Public Documents Committee.

Many of the bibliographies from the University of Illinois Library School are unpublished, but because they are part of the bibliographical record of the state, they are included in retrospective lists of bibliographic works. For example, Palic lists a number of theses as being available at the Library of Congress. The Clearing House, established by the National Association of State Libraries, published a number of checklists—on session laws, legislative journals, and statutes—that were highly regarded and served as the basis for supplementary lists. The original lists were meticulously prepared by Grace Macdonald, but they and the works that supplemented them have been superseded by checklists compiled by Meira

---

3. Thomas Tanselle, *A Guide to the Study of United States Imprints* (Cambridge, Mass.: Harvard University Press, Belknap Press, 1971); Vladimir M. Polic, *Government Publications: A Guide to Bibliographic Tools,* 4th ed. (Washington, D.C.: Library of Congress, 1975). These bibliographies are discussed in the "Guides to Checklists" section of this chapter.

Pimsleur.[4] Pimsleur's checklists are published in loose-leaf form and kept up-to-date.

In his account Palic highlights the efforts of the Documents Committee of the American Library Association to obtain greater bibliographical control in the field of state documents during the years 1933 through 1937. One chairman of the committee during the 1930s, A. F. Kuhlman, wrote and spoke extensively about the need to collect and preserve state documents and, as a corollary, the need for state checklists.

Prior to World War II only eight states issued periodic checklists; during the war twenty-two states were issuing checklists; and in the postwar period the number rose to forty-four.[5]

A resurgence of interest in producing checklists occurred in the early 1950s and 1960s, attributable perhaps to legislation establishing state depository programs and requiring the publication of checklists. The statutory provisions requiring the issuance of checklists show that in 1980 at least thirty states had a duty to issue a checklist.[6] The statutes vary from very general instructions, "The center shall quarterly publish an index to state publications . . ." (Connecticut) to the very specific instructions specifying that the list should show "the author, title, major subject content, and other appropriate catalogue information for any such publication" (Kansas).

State checklists were described in detail in a 1966 article comparing titles, frequency, content of the checklist, and details of the individual entries.[7] The plan adopted in Nebraska in the 1970s is an example of the importance attached to the state checklist in a documents distribution program. Following the enactment of a new documents law in Nebraska, the first step was to compile and publish a checklist. Once the checklist was firmly launched, then depository libraries were established.

Little change in the physical format of the checklists and the content of the entries occurred until about the 1970s. Examples of these changes are cited at the end of this chapter.

The historical record of an individual checklist is given in "Checklist Exhibit," found in the Wisconsin section of the *Documents on Documents Collection.* The captions and descriptions for the exhibit chronicle the Wisconsin list from 1917 (it was one of the first) to 1979.

4. Meira G. Pimsleur, ed., *Checklists of Basic American Legal Publications,* American Association of Law Libraries Publications Series, no. 4 (South Hackensack, N.J.: Rothman, 1962+). Loose-leaf.

5. Vladimar M. Palic, *Government Publications: A Guide to Bibliographic Tools,* 4th ed. (Washington, D.C.: Library of Congress, 1975).

6. Margaret T. Lane, *State Publications and Depository Libraries* (Westport, Conn.: Greenwood Press, 1981), 162–66.

7. Margaret T. Lane, "State Documents Checklists," *Library Trends* 15 (July 1966): 117–34.

Highlights in the Development of Wisconsin Public Documents

1917 Began as a useful innovation by Milo M. Quaife, Superintendent of Wisconsin State Historical Society.

1949 Statutory authorization received for producing a checklist.

1968 Annual cumulating and indexing of checklist began.

1978 Adopted full cataloging for record as provided by OCLC input.

1979 Provided name authority documentation.[8]

A survey of the literature on state checklists reports that articles on the preparation and function of state checklists are out of date, with the exception of Haselhuhn's analysis in 1980 and Woolley's article on implications for future development.[9] Haselhuhn made comparisons between checklist issuance in 1970 and 1980, discussing responsibility for issuance, titles, coverage, frequency, arangement, use of cataloging data, and other details.[10] Woolley saw checklists as "a reflection of the bibliographic control exercised by your state as part of a much larger effort [that is, participation in a bibliographic utility]."[11]

Guides to the Checklists

The early guides—Reece, published in 1915, is credited with being the first[12]—are now superseded. The Childs bibliographies, which had a chapter on state publications or documents and state-by-state status reports, were published in 1927, 1930, and 1942. The 1927 edition, titled *Government Document Bibliography in the United States and Elsewhere*, has been described as "a pioneer work in the broad field of guides to bibliographies of official publications."[13]

In 1940, the listing by Wilcox in *Manual on the Use of State Publications* combined the lists from the earlier guides and brought them up to date. In addition to Reece and Childs, and of course Bowker and Hasse, Wilcox mentions Kuhlman and Beers as compilers of guides to state document bibliography.[14] The list in the *Manual* was supplemented by four lists com-

8. "Checklist Exhibit" in *Documents on Documents Collection, 1980–1983*, item WI:M.

9. Lane, *State Publications and Depository Libraries*, 208–10.

10. Ronald P. Haselhuhn, "Bibliographic Control and Distribution of State Documents," *RQ* 20 (Fall 1980): 19–23.

11. Robert D. Woolley, "State Documents Checklists: Implications for Future Development," *Documents to the People* 5 (November 1977): 236–37.

12. Ernest J. Reece, *State Documents for Libraries*, University of Illinois Bulletin 12, no. 36 (Urbana, Ill.: University of Illinois, 1915).

13. Palic, *Government Publications*, 3.

14. The items listed by Wilcox have been previously cited, except: Henry Putney Beers, "States," in *Bibliographies in American History; Guide to Materials for Research* (New York: Wilson, 1938), 226–94. The Beers list is not limited to state documents bibliographies and does not identify them as a group.

piled by Wilcox and published between 1940 and 1945,[15] and by Gwendolyn Lloyd's article, "The Status of State Document Bibliography."[16] The Tanselle list, published in 1971, although valuable for its chronological arrangement, is no longer up to date.

CURRENT GUIDES

For a current guide to state document checklists, the most comprehensive source is *Government Publications: A Guide to Bibliographic Tools*, by Vladimir Palic. This work is a descendant of the Childs bibliographies, and like the three editions of the works by Childs, was published by the Library of Congress. The chapter in Palic on state document bibliography begins with the general tools that cover all or most of the states and then gives state-by-state reports. In each part, the bibliographical records are in separate lists for current and retrospective titles. Palic gives full bibliographic data for each title, including imprint; collation; series title and number, if any; frequency for periodicals; and the Library of Congress classification number. Descriptive notes, particularly for the publications listed in the "current" section, indicate relationship to earlier titles and explain the scope of the checklist. For example, Palic tells that the current Connecticut list, *Checklist of Publications of Connecticut State Agencies*, "includes publications of temporary commissions and committees and those of the University of Connecticut."

The list in Palic begins with the *Monthly Checklist of State Publications*.[17] The *Monthly Checklist* is, at the present time, the only current listing for all the states. The *Public Affairs Information Service Bulletin* is given as a source for information, but it is not limited to state publications. The retrospective section for general bibliographies lists six works: the *American Catalog*, Bowker, Childs, Hasse, the NASL publication on collected documents, and the guide to the microfilm collection on early state documents.

The section on the individual states gives the origin of the state and date of statehood, the current checklists and then retrospective works.

Bibliographic entries to bring Palic up to date are scattered. Parish, published in 1981, adds ten years to the coverage in Palic. The only new major retrospective bibliography in Parish's chapter, "Official State Bib-

15. Jerome K. Wilcox, "Aids to Public Document Use since 1937," *Special Libraries* 31 (November 1940): 389–95; "Guides and Aids to Public Documents, 1941," *Special Libraries* 33 (March 1942): 79–84 and (April 1942): 124–26; "New Guides and Aids to Public Documents, 1942–43," *Special Libraries* 35 (February 1944): 55–59; "New Guides and Aids to Public Documents, 1944," *Special Libraries* 36 (December 1945): 474–78.

16. Gwendolyn Lloyd, "The Status of State Document Bibliography," *Library Quarterly* 18 (July 1948): 192–99.

17. Palic, *Government Publications*, 84. Palic lists a GPO price list, no. 87, *States and Territories of the United States and Their Resources, Including Beautification, Public Buildings and Lands, Recreational Resources*, as being a current list, but this is now out of date.

liography," is Swanson's *Union Bibliography of Ohio Printed Documents, 1803–1970*. The new annual list for Alabama for the year 1973 is included. Parish also lists the reprint of Foote's Louisiana bibliography. Cumulations of periodically issued checklists are reported for Alaska, Colorado, New York, and Washington. The Alaska volume has a companion supplemental volume for publications not previously listed. Cumulations designed to provide additional access points for the checklists were published in Missouri (an author, title and keyword index for 1972–1978), New York (an author index for 1947–1969), and Wisconsin (a microfiche keyword index). Cumulations limited to special categories of publications include the New York listing of joint legislative committee and selected temporary state commission publications for 1900–1950, the Oregon cumulative list on legislative research publications, and the New York guide to statistics. Parish also lists the New York guide to official publications by Dorothy Butch, an essay-style bibliography.

Other additions to Palic's listings can be gleaned from Parish's *Bibliography of State Bibliographies*, published in 1985. Significant items are two Louisiana cumulations, special subject listings on legislative research (Kansas, Oregon, and South Dakota), and statistics (Kansas and South Dakota). New Jersey's list of popular names, although not a major publication in size, is a useful contribution as well.

Several publications cited in *State Publications: Depository Distribution and Bibliographical Programs* also supplement the entries in Palic:

> Lu, Joseph. *Government Publications About Idaho: A Guide to Information Sources.* 1978. 80 p.
> *Idaho State Documents Catalog.* (22,632 cards on 38 microfiche cards.) Covers 1863–1980.
> Bardhan, Gail. *Guide to Illinois Government Agencies and Their Publications, 1818–1973.* Evanston, Ill.: Northwestern University Library, May 1974.

The new semiannual bibliographical series begun by the ALA GODORT State and Local Documents Task Force lists new works that come to the attention of Marilyn Moody at Iowa State University, Ames. In the three issues that have appeared since June 1984, the following bibliographical lists appear:

> *State Documents of Kansas Catalog.* 1977+. (quarterly, on microfiche; each issue completely supersedes the previous issue.) $6.00/year.
> New York. State Library. *Dictionary Catalog of Official Publications of the State of New York.* Albany, N.Y.: State Library, 1984.
> California. California State Legislature. *Joint Publications Catalogue.* 1984. 29 p.

Moody also includes state bookstore catalogs from Minnesota and Pennsylvania.

Still another source is the unpublished study by Yvonne Boyer, "State Checklists." Updates to Palic are indicated by an asterisk.[18]

GUIDES TO CURRENT CHECKLISTS

The most recent list of current checklists for the individual states is the chapter titled "Official State Bibliography" in *State Government Reference Publications,* by David W. Parish. This list provides "current information on all state official checklists." Addresses of state agencies are included in an appendix.

State checklists, identified by an asterisk, are listed in the June and December issues of the *Monthly Checklist* in the periodicals section. Parish recommends checking the *Monthly Checklist* for changes to his listing. From 1973 to 1975 a list of the current checklists appeared as a regular feature in *Government Publications Review.*[19] This list and other similar lists that preceded it serve as a means for inventorying state checklist collections. The list also provides notice of new, ceased, or changed checklists that is not easily found in a single source.

Chronological Coverage of Checklists and Bibliographies

In her 1948 survey of state documents checklists, Gwendolyn Lloyd reported the lack of "a complete and effective *printed* bibliographic record of official state publications" for even a single state.[20] A little over twenty years later, the record had improved. Scanning the entries in Tanselle (where the bibliographical records for each state are arranged in chronological order by the period covered) indicates that a number of states, including Louisiana, New Jersey, and Virginia, have a complete bibliographic record of official publications from territorial or colonial times to the present month or year. The bibliographical record of Virginia documents, dating from 1766 to the current quarterly list, is impressive. The editors of the annual Virginia checklist follow the policy of including and identifying items not previously listed. In addition to these three states, Ohio published a major retrospective bibliography in 1973, covering 1803–1970. The current list issued in Ohio has a stated policy of serving as a supplement to this bibliography.

18. Yvonne Boyer, "State Checklists: A Survey," (Master's paper, University of North Carolina, 1981).

19. Barbara Nelson, "Current Checklists of State Publications," *Government Publications Review* 1 (Fall 1973): 109–15; *Government Publications Review* 1 (Spring 1974): 295–301; and *Government Publications Review* 2 (Winter 1975): 83–90.

20. Lloyd, "The Status of State Document Bibliography," 195.

More recently Idaho has published a microfiche edition of a state documents catalog covering 1863–1980, which gives the state complete coverage from the establishment of the Idaho Territory to the present when brought up to date with the current entries in the *Idaho Librarian*.[21] Nevada has gone even further and has entered all official publications into a database that is available online to several libraries in that state. Librarians in Nevada report that although a current checklist is prepared, it is not widely used because it is so much easier to verify a listing on the computer.

One advantage of an online list is that it provides the single access point for the entire period encompassed by the database, including the most recent publications. A printed checklist or bibliographical listing covering a substantial period of the state's history, such as the Ohio union list, is a practical alternative if older publications are sought. For current publications, bibliographical searching is limited to the monthly, quarterly, and annual issues of the checklist in the absence of an online system.

Most of the thirteen states for which Hasse compiled state documents lists have a gap after coverage by Hasse ceased in 1904. In these states more general works, local history bibliographies, imprint lists, and union catalogs are used to identify state documents. Works limited to a particular type of document, such as laws or legislative journals; in a particular format, such as serials (Pennsylvania[22]) or periodicals (Massachusetts[23]); or documents relating to a particular subject or agency, such as agricultural experiment station publications (Connecticut[24]), are also useful. Some states have a gap during the 1930s and 1940s when the depression and World War II dominated the economy. North Carolina lacks bibliographic coverage for state documents issued from 1947 to 1952 and Oregon, from 1926 to 1950.

Purposes of Checklists

Checklists serve both the individuals who use the information contained in the documents listed and the librarians who acquire the documents and make them available to these individuals.

Those who use documents as information sources include all segments of the general public. For those involved in state government administra-

21. Lane, *State Publications: Depository Distribution*, 10.

22. Robert C. Stewart, *Union List of Selected Pennsylvania Serial Documents in Pennsylvania Libraries* (Pittsburgh, Pa.: Pennsylvania Library Association, 1971).

23. Massachusetts Executive Office for Administration and Finance, Office of Planning and Program Coordination, *Massachusetts Inventory of State Agency Periodicals* ([Boston]: 1970).

24. Mohini Mundkur, "Subject and Author Index for Bulletins of the Storrs Agricultural Experiment Station," Connecticut Agricultural Experiment Station Bulletin 453 (Storrs, Conn.: 1979).

tion and for those who study and observe state government, the state checklist is a vital current awareness tool. It is also useful in identifying titles. To be fully useful, however, multiple approaches to the individual items are needed. The arrangement of the checklist, usually by corporate author, even if enhanced with cross references, is not enough to achieve maximum efficiency. Multiple approaches to individual documents by corporate and personal author, title, subjects, and series are needed. Contents notes and analytics for individual documents make even more information available.

Another feature of checklists that is important to the individual user is timeliness. A current list provides access to up-to-date data and may have the added value of alerting the user to documents before they go out of print.

Still another purpose that is of direct benefit to the individual user of checklists is that checklists are a record of what has been published—that is, what is available.

For the student or researcher in the field of state government, the publications of a state agency reveal the mission of the agency, problems encountered and proposed solutions, goals and objectives of the agency, and services provided to the general public.

A significant purpose served by checklists is as a historical record of the publications of the state. On a current basis, this record serves as an announcement of what is available and, for historians, the publication record is part of the history of the state.

For librarians, too, checklists serve multiple purposes; they are tools for acquisition, bibliographical control, and reference.

In the thinking of many state documents librarians, the primary purpose of a state documents checklist is to serve as a selection tool; that is, as an acquisitions aid. This is true because in a number of states the checklist is just that—a list with only enough information for the identification of the titles. For example, at one time the West Virginia list was titled *Short Title Checklist, West Virginia Publications*. Other checklists also have only a minimum of information. Annotations and abstracts, which give added details about the individual titles, are features found in the best checklists. Checklist editors are recognizing that for a checklist to be most useful as a selection tool, the inclusion of availability and ordering information is important. Addresses of state agencies, prices, symbols for depository copies, and notes on the availability of microfiche are often found.

When a publication is no longer available from the issuing agency, borrowing from a library is often the last resort. The S&LDTF "State Documents Checklist Guidelines" commentary (7B) suggests that lists of depository libraries be published at least annually to indicate availability in a library and to facilitate interlibrary loans.

While checklists may function as aids to bibliographic control, they were never intended as an unqualified substitute for cataloging but rather as an alternative. However, many can be used as a source for cataloging data. Checklists often have entries which have been established according to the cataloging rules and may even have tracings (catalogers' notes indicating additional access points such as title, subjects, and series). California at one time included the tracings as part of the checklist entry. Arkansas reproduced the entire catalog card, including the tracings. Since the advent of the major bibliographic utilities, the record numbers assigned by those databases for the individual titles have been added to the checklist entries in some states. Utah, as an extra helpful feature, includes both OCLC and RLIN numbers. Another bit of technical information, a classification number, is often included in the checklist entry. In some states this number is the organization scheme of the list.

In order for a checklist to be most useful for reference work, it must have multiple approaches to the individual entries to provide convenient access to the documents. Indexing by corporate author, individual author, title, and subject is found in many checklists. Keyword-in-context (KWIC) and keyword-out-of-context (KWOC) indexes, which require less professional advice than indexes based on a thesaurus and which are usually computer-generated, are the suggested minimum according to the commentary for the "Checklist Guidelines" of ALA GODORT State and Local Documents Task Force.

A 1986 survey conducted by the Government Printing Office of users of the federal documents checklist, the *Monthly Catalog of United States Government Publications,* reported that reference was by far the most popular use.[25] Of the subscribers to the *Monthly Catalog,* 89 percent used it for reference, compared to 53 percent for acquisitions. Although no such survey is available for state documents, David Parish states unequivocally that checklists "are not considered very useful as a reference source."[26] It is the lack of comprehensive indexes in state checklists that gives rise to his statement. In his survey Parish found only 38 percent of his respondents selecting state checklists as an important reference source, compared to 100 percent selecting blue books. He found only nineteen states listing checklists as important.

Different purposes served by various elements found in state checklists are outlined in Table 6. The document user (the person interested in the information in the documents) is primarily interested in the selection/current awareness and the reference/interlibrary loan purposes of the checklist. According to Table 6, most of the elements of the checklist are

25. "Final Report, Monthly Catalog Users Survey, April 4, 1986," *Administrative Notes* 7, no. 7 (May 1986): 12. This survey was made at the request of the Depository Library Council to the Public Printer, *Administrative Notes* 7, no. 1 (January 1986): 13.

26. David W. Parish, "Into the 1980s: The Ideal State Document Reference Collection," *Government Publications Review* 10 (March–April 1983): 214.

Table 6. Characteristics and Purposes Served by State Documents Checklists

CHARACTERISTICS	PURPOSES			
CONTENT OF LIST	ACQUISITION/ CURRENT AWARENESS	CATALOGING	REFERENCE/ INTERLIBRARY LOAN	INVENTORY/ COLLECTION DEVELOPMENT
Addresses of state agencies	x			
Availability symbols	x			
Ordering identification symbols	x			
Availability of microforms	x			
Price	x	x		
State agency histories			x	
Indexes (title, subject)			x	
Individual periodical issues				x
Regional, municipal, U.S.			x	
CONTENT OF INDIVIDUAL ENTRIES				
Classification numbers		x		
Corporate entry		x	x	x
AACR main entry		x		
MARC format		x		
Tracings		x		
OCLC, RLIN, WLN numbers		x		
Annotations or abstracts	x		x	
Contents notes for journals			x	x
Irregularity data for journals		x		x
Series entry				

designed to meet these needs. The catalog/classification and the collection development/inventory categories are principally of interest to librarians.

In most instances each particular characteristic serves more than one purpose. Addresses, ordering information, and price are characteristics limited to the use of the checklist as a selection tool. On the other hand, contents notes are probably most useful in reference work, and such features as AACR main entry and MARC format are intended for catalogers. However, adherence to AACR and MARC standards is advantageous for librarians doing reference work because the librarian has a basic familiarity with those standards, and addresses of state agencies are sometimes the answer to a reference question.

Checklist Guidelines

The "Guidelines for State Document Checklists," drafted by a work group of the ALA GODORT State and Local Documents Task Force (S&LDTF), were adopted by the ALA Council in 1982. They were based on a survey conducted in 1975.[27] The tabulation of this survey and the individual responses, from all states except Colorado, Delaware, Georgia, and Oklahoma, are available in the GODORT archives.

Although designed for use by editors of state checklists, the guidelines are of interest to others as standards against which home-state checklists can be measured. The guidelines set only minimum standards in order to "provide an opportunity for all states to cooperate in achieving uniformity in reporting the existence of state documents—furthering the goal of nationwide bibliographic control."[28] Although the guidelines and the accompanying commentary are intended to be self-explanatory, some background and elaboration will prove helpful.

BACKGROUND

The survey conducted by the S&LDTF resulted in checklist rules more extensive than the fifty-year-old precedent set by Kuhlman.[29] Kuhlman's rules, except for the ninth rule, were limited to the form and the content of the entries. The ninth rule required biographical notes for each agency.

Kuhlman's rules provided that Library of Congress cataloging practices should be followed with certain exceptions. Perhaps the most sig-

27. The questionnaire and survey were not published. The responses are in the ALA GODORT S&LDTF archives, administered by Sharon Egan, Documents Department, Edmon Low Library, Oklahoma State University, Stillwater, OK 74078. The responses for eleven states were tabulated in *The State of State Documents*, 42-43.

28. See Appendix A, "Guidelines for State Documents Checklists," Commentary, paragraph 1.

29. Kuhlman, "The Need for a Comprehensive Check-List Bibliography," 52–58.

nificant of these exceptions was that all entries should be corporate. Even fifty years ago some state documents were cataloged under individual author if the individual had made a substantial contribution. The details of these old rules are not important except as evidence of the insistence on following established cataloging rules insofar as possible.

Kuhlman's rules did not make provision for indexes to the checklists. He attempted to provide an alternative approach by providing for alphabetizing under the key word or the corporate name. With the key word italicized or capitalized to facilitate this, cross-references were to be used if more than one word might be considered the key word.

Other rules, some of which have been carried forward into the S&LDTF guidelines, are:

1. Include place or publisher only if other than the state capital.
2. Omit name of printer.
3. Use the virgule (/) and the en dash (-) to distinguish fiscal years from calendar years, and in general, follow the method employed by the *Union List of Serials*.

PREAMBLE

The preamble to the S&LDTF guidelines states that checklists are necessary for bibliographic control. Woolley's thesis that checklists should be the reflection, not the instrument, of bibliographical control questions this assumption and anticipates the mainstreaming of documents into general cataloging utilities. This proposition recognizes the legacy from Kuhlman's rules requiring adherence to standard cataloging rules. Woolley emphasizes the idea that bibliographical control can be achieved at the time of the original entry of a document into a bibliographical utility, with documents checklists merely one of several possible by-products from the bibliographical file.[30]

However, even today, not all states input their state documents into a database, and of those that do so, not all have the ability (software or financial) to produce a checklist from the database. Checklists still serve a useful purpose and at least for the short term, will continue to be prepared and used. Nevertheless, some progress has been made toward the goals outlined by Woolley. For example, California produces its checklist from RLIN (Research Libraries Information Network) tapes, and Colorado, from OCLC (Online Computer Library Center) records.

LEGAL BASIS

The first checklist guideline provides that state checklists should be required by law. The trend toward requiring justification for all state pub-

---

30. Woolley, "State Documents Checklists," 236–37.

lications and even requiring that this justification be printed on the documents makes a statutory provision practically indispensable. The primary advantage of statutory mandate is to increase the probability of the list being published. If a law provides for the publication of a list, that in itself gives the list a semblance of official character and makes it more difficult to discontinue publication. Yvonne Boyer, in her study of state checklists, observes that legislation is necessary to ensure that quality is not reduced by budgetary restraints. She found that legislation has a positive effect on the quality of the checklists. The twenty-four states having statutes do slightly better in meeting the checklist guidelines than those without a legislative mandate.[31]

CONTENT AND FORMAT REQUIREMENTS

The gist of the next five guidelines can be consolidated into a single sentence: A complete current list, conforming to the standard periodical format, issued at least quarterly, with an annual index, adequately and appropriately distributed, should be prepared under the supervision of professional personnel. Completeness is a goal that should not be compromised, although this is one of the most difficult tasks facing the checklist editor. Two things making it difficult are the problem of acquiring the documents and the need to have as broad an inclusion policy as possible. Completeness may be more difficult to achieve in the future if the checklist is a by-product of cataloging. The question of whether state documents are worthy of being cataloged has a direct bearing on the completeness of the checklist when the checklist is a by-product of cataloging. The question arises: Will public relations flyers, press releases, and meeting announcements no longer be listed in state checklists because they are not eligible for cataloging?

The commentary on the scope of the checklist, in addition to stressing completeness, advises the inclusion of older, newly discovered titles. With more states having comprehensive retrospective listings of state documents, the opportunity to keep these retrospective lists up to date should not be overlooked. The Ohio policy of including old but newly identified documents in the current checklist is an admirable example.[32]

The reference in the third guideline, to format is a recognition by checklist editors of the needs of librarians. A checklist prepared by librarians should adhere to the recognized formulas for producing a publication that will not add to the burdens of serials librarians.

The statement on frequency may be more liberally interpreted if a shipping list is distributed to a representative number of libraries over the state. According to the 1975 survey on which the guidelines were based,

31. Boyer, "State Checklists," 18.
32. Parish, *State Government Reference Publications*, 2d ed., 20.

eleven states published shipping lists.[33] The relationship of these shipping lists to the checklists is not clear in the survey summary. The shipping lists in some states may be the same as the monthly checklist in other states. This is true in Louisiana, where the shipping list entries are used in the semiannual checklist. In other states, as shown in the earlier Texas example, the shipping list entry is not a full bibliographical entry.

The format of the list also has a bearing on frequency of publication. If bibliographical information about state documents is available in a cataloging database, and libraries in the state have online access, the printed checklist is no longer needed as an identification tool, and its frequency is of less consequence. This is the situation in Nebraska and Nevada, where the index to state documents is online.

Issuance of the index to the checklist on an annual basis is the minimum acceptable frequency. Making the statement requiring an index, as the guideline on frequency does, is an indication that effective use requires a timely index and a tacit assumption that an index is essential.

Like the guideline on frequency, the guideline on distribution is affected by the format of the list. At the time the guidelines were drafted, microform checklists, much less databases, were not contemplated. Microfiche, of course, can be distributed like paper copy, but a checklist that is electronically online is not distributable in the same way.

The commentary says that preparation by a professional is necessary for accurate bibliographical entries and for publication of a quality index. Even if state agencies are required to submit lists of their publications to serve as a basis for the checklist (as in Louisiana, Texas, and other states), these lists need editorial attention from librarians. The standards for bibliographical entry must be uniformly and consistently applied.

PRELIMINARY PAGES OF CHECKLISTS

The seventh guideline relates to statements needed in preliminary pages of the checklist to explain the inclusions and exclusions of the list, its arrangement, availability of the documents listed, and cross-references within the list. These statements are particularly necessary for out-of-state use of the checklist. One quickly becomes accustomed to the parameters and limitations of the checklist in one's home state, but an out-of-state checklist may have entirely different coverage. There is considerable variance among the state checklists in the preliminary statements.[34] An indication of the period covered is the most usual statement on the scope of the checklist, and for most states, the coverage is for publications re-

---

33. The questionnaire and survey were not published. The responses are in the ALA GODORT archives. The responses for eleven states were tabulated in *The State of State Documents*, 42–43.

34. Lane, "State Documents Checklists," 117–34.

ceived, not for publications issued, during the period. Types of publications included is a more frequent statement than kinds of agencies. Checklist editors should realize that users want to know whether judicial publications or state university publications are within the scope of the checklist and should include such information in the preface or preliminary statements.

BIBLIOGRAPHICAL CONTENT OF ENTRIES

Bibliographical content of the individual entries is the area that Kuhlman addressed. The checklist guidelines do not specify that checklist editors use the catalogers' main entry, but if documents are entered in a catalog database, the librarian has no choice. All three bibliographical utilities require cataloging according to *AACR2* and the MARC format. This means that the option given by guideline 8A of omitting the name of the state cannot be exercised (unless the checklist software program makes provision for suppressing the name of the state). Likewise, the note in the commentary to 8A, that full hierarchy should be given, cannot be followed. Guideline 8E, the commentary suggesting the omission of the place of publication (again a rule dating back to Kuhlman's time), cannot be followed because the rules of the bibliographical utilities supersede the guideline.

CONCLUDING REQUIREMENTS

The checklist guidelines end with requirements that (1) mailing addresses of state agencies be made known (if not in the checklist, at least by reference); (2) distribution mailing lists updated only after due notice; and (3) entries for new agencies include a citation for their creation and a brief history. These additional information items are all designed to enable librarians to serve the state document user more effectively.

BOYER SURVEY

In 1981, a student paper by Yvonne Boyer at the University of North Carolina compared 1977 and 1979 checklists to determine the influence of the guidelines. From her survey Boyer concluded:

> While some improvements have been made in state checklists, an average of only 56.71% of the "Guidelines" are currently met. The bibliographical content of the entries usually meet the guidelines. Areas in need of improvement appear to be the physical features of the checklists (i.e., frequency) and the general information included in the checklists (i.e., indexing).[35]

35. Boyer, "State Checklists," abstract.

Bibliographical content, the area in which more state checklists meet the guidelines according to Boyer's findings, is the area for which Kuhlman prepared rules in 1935. It is possible that the Kuhlman rules for checklists published in 1935—which are not substantially different from Checklist Guideline 8 on bibliographical content of entries—have had a lasting influence on checklist bibliography. Perhaps Boyer's study, conducted only two-and-a-half years after the adoption of the guidelines by the S&LDTF, came too soon after their adoption for them to have made an impact. Boyer attributes the meeting of the bibliographical content of the entries to "expansion of cataloging networks and the increase in computerized production of the checklists."[36]

Changes and Trends in Checklists

Changes in state checklists can be seen in the physical appearance of the lists, resulting from the constraints of computer output, and in the individual entries of the checklists that no longer invariably have a government author as the main entry, but often a personal author.

CHECKLISTS TODAY

Substantial changes in state document checklists since 1970 can be traced in part to the impact of the new bibliographical utilities and possibilities presented by advances in technology. Some checklists are examples of the adoption of new procedures and techniques, while for other checklists these changes are still in the future.

A development that has significantly influenced state checklists in recent years was the adoption of new catalog rules. This development affects the individual entries rather than the format of the list. *AACR* in 1970 and *AACR2* in 1978 changed the rules for entry. Another, perhaps lesser, influence on the format and content of the checklists was the adoption of the checklist guidelines.

CHANGES IN PHYSICAL FEATURES

Changes in the physical features of checklists vary from those immediately apparent, such as changes in format, to small details, such as inclusion of the international standard serial number (ISSN) and cataloging in publication (CIP).

In some states, Iowa for example, the entries for the checklist are input as an independent file. In other states, such as Colorado, the checklist entries come from catalog tapes (OCLC) generated by the library and

36. Ibid., 17.

manipulated by a special checklist program. The Colorado list is produced by a commercial company, Marcive.[37] The California checklist, to provide another example, is based on RLIN tapes, and the program producing the checklist was developed by RLIN.

Small changes in the physical features of the checklist worthy of comment include the ISSN on the cover (Kentucky), CIP on the verso of the title page (Washington), use of multiple type sizes (Texas uses three), and reduction of the text (Nevada and Louisiana).

Major changes in format occur with the adoption of computer compilation of the checklist. Computer output in microform (COM) is the most radical change. A 1983 ALA GODORT State and Local Documents Task Force survey reported that seven states issued a checklist in microfiche (Delaware, Michigan, Minnesota, Nebraska, Nevada, Oregon, and Washington), and six states had plans for future listings in a microfiche format.[38]

The content of the checklists has been augmented to include addresses (Massachusetts, New Mexico, Oklahoma), creation and cessation of agencies (New York), regional documents (Nevada for a long time, Texas recently), local documents (Nevada, Utah), and monthly indexes (California). Indexes issued in lieu of cumulations can also be considered a content augmentation if they are thought of as an integral part of the bibliographical service of the state. The Texas indexes are an example.

The individual entries in the checklists have been affected by both editions of the *AACR* and also by state government reorganizations. As states adopted statutes providing so-called "umbrella" departments, the hierarchy of state agencies became more extensive.

Elements in the individual entries that can be seen in recent checklists include tracings (that is, appropriate subjects and added entries); availability codes; OCLC, RLIN, or WLN record numbers; annotations; contents notes; and prices.

THE FUTURE

If the guidelines were to be rewritten today, would there be changes? The requirement for a legislative basis for the checklist will continue to be necessary. Perhaps this requirement could be stated more generally— to the effect that a bibliographical record of state publications should be required with the understanding that this record might be part of a larger record. In other words, bibliographical records of the existence of state publications should be required by law; it is not essential that these records be in a separate file.

37. Marcive, Inc., P.O. Box 47508, San Antonio, TX 78265-7508.

38. Margaret T. Lane, "Scattered Notes for State Documents Librarians," *Documents to the People* 11 (May 1983): 57–58.

The guideline on the scope of the checklist, with its emphasis on completeness, is likewise of continuing importance because of the value of the checklist as a historical record.

Format, frequency, distribution, and the statements required in the checklist content guideline are attributes that might vary with changed circumstances, such as computer production of the lists.

The content of the entry should be closely related to standard cataloging practices, as Kuhlman indicated long ago. The ALA GODORT State and Local Documents Task Force "Guideline on Data Bases" addresses the issue of inputting state documents into databases.[39] As more states adopt the practice of cataloging state documents first and then producing a checklist as a subsidiary product, the importance of the individual elements of an entry will decrease because they will be determined by the requirements of the bibliographical utilities for adherence to the standards.

Surely if new checklist guidelines were written, new formats, particularly online databases would have to be accommodated. Nebraska, which has an online state documents checklist, has a publication providing instructions for the use of the checklist and several other databases available through the same program. The Nebraska database is menu-driven and lists the following options:

1. State Publications Checklist
2. Nebraska Statutes
3. Introduced Bills
4. Nebraska Film Locator.

The Nebraska State Publications Checklist database can be searched by single words, phrases, or Boolean constructs using the IBM database management package, STAIRS.

The checklist database provides access by subject, author, title, series, and issuing agency. It identifies new publications and gives ordering information for them. The full text of the checklist entries is included in the database. There are sixteen fields for each entry:

> Computer record number
> State Documents Classification
> Checklist issue number
> Alternate agency name flag
> Document title
> Document personal/joint corporate author(s)
> Publication date/Clearinghouse holdings
> Pagination information & State Depository flag
> Special contents notes (illus., maps, etc.)
> Frequency of publication (for serials only)
> Availability/ordering information

39. See Appendix A, "Guidelines for Inputting State Documents into Data Bases."

Series title
Series number
Annotation
LC subject headings (separated by semi-colons)
Subject, title, author, series cross-references.[40]

Conclusion

The individual state checklists and bibliographies are the most important tools for acquiring and using the documents of a single state. The checklists vary widely from state to state in scope, format, and content.

Preparation of checklists has a history dating back to colonial times. State-by-state lists of these checklists have been compiled since Reece published his list in 1915.[41] Today the basic list of checklists and bibliographies, both all-state and for the individual states, is Palic.[42]

Bibliographical control of state publications, as evidenced by the issuance of state checklists, has increased in the past few years. Comparison of the list in the Wilcox *Manual* with that in Palic illustrates this trend. The updates to Palic cited in this text are a further indication of added bibliographical control. More checklists and more documents entered in the bibliographical utilities have combined to provide more bibliographical control.

The checklist guidelines provide guidance for checklists as we have known them in the past. Today the possibilities of cooperation between the checklist editor and the cataloger have lessened the independent work of the checklist editor. By using data created by catalogers, the checklist editor's preparation of bibliographical records for state publications can be limited to publications that are not cataloged. Records for publications that are cataloged can be retrieved, arranged, and reproduced as a checklist. For the future, Nevada, with records for *all* its documents online, and Nebraska, with current bibliographic records online, serve as an inspiration.

40. Nebraska Library Commission, "Online Database Users Guide: Dial-Access Instructions," rev. February, 1984–date, in *Docs on Docs*, item NE85:M1.

41. Reece, *State Documents for Libraries.*

42. Palic, *Government Publications.*

8

INFORMATION

SERVICES

Guiding library patrons in locating state publications and information in state publications calls for special skills and bibliographic knowledge over and above standard reference skills. Querying the patron to find out exactly what publication or information is needed, determining how much searching the patron is willing to do, and sensing when to abandon the quest are all part of good reference service. Reference service for state documents also requires skills necessary for work with documents in general along with a few other skills specific to state documents. The special skills necessary for work with state documents and the particular tools needed are the subjects of this chapter.

State Documents Reference Librarians

State documents reference librarians are treated here as though a single individual exercises these responsibilities. In the "real world," these individuals do not devote their full time to state documents work, and sometimes more than one staff member discharges the functions of the state document reference librarians.

EDUCATION

Formal courses on state documents for library school students are few. In most library schools, state documents are usually taught as a small segment of the general government publications course.[1] Some library schools, however, offer a separate documents course on state publications,

---

1. Fred J. Heinritz, "The Present State of the Teaching of Government Publications in Library Schools," *Library Trends* 15 (July 1966): 157–66. The published literature on the teaching of government publications is noted in John V. Richardson, Jr., "Paradigmatic Shifts in the Teaching of Government Publications, 1895–1985," *Journal of Education and Information Science* 26 (Spring 1986): 263, n. 2.

although as one professor has written, "This area of study is not all wine and roses."[2]

A course outline and bibliography limited to state publications were drafted by the Education Committee of the ALA GODORT State Documents Task Force in 1977. The outline is divided into six parts: (1) State Government Origin, (2) Basic State Publications—Source and Use, (3) State Intergovernmental Relations, (4) Bibliographic Guides and Indexes, (5) Reference Use and Comparative Statistics, and (6) Administration of State Document Collections.[3] A bibliography prepared by the work group was published in *Documents to the People.*[4]

The ALA GODORT Education Task Force prepared a "Draft Syllabus of Resources for Teaching Government Publications" in 1976. The state document section consists of a well-selected bibliography, arranged by topics and a list of state checklists. The bibliography topics are: (1) Early Records of State Documents, (2) State Government, Laws and Legislation, (3) Introductory Readings, (4) Manuals and Guides, (5) Selection and Acquisition, (6) Checklists of State Publications, and (7) Cataloging, Classification, Arrangement.[5]

Textbooks for government documents have been reviewed by John Richardson, who found that although Wyer, the first textbook in the documents field, encompassed the three levels of government, until recently other writers limited their texts to publications of the federal government. Hernon and McClure in *Public Access to Government Information* return to the multilevel concept and include a chapter, "Exploiting State and Local Information Resources." Hernon and McClure's work represents, according to Richardson, another break with traditional document textbook organization, a "paradigmatic shift" from the source of issue approach to "issues, and trends and strategies."[6] Hernon and McClure's chapter "The Education of the Government Documents Professional" makes few references to state documents librarianship.

Informal continuing education is offered at the state level through workshops and newsletters. The New Mexico example is noteworthy because a formal certificate was awarded. Basic training in state documents was offered in New Mexico in 1979 and 1980. The training was a workshop exercise of twenty-six test questions to be answered from fourteen items

2. Joe Morehead, "The Challenges of Teaching State and Local Government Publications," *Documents to the People* 13 (July-August 1986): 543.

3. ALA GODORT State Documents Task Force Education Committee, "Syllabus for the Teaching of State Publications," Working Draft. May 1977.

4. "Bibliography for State Documents Syllabus," *Documents to the People* 6 (January 1978): 54–63.

5. ALA GODORT Education Task Force, Optimal Syllabus Committee, "Draft Syllabus of Resources for Teaching Government Publications," M. Dean Trivette, Coordinator. July 18, 1976.

6. Richardson, "Paradigmatic Shifts," 249–66.

on an annotated bibliography. The answers required were titles of publications only, not specific data. The 1980 follow-up consisted of twenty-nine questions based on a fifteen-title bibliography of reference items distributed to depository librarians in the previous eighteen months. The 1980 exercise was conducted on an honor basis, with test questions and answers (in sealed envelopes) mailed to depository librarians. Corrected tests were mailed to the state library for certificates.[7]

SPECIAL SKILLS

A reference librarian who specializes in state documents must remember that the patron may not know that a state document can answer his or her question and may not be familiar with the indexing or other special features of the tools that should be used to find the answer. The librarian's offer to help must be volunteered more spontaneously and more frequently than might be customary in general reference work.

One must first be aware of the possibility that information which meets a user's need can be found in a state publication. This is the point at which it is vital that the general reference staff remember what types of information can be found in documents. Here the staff should either guide the patrons to the appropriate bibliographic tools or refer them to the documents department or documents specialist.

The study, *Improving the Quality of Reference Service for Government Publications*, by McClure and Hernon reports that a survey based on federal documents questions found only 37 percent of the survey questions were answered correctly. As a means of improving this distressing situation, the authors emphasize better integration of documents reference service with the reference service of the library as a whole.[8] Administrative support, a "positive staff attitude," and written policy statements are necessary for effective reference use of government publications, according to the authors. McClure and Hernon mention the likelihood that "the individual library staff member is *the single most significant factor* affecting the quality of reference service for documents."[9]

Kathleen Heim, addressing government documents librarians in 1984, outlined requirements for success as a government information specialist:

> Five characteristics of successful government information professionals are political awareness, skill in identifying sources of information, ability

7. All the items for the training course are in the *Documents on Documents Collection* together with letters of transmittal and agendas. The certificate is *Docs on Docs*, 1973–1979, NM:M4; the bibliographies and test questions are *Docs on Docs*, 1973–1979, item NM:M2 and *Docs on Docs*, 1980–1983, item NM:M7.

8. Charles R. McClure and Peter Hernon, *Improving the Quality of Reference Service for Government Publications* (Chicago: American Library Association, 1983).

9. Ibid., 111.

to elicit information, capacity to convey information, and commitment to disseminate information with an advocacy stance.[10]

Librarians using state documents must have or develop a background in state history and a knowledge of the structure of state government. In addition, they must understand the importance of current information. The patron who has read about a publication in a newspaper expects the librarian to be able to produce it. The issues facing the legislature (perhaps a state lottery or a proposed dam), the timing of elections and of the meeting of the legislature, and economic conditions in the state are all part of the political, social and economic awareness that a state documents reference librarian must cultivate. The importance of familiarity with microforms (as stressed by Zink) and knowledge of computers and database searching (as advocated by Heim) must not be overlooked.[11]

The variances among the states in the subjects on which information is needed, the tools available to locate the information, and the varying formats in which the information appears all require interpretation by librarians. Familiarity with the publications of one state is frequently an advantage in attempting to use the publications of another.

The general reference tools for state documents are, in many instances, the tools that are used for acquisition of documents. The *Monthly Checklist of State Publications* is the mainstay of many documents librarians, although the lack of a current index makes reference use somewhat inconvenient.[12]

To search for a particular state publication in a library, the patron may rely on the card catalog or a database of library holdings. If the collection is separate from the main collection and not classified by the same scheme as the general collection, reliance on the guidance of the library staff is critical. First-time users of local classification schemes should receive directions and guidance in the use of the scheme, either in the form of signs, handouts, or verbal directions from library staff.

Locating information within state publications can also be a problem. For example, those state publications that are primary sources, that is, the legal materials, are chronological by nature. Court reports, session laws, administrative rulings and decisions are all published on a continuing basis,

10. Kathleen Heim, "Attitudinal and Operational Considerations for Education in the Provision of Government Information," *Government Publications Review* 12 (July-August 1985): 131.

11. Steven D. Zink, "The Impending Crisis in Government Publications Reference Service," *Microform Review* 11 (Spring 1982): 106–11; Kathleen M. Heim, "Government-Produced Machine-Readable Statistical Data as a Component of the Social Science Information System: An Examination of Federal Policy and Strategies for Access" in *Communicating Public Access to Government Information; Proceedings of the Second Annual Library Government Documents and Information Conference*, ed. Peter Hernon (Westport, Conn.: Meckler Publishing, 1983), 33–74.

12. *Monthly Checklist of State Publications* (Washington, D.C.: GPO) v. 1 +, 1910 +. Monthly.

year by year. The volumes for individual years may be indexed, but each volume is a separate unit. To find information by subject, it is necessary to consult digests or compiled statutes. Most of these legal finding tools are commercially published, although a few states do issue official editions of their statutes. Commercially available legal databases (the major ones are WESTLAW and LEXIS) make information in court reports available through computer searches, an alternative way of locating information. It is the librarian who can guide the user to these tools and, through them, help the patron locate the needed information.

Nonlegal publications, which include most executive branch publications, do not always have a table of contents or an index because they are prepared by part-time publishers. Interpretation of statistical tables by a reference librarian and a reminder that more up-to-date information might be available through another source, such as a telephone call to a state agency, may be needed.

Librarians have many different reasons for using state documents and use different tools for all-state and for in-state approaches. For example, if the issuing agency is known, the *Monthly Checklist of State Publications* is used for an all-state or out-of-state search, and the local state checklist for an in-state approach. Retrospective searches by issuing agency rely on the same tools, but the searches are more tedious with a year-by-year search required in the *Monthly Checklist of State Publications* and for most states, various local bibliographies.

Searches by subject use *PAIS* or the *State Government Research Checklist* for all-state searches and the index to the state checklist, if there is such an index, for in-state searches.[13] Some subjects (agriculture, geology, medicine) have comprehensive indexes that include state documents. If available, these are useful. They can be supplemented with listings made by state agencies. David Parish's *Bibliography* is a current guide to bibliographies issued by state agencies.[14] His listing of 1031 titles is an indication of the quantity of publications in this area. Searching for laws by subject is facilitated by the Foster and Boast and the Nyberg and Boast compilations for all-state searches.[15] In-state searches for laws by subject use the index to state codes or revised statutes. When state statutes become available on WESTLAW, subject searches for current legislation will be possible for any subject, will be up-to-date, and can be supplemented easily.

13. *Public Affairs Information Service Bulletin* (New York: PAIS) v. 1+ 1915+. Weekly; *State Government Research Checklist* (Lexington, Ky.: Council of State Governments, 1947+). Bimonthly.

14. David W. Parish, *A Bibliography of State Bibliographies, 1970–1982* (Littleton, Colo.: Libraries Unlimited, 1985).

15. Lynn Foster and Carol Boast, *Subject Compilations of State Laws: Research Guide and Annotated Bibliography* (Westport, Conn.: Greenwood Press, 1981); Cheryl Nyberg and Carol Boast, *Subject Compilations of State Laws, 1979–83: Research Guide and Annotated Bibliography* (Westport, Conn.: Greenwood Press, 1984).

Searches for statistics use the *Statistical Reference Index* for all-state searches and the state statistical abstract for the in-state approach.[16]

Tools appropriate for special groups or for special formats are available in some fields. State compilations for high school librarians or law librarians meet the state needs for these groups. The listing in *State Atlases* is an all-state tool for maps.[17] Some recent state map compilations are listed in footnote 46.

Types of Special Reference Tools

Reference tools can be divided into two broad groups: conventional reference tools and all other publications.[18] Those produced as reference tools—checklists, statistical abstracts, directories, and the like—are often listed in guides having entries for each of the fifty states. Seven of the eleven types of state government publications of reference value, as listed in articles by Ford and Nakata and by Gary Purcell are in the group of tools produced as reference tools.[19] Statistical information, legislative calendars and indexes, information about government, business and commercial information, judicial or administrative court reports, administrative rules and regulations, and maps all fall in this category.

The other four categories listed in the same articles—recreational information, research reports, administrative or regulatory agency reports, and agriculture and gardening—cover a multitude of topics. These groups of reference tools are issued both as serials and as monographs and are not usually listed by category. Guides to state documents in these categories are selective and cite representative or new titles. Although Parish in his reference guide has a section on tourist guides, he indicates that those listed are representative only, because "the vacation tourist guide is an ever-changing type of state document."[20]

Sources for providing reference use of home state publications were evaluated by academic librarians and public librarians in 1983 to ascertain preferred sources. The results are given in Table 7.

The reference value of some types of state documents was also analyzed by the same writers; the results are presented in Table 8. For both academic

16. *Statistical Reference Index (SRI)* (Washington, D.C.: Congressional Information Service, 1980+).

17. *State Atlases: An Annotated Bibliography*, no. 108 (Chicago: Council of Planning Libraries, 1983).

18. Marilyn Moody, "State Documents: Basic Selection Sources," *Collection Building* 7 (Spring 1985): 41.

19. Barbara J. Ford and Yuri Nakata, "Reference Use of State Government Information in Academic Libraries," *Government Publications Review* 10 (March-April 1983): 189–99; Gary R. Purcell, "Reference Use of State Government Information in Public Libraries," *Government Publications Review* 10 (March-April 1983): 173–87.

20. David W. Parish, *State Government Reference Publications: An Annotated Bibliography*, 2d ed. (Littleton, Colo.: Libraries Unlimited, 1981), 164.

Table 7. *Preferred Sources for Reference Access*

	ACADEMIC LIBRARIES[a]	PUBLIC LIBRARIES[b]
Home state documents checklist	1	2
State depository distribution	2	1
State agency mailing lists	3	3
Monthly Checklist of State Publications	4	5
Statistical Reference Index	5	7
State newspapers	6	4
Bibliographies	7	6

[a] Barbara J. Ford and Yuri Nakata, "Reference Use of State Government Information in Academic Libraries," *Government Publications Review* 10 (March–April 1983): 193.
[b] Gary R. Purcell, "Reference Use of State Government Information in Public Libraries," *Government Publications Review* 10 (March–April 1983): 181.

Table 8. *Reference Value of State Documents*

	ACADEMIC LIBRARIES[a]	PUBLIC LIBRARIES[b]
Statistical information	1	1
Legislative publications	2	2
Information about government	3	3
Business or commercial information	4	4
Research reports	5	5
Judicial or administrative court reports	6	11
Maps	7	4
Administrative or regulatory reports	8	10
Administrative rules and regulations	9	8
Recreational information	10	5
Agricultural or gardening information	11	7

[a] Barbara J. Ford and Yuri Nakata, "Reference Use of State Government Information in Academic Libraries," *Government Publications Review* 10 (March–April 1983): 193.
[b] Gary R. Purcell, "Reference Use of State Government Information in Public Libraries," *Government Publications Review* 10 (March–April 1983): 181.

and public libraries the categories of state publications having the highest reference value were statistical information, legislative publications, and information about government (its structure, activities, and personnel). The lowest perceived value for academic libraries was for recreational information and agricultural and gardening information; for public libraries the lowest value was administrative or regulatory agency reports and judicial or administrative court reports.

GUIDES TO THE STATUTES

A wealth of information on research techniques relating to state laws is given in *Subject Compilations of State Laws*. The "Research Guide" in this work is a detailed, separately indexed, discussion of state legislation beginning with definitions for bill, slip law, session laws, state code, and annotated code. The listings of legal research manuals (both general and for individual states), state codes and publishers, and research aids all provide guidance for the reference librarian. Although tools for current research are stressed, information for those doing retrospective searches is provided.

The principal purpose of this work is to list those publications that answer the question, "What are the state laws on ————?" The 1,242 bibliographic entries are for publications published between 1960 and 1979 and are arranged under 403 subjects. Cross-references, an author index, and a directory of publishers added to the usefulness of the lists. This work has been supplemented by a volume, published in 1984, covering 1979–1983 and by a privately published work for 1983–1985. Freedom of information, open meetings, and sunset laws are only a few of the topics for which these books list compilations of state laws.

A similar list is found in Schmeckebier and Eastin, *Government Publications and Their Use.*[21] The Schmeckebier and Eastin list is limited to compilations published as federal publications. The authors suggest that those interested in state legislation should apply to the federal agency operating in their field of interest. For example, the first compilation cited for a specific field is the Civil Aeronautics Authority "Survey of State Airport Zone Legislation."

A current source suggested by Foster and Boast for federally published state compilations is the *CIS Annual Index and Abstracts.*[22] The *CIS Index* covers all publications of the U.S. Congress and since 1979 has used the heading "State Laws" to identify compilations of state laws.

Martindale-Hubbell Law Directory has digests of state laws by subject in volume 7.[23] This annual publication provides citations to the state statutes, which are summarized. For a brief statement of the law of a particular state, *Martindale-Hubbell* is the first choice. Because the subject headings are consistent from state to state, comparisons of the laws of all the states on a particular subject can be made.

21. Laurence F. Schmeckebier and Roy B. Eastin, *Government Publications and Their Use,* 2d rev. ed. (Washington, D.C.: Brookings Institution, 1969).

22. *CIS Annual Abstracts and Index* (Washington, D.C.: Congressional Information Service, 1970+).

23. *Martindale-Hubbell Law Directory,* v. 7 (Summit, N.J.: Martindale-Hubbell). Annual.

Shepard's Acts and Cases by Popular Names, Federal and State is another tool that locates state legislation that is known by a popular name.[24] If a state statute has a popular name, such as "right to work," citations are given for all states having legislation so designated. Users who are making a search by subject must remember that the statute must have been referred to by a popular name; thus the list may not be complete for the subject matter. Moreover, because both "bad check law" and "worthless check law" are popular names, the laws on this subject are not listed in one place. Foster and Boast say that the majority of entries for acts are for state acts.[25] Semiannual pocket parts keep the volume up to date.

West Publishing Company has announced a major new program to include the text of state statutes in its WESTLAW database. Information from the WESTLAW representative at (800) 328-0109 is that the plans include an access program that would permit an all-state search by topic. In September 1986, when the announcement was published in the *American Bar Association Journal,* the Illinois statutes were online and several additional states were to be added by the end of the year.

GUIDES TO OTHER LEGISLATIVE MATERIALS

Guide to State Legislative Materials, by Mary L. Fisher, is intended to be an introductory guide to the sources of state legislative and selected administrative materials.[26] From these sources one can acquire and pursue the status of pending legislation, legislative intent of enactment, regulation, attorney general opinions construing the statutes, and executive pronouncements which have the force and effect of law.

State Legislative Sourcebook is arranged by state, with consistent subheadings thereunder for (1) legislative organization and process, (2) information about individual legislators, (3) where to get bills, bill status, and session-related information, (4) interim study information, (5) lobbying information, and (6) sources of general information for each state's government.[27]

Legislative history for state legislation is not usually available. The Missouri situation is typical: "It is evident from the comparison of the resources available for tracking federal legislation to those available in Missouri that Missouri has little to offer."[28]

24. *Shepard's Acts and Cases by Popular Names, Federal and State.* 3d ed. (Colorado Springs, Colo.: Shepard's McGraw-Hill, 1986). 2 v. Semiannual supplements.

25. Foster and Boast, *Subject Compilations,* 29.

26. Mary L. Fisher, ed., *Guide to State Legislative Materials,* 3d ed. AALL (American Association of Law Libraries) Publications Series, no. 15. (Littleton, Colo.: Rothman, 1985). Loose-leaf.

27. *State Legislative Sourcebook: A Resource Guide to Legislative Information in the Fifty States* (Topeka, Kans.: Government Research Service, 1985). Loose-leaf.

28. D. A. Divilbiss, "Missouri Sources for Status Reports and Legislative Histories," *Show-Me Libraries* 35 (December 1983): 10.

STATISTICAL INFORMATION

Statistical Reference Index (SRI) indexes ten to fifteen statistical titles from each state, including the statistical abstract, if published. Indexing is by subjects, names, title and issuing sources. A microfiche copy of the documents indexed is available (with minor exceptions) as a full set or for individual state governments. Fiche for individual titles is not available.

A state publication worthy of duplication in other states is Redmond's *Guide to Statistics in Illinois State Documents.*[29] This publication is patterned after the U.S. Census Bureau, *Directory of Federal Statistics for States: A Guide to Sources, 1967.* It serves as a supplement to the state statistical abstract, making it much easier to find "hidden" statistical data, according to an enthusiastic review by Michele Strange.[30] The list includes 150 sources, arranged by subject.

A good source for state statistics in a federal publication is the *State and Metropolitan Data Book.*[31] Two editions have appeared, in 1979 and 1982. Statistics for births, deaths, health, education, employment, personal wealth, crime, housing, business and commerce are provided.

INFORMATION ABOUT GOVERNMENT

Information about government includes its structure, activities and personnel.

The *Book of the States* has chapters by experts, directory information for each state, and many tables.[32] Its wide scope and biennial publication pattern make it a widely known ready reference tool.

The Council of State Governments publication *State Blue Books and Reference Publications* lists state documents reference items for the individual states, including blue books, legislative manuals, directories, statistical abstracts, and other reference works.[33]

Directories have been listed in the state agency chapter and checklists, in that chapter.

29. Mary Redmond, *Guide to Statistics in Illinois State Documents* (Springfield, Ill.: Illinois State Library, 1976).

30. Michele Strange, review of *Guide to Statistics in Illinois State Documents* by Mary Redmond, *Government Publications Review* 4 (Spring 1979): 43–44.

31. U.S. Bureau of the Census, *State and Metropolitan Area Data Book: A Supplement to the Statistical Abstract* (Washington, D.C.: GPO, 1979, 1982). Earlier Census Bureau publications with state statistics include: *Directory of Federal Statistics*; *Directory of Non-federal Statistics for States and Local Areas: A Guide to Sources, 1969*, prepared by Francine E. Shacter (Washington, D.C.: GPO, 1970); *State Reports on State and Local Government Finances.* Census of Governments 1972, vol. 6, no. 2 (Washington, D.C.: GPO, 1973).

32. *Book of the States* (Lexington, Ky.: Council of State Governments, 1935+). Biennial.

33. *State Blue Books and Reference Publications: A Selected Bibliography*, rev. and annotated ed. (Lexington, Ky.: Council of State Governments, 1983). (RM-526)

STATE LEGAL RESEARCH GUIDES

Legal research guides provide an introduction to legislative and judicial materials used by the legal profession.[34]

Such materials are part of the state documents collection in some states. Also included in these guides are the administrative materials issued by executive agencies, which include both rules and regulations and opinions. Foster and Boast include a list of these guides.[35]

Recent additions to this list have been published by Louisiana and Minnesota. *Louisiana Legal Research,* by Win-Shin S. Chiang, is intended for research in current Louisiana law.[36] It does not supersede the earlier Louisiana guides used for historical research. *Minnesota Legal Research Guide,* by Arlette M. Soderberg and Barbara L. Golden is another recent guide.[37]

Other guides prepared for individual states include the AALL guides, now published for twenty-three states, listed in Appendix D. These guides are an unnumbered series prepared by law librarians, and each guide is different. A current listing of these titles with ordering information is found from time to time in *Jurisdocs,* the newsletter of the Government Documents Special Interest Section of the American Association of Law Libraries.

GUIDES FOR INDIVIDUAL STATES

For most states, guides to state publications are a few pages in the depository manual, if the state has one. Examples of more extensive guides are those from New York and Texas. These bear some explanation as they are excellent models that all states might wish to emulate.

New York

One of the best individual guides to state publications is that written by Dorothy Butch and published for New York State, *Official Publications of New York State: A Bibliographic Guide to Their Use.*[38] This is not a typical guide prepared by law librarians explaining the use of the court reports, session laws, and statutes. In fact, topics specifically excluded are "statutes,

34. Morris L. Cohen, *Legal Research in a Nutshell,* 3d ed. (St. Paul, Minn.: West Publishing, 1978), is a brief, introductory text.

35. Foster and Boast, *Subject Compilations,* 14–17.

36. Win-Shin S. Chiang, *Louisiana Legal Research* (Austin, Tex.: Butterworth Legal Publishers, 1985).

37. Arlette M. Soderberg and Barbara L. Golden, *Minnesota Legal Research Guide* (Buffalo, N.Y.: William S. Hein, 1985).

38. Dorothy Butch, *Official Publications of New York State: A Bibliographic Guide to Their Use,* rev. August 1980. (Albany, N.Y.: New York State Library, Cultural Education Center, 1981).

administrative law, judicial decisions, and legislative history."[39] Rather this guide is a five-part bibliographical text that demonstrates the extensive background of its author in servicing New York state documents and the many details that librarians who service state documents must have at their fingertips.

A running commentary ties together the 179 titles cited. The text begins with the caution that not all New York state documents are in the catalog at the State Library and lists the checklists that supplement the catalog. General history and government texts are listed, followed by a brief statement on the constitutions which the state has had. These constitutions are not listed, but the works that amplify and supplement the constitutional history of the state are given with evaluations of their usefulness. At the end of Part 1 are five titles listed under the heading, "Nineteenth Century: Elusive Governmental, Biographical and Political Information." Part 2 covers the legislative branch of government and Part 3, the longest part, the executive branch. Advice in the text that press releases of the biographies of gubernatorial nominees are excluded from the *Public Papers* and should be retained if a comprehensive Executive Chamber collection is desired is obviously addressed to librarians.[40] Here again, the text reveals the author's expertise, referring to a "frequently reorganized agency" (p. 14) and "the most authoritative work" (p. 21).

Part 4 on the judicial branch is a mini-history of court reform in the state, and Part 5 lists "Selected Sources of Statistical and Fiscal Information." The text that ties this bibliographical listing together is so full of practical advice on the use of materials in the New York State Library (references to nonpublic files in the reference department, p. 2), on policies for other libraries (retain the press releases of gubernatorial nominees) and guidance for researchers in general ("other useful materials include" and "an interesting history") that it can almost be read as an essay. The inclusion of popular names of commissions and their reports will arouse a favorable response from many readers. This unique guide should serve as a model for other states. An expanded version is in preparation.

Texas

The Texas primer is similar to the New York guide but has more elementary information. *Texas State Documents: A Primer for Librarians* begins with an explanation of the three branches of government, to which the author, Brenda Olds, adds a suggested fourth branch, higher education. Olds says:

> Universities enjoy more private funding than do agencies, have more self-supporting enterprises. Financial accountability in published format is

39. Ibid., iii.
40. Ibid., 12.

much more detailed than for agencies; universities must publish an annual financial report and a detailed budget (which agencies do not normally publish). There is no central control over publishing within a university and most departments publish and distribute their own publications.[41]

The same types of advice to librarians given in the New York guide is found: warnings to keep back issues, tools to use as supplements, and sources for bringing information up-to-date. The Texas primer serves not only as a guide for the uninitiated but as a general review for experienced state documents librarians in Texas.

MAPS

Maps have attained a new visibility in libraries due to the current federal distribution program and to the establishment of a new ALA round table, MAGERT (Map and Geography Round Table), in 1980. An oft-repeated figure is that 80 percent of all maps are produced by governmental units.[42] The states are responsible for some of that number and are often involved on a cooperative basis with the federal government.

Charles Seavey, a map librarian, indicates that state maps are not as good as federal maps. He says that they present acquisition problems because they are documents; bibliographical control problems because they are documents and because of their format; and use problems because of their format.[43]

The 1983 survey by Sandra Faull reported on the different types of state agencies that publish maps.[44] State geological surveys, which have a history of issuing publications in cooperation with other agencies, both state and federal, produce many maps and usually have catalogs of their current publications. These catalogs, mostly available without charge, are "the most complete readily available mapping information on a state," according to Faull.

In addition to state geological surveys, units of state government that produce maps in most states include highway and transportation agencies, and natural resources and environment agencies. Other types of agencies that Faull reported as issuing maps include planning, commerce and development, public lands, and parks.

41. Brenda F. Olds, *Texas State Documents: A Primer for Librarians* (Austin: Legislative Reference Library, 1975), ii. In *Docs on Docs*, 1973–1979, item TX:H.

42. Charles A. Seavey, "Government Map Publications: An Overview" in *Communicating Public Access to Government Information; Proceedings of the Second Annual Library Government Documents and Information Conference*, ed. Peter Hernon (Westport, Conn.: Meckler Publishing, 1983), 75.

43. Ibid., 88.

44. Sandra K. Faull, "State and Local Map Publishing in the United States," *Government Publications Review* 10 (July-August 1983): 375–80.

Faull reported that three states have a specific map depository program; fourteen states that have a depository library program include the distribution of maps in that program. These figures are based on a survey response from twenty-eight states.

The National Cartographic Information Center (NCIC), a unit of the National Mapping Program of the United States Geological Survey, has plans to establish NCIC affiliates in each state. These affiliates would assist the NCIC in collecting state and local data and in responding to inquiries. Texas already has a state affiliate in the Department of Natural Resources and Illinois has a cooperative arrangement between the Illinois State Geological Survey and the Map and Geography Library of the University of Illinois, Champaign-Urbana.[45]

Recent bibliographic guides include *State Atlases: An Annotated Bibliography*, and those from Georgia, Michigan, and Washington.[46] The state map information center at the University of Illinois, Champaign-Urbana is an agency that should be included in such a directory.

Nonpublished Formats for State Information

Reference service for state publications, like all reference service, is governed by the need for the information; that is, different information is needed by different persons. The information needed for a school paper on cows is much less specific than the information needed by the farmer whose milk cows have eaten contaminated feed.

State publications in printed form are useful for some reference purposes. In many situations, however, it is no longer possible to rely on printed publications. The latest information may be available only by telephone or in a computer database. Printed publications and directories are guides for the librarian in identifying the agency to be contacted for up-to-date information.

Many states have general purpose telephone numbers for responding to citizen inquiries. In addition, special purpose lines are available for questions on utility services, state regulations and licenses, insurance problems, energy conservation, and many more topics. Michigan listed fifteen such lines in a documents newsletter.[47] Most states have special legislative

45. Arlyn Sherwood, "National Cartographic Information Center," *Illinois Libraries* 64 (October 1982): 1016–17.

46. Gayle R. Christian, "Bibliography of Georgia Maps from State Agencies," *The Georgia Librarian* 22 (November 1985): 90–91; James M. Walsh, "A Michigan Carto-Bibliography: An Annotated Guide to Sources Pertaining to Michigan Maps, Atlases, and Related Cartographic Materials" (January 1983). ERIC microfiche ED 230 482; Peter Stark, *Purchasing Maps of Washington: A Popular Guide* (Ellensburg, Wash.: Central Washington University Library, 1981).

47. F. Anne Diamond, "State Toll-Free 'Hot Lines'," *Red Tape* no. 4 (July-August 1979): 5.

hotlines that operate during the time the legislature is in session. The reference librarian handling state documents must evaluate the need for the information and if appropriate, bring the printed information up to date through correspondence and telephone inquiries.

REFERRAL

If needed information is not available to the patron at the first point of inquiry in the library, referral is an appropriate step. In a survey of U.S. academic depository libraries, Hernon and McClure found that referral service was both infrequent and limited.[48] The authors recommended a referral file encompassing individuals, specific information sources, organizations or agencies, departments or areas of the library, and techniques or processes. The authors go so far as to say that if such a file is accurate and current, it may be "essential for the provision of high-quality reference work."

For state documents, referral may be a practice employed more frequently than for federal documents, particularly by libraries located at the state capital. These libraries have contacts at state agencies for the acquisition of state documents and it is only reasonable to suppose that the same contacts are used when answers to reference questions are needed. The state library agency in the various states often serves as a backup library for public libraries of the state and has many reference questions referred from those libraries. Academic libraries, particularly if they are depositories for state documents, also have an ongoing relationship with the state library, with referrals a natural outgrowth. Whether libraries in various parts of the state take advantage of the services of a library at the state capital, or whether they contact the appropriate state agency directly, depends on the information sought and the needs of the particular patron.

No investigation of the extent of referrals for in-state information has been written up in the literature. Nor is there information on out-of-state referrals. For out-of-state referrals, the librarians listed in the "State Document Authorities" section of the *Directory of Government Document Collections and Librarians* should be helpful.[49] A hint from a state documents librarian in Texas is worth observing: "if you call, rather than suggest the patron call, chances are that the information will benefit the library as well—either in another contact, publication(s) or both."[50] Organizations

48. Peter Hernon and Charles R. McClure, "Referral Services in U.S. Academic Depository Libraries: Findings, Implications, and Research Needs," *RQ* 22 (Winter 1982): 161.

49. American Library Association, Government Documents Round Table, *Directory of Government Document Collections and Librarians*, 4th ed. (Bethesda, Md.: Congressional Information Service, 1984), 643–47.

50. American Library Association, Government Documents Round Table, State and Local Documents Task Force Education Committee, "Syllabus for the Teaching of State Publications; Working Draft," (May 1977), 54.

and agencies to which referrals might be made are listed in the standard reference tools. Referrals to online bibliographic databases and cataloging utilities are also appropriate, although none are devoted exclusively to state documents.

STATE CENSUS DATA CENTERS

State Data Centers (SDC) were established as referral centers for data from the 1980 census. The Census Bureau relies on the SDC to disseminate census information to all users. Some libraries serve as SDCs and other libraries have an affiliate status. The availability of census information from this source should not be overlooked. Major reports from state data centers are included in *Statistical Reference Index*.

INFORMATION AVAILABLE ON DATABASES

On a national basis, state information in databases is limited to legislation, particularly bills. Services such as The Commerce Clearing House's Electronic Legislative Search System provide individualized reports based on a profile developed for a particular customer.[51]

Special subject services, such as Insurance Law or Environmental Law, include state legislation and administrative rules and rulings (Bureau of National Affairs' *Family Law Reporter* has summaries of state divorce laws, for example) but such information is buried.

Bibliographic data for state publications were available on Bibliographic Retrieval Service (BRS) for a short time in the late seventies when the *State Publications Index* was online. Since then, there has been no nationwide availability of such data, except insofar as it can be identified through OCLC, RLIN, or WLN. Statewide access to home-state documents is available in several states. In Nebraska, a documents checklist database of bibliographic records, a film catalog, the text of the current Revised Statutes, and the text of current legislative bills are all available online. Nevada has bibliographic records for all state documents online, including the retrospective collection at the state library.

Bibliographical Possibilities in the State

The foremost bibliographical need in a state is a checklist. Almost all the states now have a current checklist. The most recent list of current state checklists is that in Parish, *State Government Reference Publications*. The importance of checklists justified a full chapter of discussion earlier in this volume.

---

51. Commerce Clearing House, *Electronic Legislative Search System* (Chicago: CCH, 1982+).

Equally important is a bibliography of the sources to search for state publications over the years, a bibliography of bibliographies or checklists. For states with a comprehensive basic volume and regularly issued current checklists, the listing is a mere formality. For states relying on Bowker or Hasse or on a checklist without a long history for their early bibliographic record, the works covering the intervening period should be listed.[52] Examples are found in the bibliography section (Section A) of the *Documents on Documents* guides.[53] The bibliographies of bibliographies can, of course, be arranged in alphabetical order. However, a chronological order, based on the period covered, is helpful for this type of listing. The listing should begin with the date of statehood (again knowledge of the history and government of the state is pertinent!). Tanselle has chronological lists for all of the states.[54]

Author heading lists, that is, lists of the names of state agencies and brief histories of the agencies, are a major tool comparable in importance to the checklists. A listing of the early author heading lists is given in Lane.[55] Today the Library of Congress is monitoring the establishment of name authorities and is making its authority file available online. Librarians from several states have received training at the Library of Congress and are contributing to this database. This is the NACO project discussed in Chapter 10.

Union lists, as such, are not widely available for the individual states. In some states, the major bibliographic listing of the documents gives holdings. This is true in Louisiana and Ohio. In one sense, the major bibliographic tools for earlier years are union lists because they were based on the collections in the major libraries of the state. A union list of holdings is unnecessary for current publications if the state has a state documents program. The complete depositories have the items on the current lists.

A subject guide to documents collections in the state is a specialized type of union list. Such lists are usually limited to broad subjects (agriculture or health, for example), particularly for retrospective subject guides. For current subject guides the detail possible is governed by the detail permitted in the selection lists used in the depository library program. As

52. Richard R. Bowker, *State Publications: A Provisional Checklist of the Official Publications of the Several States from Their Organization* (New York: Publishers' Weekly, 1899–1908); Adelaide R. Hasse, *Index of Economic Material in Documents of the States of the United States* (Washington, D.C.: Carnegie Institution, 1907–1922).

53. Margaret T. Lane, comp. *A Guide to the Documents on Documents Collection, 1973–1979* and *1980–1983*. 2 vols. (Chicago: American Library Association, Government Documents Round Table, State and Local Documents Task Force, 1984). ERIC microfiche ED 247 939 and ED 263 922. Hard copy available from Margaret T. Lane, P.O. Box 3335, Baton Rouge, LA 70821; $3.00 prepaid; checks payable to ALA GODORT.

54. Thomas Tanselle, *A Guide to the Study of United States Imprints* (Cambridge, Mass.: Harvard University Press, Belknap Press, 1971).

55. Margaret T. Lane, *State Publications and Depository Libraries* (Westport, Conn.: Greenwood Press, 1981), 214.

mentioned in discussing depository libraries in Chapter 5, states cannot permit selection in the detail that is possible on the national level, and some states do not permit any selection at all. In Louisiana, the current selection list has thirty categories and it would be easy to list the libraries that selected each category.

A listing of the holdings of individual titles, as is sometimes done for expensive and extensive federal titles, would be appropriate at the state level for only a very few titles. The major, extensive bibliographic tool is the *Monthly Checklist of State Publications,* and one can assume that the federal regional depository would have a complete file. Perhaps the libraries in the state might be surveyed to see who has the *State Government Research Checklist,* Bowker, Hasse, *SRI,* or the early state records filmed by Jenkins.[56]

Possibly more pertinent at the state level is a listing of specialized unpublished files or records, if any. Publication of a list of bibliographies in state agency publications or a list of state agency catalogs is another possibility. A union list of state documents available on microfiche in the state would also be useful. Still another possibility is a list of federal documents with state detail or relating specifically to the individual state.

In some states with depository library programs, manuals have been prepared for the use of librarians in the state. Those states contributing manuals to the *Documents on Documents Collection* are listed in Appendix C. One section of a state documents manual should list all of the tools available for the state. This bibliographic section should begin with an entry for the checklist (and how to acquire it), continue with the bibliography of bibliographic listings for the state and other types of publications mentioned here and conclude with a listing of journal articles on documents on the state. Specialized manuals are often prepared for the use of state agencies. These repeat much of the material in the librarians' manuals. They reproduce the forms that are required of the state agencies. Colorado and Missouri are examples of state agency manuals in the *Documents on Documents Collection.*[57]

Another type of manual is prepared for the use of the administrator of the state documents program and contains all the material in the depository librarians' manual and in the state agency manual as well as additional, detailed materials. For example, this manual would contain procedures for creating a new depository library or for terminating one; step-by-step preparation of the monthly list, and the cumulations; details on the subject index; office routines, such as opening mail and packaging

56. U.S. Library of Congress, *A Guide to the Microfilm Collection of Early State Records,* William S. Jenkins (Washington, D.C.: Library of Congress, Photoduplication Service, 1950) and Supplement (1951).

57. *Manual of Guidelines for Colorado State Agencies* (August 1981). In *Docs on Docs,* item CO85:H; Missouri, *Depository Library Handbook* (January, 1980). In *Docs on Docs,* item MO:H4.

for depositories; forms used for requesting publications; and a calendar for regular activities.

Some of the pages from the administrator's manual can be reproduced and used as a clerical or student workers' manual for the office. It might even be that the workers' manual is prepared first and incorporated into the more extensive administrator's manual. The assistants in the department need detailed instruction on opening packages, dating publications, recording receipt, and other day-by-day tasks. Duties that require the exercise of professional discretion—the creation and termination of depositories; ideas that were tried and abandoned (in Louisiana selection by five broad categories did not work because it substantially increased the number of copies required for distribution); the rationale behind decisions to use a particular classification scheme or subject heading list; and historical data on the depository libraries, their creation date, changes in their status, their selection history, and special considerations (for example, the Library of Congress will supply franked labels for documents shipments)—all these are appropriate in the administrator's manual.

Directory-type information should also be collected for the state. First, a list of the depository libraries should be available. It is often convenient to include this in the preliminary pages of the checklist. This list would also be available in all the manuals mentioned above.

Publicity materials are discussed last because, obviously, one must not generate enthusiasm for documents without first having them organized, listed, and ready for use. First, one needs a checklist, a depository program, and some helpful librarians.

Publicity can take many forms. Some items can most appropriately be prepared at the state level and made available for use throughout the state. Examples are lists of depository libraries, maps locating the depository libraries (New Mexico has one in poster format), brochures on the depository library program, brochures on the checklist, and brochures on the importance of documents in general or in a subject area. The North Carolina bookmark provides telephone numbers for current information in convenient format (see Figure 7).

In the individual library, bibliographies addressed to a specific group (law librarians, for example) or to school librarians are effective means of making documents known to those who can use them.

Citations

An author referring to a state document hopes that the reader will be able to identify that document, to locate it, and to distinguish it from similar documents. This process is what citation work is all about. Citing state documents may have two other purposes: to indicate the quality of the documents (whether a popular bulletin or a technical report) and to

NORTH CAROLINA GOVERNMENT INFORMATION SOURCES
(Legislation, Rules, Regulations, Opinions, Decisions, Codes)

Libraries may call INWATS for
this information.

LEGISLATIVE

Bill status and history
Legislative Library
919/733-7779
Library, Institute of Government
919/966-4130

Copy of a bill from current session
Legislative Bills Office
919/733-5648

Copy of a bill from past sessions
Documents Branch Library
919/733-3343
North Carolina Collection
Wilson Library
919/962-1172
Library, Institute of Government
919/966-4130

Votes on bills (since 1977 session)
Legislative Library
919/733-7778

ADMINISTRATIVE

**Rules and regulations of
state agencies not yet published**
Administrative Procedures
Act Section,
Office of the Attorney General
919/733-4723

**Opinions of the Attorney General
not yet published**
Library, Institute of Government
919/966-4130
Law Library, UNC-Chapel Hill
919/962-1321/2
Office of the Attorney General
919/733-4618

JUDICIAL

**Decisions of the higher state courts
not yet published**
Supreme Court Library
919/733-3425
Clerk, Court of Appeals
919/733-3561
Clerk, Supreme Court
919/733-3723
Law Library, UNC-Chapel Hill
919/962-1321/2
Law Library, Wake Forest Univ.
919/761-5438
Law Library, Campbell Univ.
919/893-4111

LOCAL GOVERNMENT
**Codes of ordinances of selected
counties/municipalities in NC**
Supreme Court Library
919/733-3425
Library, Institute of Government
919/966-4130

NORTH CAROLINA LIBRARY SERVICES
Division of State Library
Documents   919/733-3343
Films   733-4376
Genealogy   733-7222
Reference   733-3270

NC Foreign Language Library
919/483-5022

Technical Information Center
919/737-2830
NCSU, D. H. Hill Library

State Data Centers
Office of State
Budget & Management
919/733-7061
IRSS, UNC-Chapel Hill
919/966-3346
Division of State Library
919/733-3343

U.S. GOVERNMENT INFORMATION SOURCES
U.S Bureau of the Census,
Charlotte   704/371-6142
U.S. International Trade Administration
919/378-5345
Dept. of Commerce, Greensboro

Federal Documents Regional
Depository
919/962-1151
UNC-CH, Davis Library

U.S. Patents, NTIS Depository
919/737-3280
NCSU, D. H. Hill Library

National Technical Information
Service   703/487-4600
Springfield, VA 22161

Federal Job Information Center,
Raleigh   919/755-4361

U.S. Internal Revenue Service,
Raleigh   919/828-6278

U.S. SENATORS FROM NORTH CAROLINA
Sen. John P. East   202/224-3154
716 Hart Bldg., Washington, DC 20510
322 Federal Bldg.   919/755-4401
310 New Bern Avenue
Raleigh, NC 27611

Sen. Jesse Helms   202/224-6342
402 Dirksen Bldg., Washington, DC
P.O. Box 2888, Raleigh, NC 27602
919/755-4630

Distributed by: Documents Section
North Carolina Library Association

Figure 7. Bookmark, front (left) and back (right). Government information in a convenient form distributed by Documents Section, North Carolina Library Association.

give credit to the ideas of other authors. Locating the cited document, what Garner and Smith, authors of a comprehensive text on citing documents, call providing "a kind of road map for research,"[58] is, however, the most important objective. For state documents, even more than for federal documents, this goal may be elusive. With fifty states involved, examples cannot apply to all situations, and individual ingenuity must be called upon to create useful citations.

Citations may be needed either for notes (footnotes, endnotes, or references) or for bibliographical lists. The most visible distinction between the two is that in notes, where the author's name is in the natural order, and in bibliographies, where the name is inverted in order to produce an alphabetical listing. Because corporate authors (which, of course, cannot be inverted) are frequently found in documents citations, this distinction is less significant in citing documents. It is not often that corporate author headings can be looked upon with favor, but that seems to be the case here.

Although citing state documents involves determining some of the same elements that are needed for cataloging, citations do not require as many different elements. Collation and notes are not as extensive in citation work as in cataloging. For documents, however, the minimum elements required for citing a trade book—author, title and facts of publication (place, publisher, and date)—may not be sufficient. For documents, series and issuing agency are always necessary. At the same time, some of the standard elements, particularly place and publisher, may be unnecessary.[59]

Manuscripts requiring the use of a particular style manual will raise the question of how extensively that manual deals with state documents. The answer is: very briefly. Even for federal documents, the coverage, although more complete than for state documents, is "superficial."[60]

It is standard practice to advise that federal examples be followed for state publications. For example, *The Chicago Manual of Style* has one paragraph on state and local documents, "Bibliography and note citations parallel the forms for federal documents."[61] Indeed, even *The Complete Guide to Citing Government Documents,* which has a whole chapter on state, local and regional documents, has cross-references to the federal section of the book.

The work in which the citation is to be used is an important consideration in determining which elements should be included. If a paper or

58. Diane L. Garner and Diane H. Smith, *The Complete Guide to Citing Government Documents: A Manual for Writers and Librarians* (Bethesda, Md.: Congressional Information Service, 1984), 1.

59. Kate L. Turabian, *A Manual for Writers of Term Papers, Theses, and Dissertations,* 4th ed. (Chicago: University of Chicago Press, 1973), sec. 9.31.

60. Garner and Smith, *Citing Government Documents,* iii.

61. *The Chicago Manual of Style,* 13th ed. (Chicago: University of Chicago Press, 1982), sec. 16.160.

a bibliography is limited to a single state, it may not be necessary to include the name of the state in the citations.

Two general rules should always be followed. Both rules are self-explanatory and both are intended as a courtesy and a convenience for the user. First, be consistent, and, second, if in doubt about a borderline element, include it.

For documents in general, the reasons for special rules and examples are: "governments do not always follow standard publication practices, and libraries do not always treat documents as they treat books."[62]

For state documents in particular, citation rules are important because, first, state publications are even less available than federal publications. Generally, only libraries within a state have more than a few documents of that state. Out-of-state documents are not widely available and are not under unified bibliographical control. Second, the differences between the states, although sometimes minor, may make creating a citation more complicated. For example, in Nebraska, a unicameral state, the citation for a legislative document would have fewer elements in the author statement than in other states.

SPECIAL STATE DOCUMENTS CITATION RULES

Some special rules, gleaned from the various style manuals, that should be emphasized in establishing a citation format for state publications include:

1. Consider omitting the name of the state in a work limited to one state, particularly in the notes. It may be advisable, however, to retain the state name in the bibliography.

2. Include all hierarchical levels. More hierarchy is necessary than with federal publications. Small state agencies, although distinctive in name and mission, may indeed be so small that they do not have a separate address or telephone listing. They may exist for only a short time. Many minor state agencies can be traced only through the departments under which they operate.

Another reason for more hierarchy for state agencies is that classification schemes and checklists often group publications first by major department and then by subordinate agency. Having all agency publications together on the shelves and in the checklists is considered convenient for the user. Citations that recognize major departments are easier to use in such libraries. For example, the Livestock Brand Book should be cited: Louisiana. Department of Agriculture. Livestock Brand Commission. Livestock brand book.

The second edition of the *Anglo-American Cataloguing Rules* requires entering without reference to the Department of Agriculture when cataloging.

---

62. Garner and Smith, *Citing Government Documents*, 2.

Still another reason for adopting full hierarchy, mentioned by Garner and Smith, is that state agencies are changeable and flexible.[63] They change names and move from department to department at the whim of the governor, the legislature, or even the wind, it seems. Tying a small agency to its parent agency by including the hierarchy helps trace an agency and its publications through such changes.

3. Give date for state constitutions only when no longer in force or if the section cited has been significantly amended. This practice relating to state constitutions is illustrated in Turabian: "N.Y. Const. . . . art. 2, sec. 6 (1894)."[64]

A more precise rule is given in the Harvard Blue Book, Rule 11:

> Cite constitutions that have been totally superseded by year of adoption; if the specific provision cited was adopted in a different year, give that year parenthetically:
> Ark. Const. of 1868, art. III, sec. 2 (1873).[65]

The examples are relevant only to state constitutions because we have had but one federal constitution in the history of the United States.

4. Use the title appearing in the state checklist or local catalog, in cases of doubt. If a document is originally located in a checklist or a microfiche collection, the title used there can be adopted. However, the caution given by Garner and Smith not to take the title from a microfiche header should be observed.[66] Titles are more difficult to recognize in state publications than in federal publications because state publications are less likely to be produced by a professional editor. Preference should be given to a true title page or a bibliographical data sheet, if available.

5. Give the issuing agency for periodical titles, if not already part of the title. For state documents for which periodical titles are even less familiar than they are for federal documents, this rule is particularly pertinent. Brightbill and Maxson place the issuing agency in parentheses following the periodical title. The Brightbill and Maxson form is:

> Author (if any). "Title of Article," *Title of Periodical* (Government Department) Volume number (Issue number, if any): Page Full date.[67]

Garner and Smith suggest a "source note" at the end of the citation giving the issuing agency:

---

63. Ibid., 67.

64. Turabian, *A Manual for Writers*, sec. 6:130.

65. *A Uniform System of Citation* (Cambridge, Mass.: Harvard Law Review Association, 1981), rule 11.

66. Garner and Smith, *Citing Government Documents*, sec. US 2.1b. and sec. SLR 2.1b.

67. George D. Brightbill and Wayne C. Maxson, *Citation Manual for United States Government Publications* (Philadelphia: Center for the Study of Federalism, 1974), 41.

Jones, Marie. "Postwar Baby Boom Shifts 80's Labor Supply," *Prairie Employer Review* 3:11(Nov. 81) p. 1. (Publication of the North Dakota Job Service).[68]

6. Include a statement on format if the publication is anything other than conventional print. When state documents are compared to federal documents, one must remember that many states do not have state printing agencies like the U.S. Government Printing Office, and that the need for multiple copies is not as great as at the federal level. Thus, the states produce more items with less than formal printing, creating a greater need to specify format. The need for format identification has become more important in the last fifty years as new formats—mimeograph, audiovisuals, film, tape, and computer printouts—have come into being. If a document has been reproduced in a different format, this information should be included in the citation. For example, state documents that have been reproduced by the ERIC Clearinghouse on Information Resources or the National Technical Information Service (NTIS) should have the ERIC or NTIS numbers as part of the citation. If the information is computerized, the appropriate general material designation is "machine-readable data file." This term is used for both computer programs and data files.[69]

Conclusion

The principal purpose of a citation, assistance to the reader, should always be foremost in the mind of the person creating a citation. The advice given by Garner and Smith, to include in the citation the elements used in locating the item being cited, is helpful. Whether the publication is to be found in a library catalog or in a microfiche collection, the person using the citation should be able to follow in the tracks of the person creating the citation.

Consistency, both for the individual items that are cited more than once and for items that are from the same agency, are of the same type, or are parts of the same series, is a sign of the careful editor. Finally, the policy of more rather than less should be followed; that is, when in doubt about the need for including a bibliographic element, include it.

That more reference service is required is the theme of an article by Steven Zink, "The Impending Crisis in Government Publications Reference Service" in which he pointed out that the federal documents collections were becoming "splintered" because of proliferation of commercial products and of GPO microfiche.[70] This is also true with respect to state

68. Garner and Smith, *Citing Government Documents*, sec. SLR 7.1.
69. Sue Dodd, *Cataloging Machine-Readable Data Files: An Interpretive Manual* (Chicago: American Library Association, 1982), 171.
70. Zink, "The Impending Crisis," 106–11.

documents collections, which also face "splintering" due to commercial products, microforms, and computer data, and for which the mix varies at least a little for each of the fifty states. Zink suggests information leaflets for each tool and one-page handouts on search strategies. Texas has already adopted the search strategy idea and has included a state document sheet in its handouts.

In 1983 Ford and Nakata made a prediction that has proven valid for the past three years:

> During the next ten years with the growing interest of state governments in computer technology and the increasing interest in state government information, academic librarians will face the challenge of integrating machine-readable formats into reference activities. The trend of transferring power to state governments will have an impact on academic curricula and increase the importance of access to information in various formats about state government activities and programs.[71]

---

71. Ford and Nakata, "Reference Use of State Government Information," 197.

PROCESSING
DOCUMENTS
IN THE LIBRARY

Documents arriving at a library often must receive special handling because they are not ordered and paid for as trade books are. They may be gift, exchange, or depository items; they may be paid for in advance or even, occasionally, accompanied by an invoice. This chapter is arranged somewhat like a procedure manual, following the state documents from their arrival at the library through the various procedures prior to final shelving. Cataloging and classification are discussed in Chapter 10. Much of the information in the chapter is taken from procedure manuals prepared in the individual states (see Appendix C). One of the last sections of this chapter discusses what the California manual calls "publications presenting special problems." The final sections of the chapter address the placement of the document function in the library structure, staffing requirements, and budget figures for operating state distribution programs.

The discussion encompasses both depository and nondepository libraries, but because depository status requires some extra attention and because depository libraries have responsibilities beyond the confines of their own institution, more emphasis is placed on depository libraries. Nondepository libraries, as a general rule, acquire fewer documents than depository libraries and in many instances are able to admit them into the library processing stream without the special attention required in depository libraries. In either case, depository or nondepository, procedures adopted for state documents must be reconciled with the general policies of the library as a whole.

Handling in Nondepository Libraries

The duties imposed on depository libraries may be assumed voluntarily by nondepository libraries. Because the materials are not received automatically but arrive individually in response to requests or orders, it may be that they can be processed more quickly into the library collections. Promoting reference service and encouraging use are not problems because the items are individually acquired for the collection. Items no longer needed can be disposed of at will, and disposal policies can rely upon the availability of depository copies in nearby depository libraries.

Special manuals prepared for the use of depository libraries in a state and other information on handling documents received through a depository system are found in the *Documents on Documents Collection* assembled by the State and Local Documents Task Force of ALA GODORT.[1] This collection is recommended as a source of examples for procedures and forms.

Documents on Documents Collection

The *Documents on Documents Collection* consists of materials produced by a state document distribution center in the administration of a state depository program. Although these materials were assembled primarily as samples for the administrators of documents programs, they have been circulated to library school faculty and students, to committees drafting depository legislation, and even to commercial firms. The collection provides an overview of the operation of state depository systems.

The collection, at least theoretically, makes it unnecessary to address requests to fifty individual states for information about the handling of state documents. State documents librarians are generous in sharing publications and ideas, as this collection proves. The collection gives an overview of the operation of state depository programs and provides a basis for comparisons. The scope of the collection is interpreted liberally to include all materials of statewide interest about state documents. For example, the publications of state documents centers, journal articles that explain and publicize the documents of the state, and workshop materials are included. The *Documents on Documents Collection* is divided into three parts according to the date the materials were incorporated into the collection. The 1973–1979 collection is the first part and is available on ERIC microfiche (ED 247 940). The 1980–1983 collection is also available on ERIC microfiche (ED 263 923). The current collection, 1984 to date, is circulated on interlibrary loan in hard copy.

Users' guides have been prepared for the first two parts of the collection and are also available on ERIC microfiche (ED 247 939 and ED 263 922).[2] Each guide lists the individual items in the collection by state

1. Margaret T. Lane, comp., *Documents on Documents Collection*, 1973–1979 and 1980–1983 (Chicago: American Library Association, Government Documents Round Table, State and Local Documents Task Force, 1984 and 1985). The 1973–1979 collection is in ERIC microfiche (ED 247 940), and the 1980–1983 collection is in ERIC microfiche (ED 263 923). The current materials may be borrowed from Lauri Sebo, University Research Library, University of California, Los Angeles, CA 90024.

2. Margaret T. Lane, comp., *A Guide to the Documents on Documents Collection, 1973–1979* and *1980–1983*. 2 vols. (Chicago: American Library Association, Government Documents Round Table, State and Local Documents Task Force, 1984). ERIC microfiche ED 247 939 and ED 263 922. Hard copy available from: Margaret T. Lane, P.O. Box 3335, Baton Rouge, LA 70821; $3.00 prepaid; checks payable to ALA GODORT.

(which is the arrangement for the collection on the microfiche), and then the guides rearrange the items by type of publication. The sections of particular interest in administering documents collections are: "D. Forms and Form Letters," "H. Manuals," and "I. Procedural Guidelines." Because *Documents on Documents Collection* contains materials relating to depository library programs, some of the items are intended for communication with state agencies; however, most are intended for use by librarians.

The forms in Section D include request letters and claim letters from several different states (Arizona, Connecticut, Illinois).

Section H on manuals includes publications that attempt to cover all or most aspects of document handling. Manuals are usually ten pages or more. Major manuals in the collection intended for depository libraries are listed in Appendix C. Materials that are too brief to be called manuals are grouped under the heading, "Procedural Guidelines." Weeding policies and disposal policies are typical examples. Such policies are usually included in a manual, if there is one, but are also available as separate publications, perhaps because they were issued before the manual was assembled, or because a separate sheet was necessary for responding to inquiries.

Arrival at the Library

Most state documents arriving at a library can go directly from the mail room to the shelf without passing through the cataloging and classification sections of the library. Because most state documents are serials, they are already represented in the library catalog and have a classification number assigned. The exceptions are monographs and new serials. The majority of state documents received are continuations of titles already captured; they can follow a direct path, with a minimum of processing, to the shelves.

The first step in the processing of state documents is their arrival at the library. Publications may arrive individually or in packages containing multiple items. Examination of the package wrapping or envelope and the address label is vital. If the library is a depository library, depository items must be identified at the moment they arrive. The address label may give a clue, either by the words, "depository librarian" as part of the address, or by adding a symbol, "D," or a depository number to the address. In Missouri all depository shipments are addressed to "MO. DEPOSITORY DOCS. LIBN." followed by the name and address of the library. Florida uses a rubber stamp: "Florida Documents, Depository Shipment." Louisiana and Mississippi at one time had printed labels citing the statutory provisions authorizing the shipments. Examples of labels used in state depository programs are included in Section E of the *Documents on Documents Collection.*

Another clue to the depository nature of the package is that depository shipments usually consist of multiple items from different state agencies in one package. Some depository items arrive as individual items, possibly because their timeliness or their content necessitated special mailing. State depository programs do not provide daily mailing as the federal program does because the quantity of material does not justify such frequency. Illinois, with weekly shipments, is exceptionally prompt in its distribution of depository materials. Exceptions may, and should, exist for the mailing of legislative materials. In some states, such as Pennsylvania, legislative mailing to depository libraries originates in the "bill room." In Louisiana bills are distributed through the depository program, and mailed on a daily basis during legislative sessions.

A shipping list in the package is a third indication that a shipment is a depository one. Shipping lists are intended as packing slips for checking the items in the depository packages. As such, they are associated with the claiming procedures which occur later in the journey of the documents to the library shelves.

Nondepository state publications that come to the library as individual items may be either gifts, exchanges, or special orders and must follow the library's standard procedure for these items. Again, the package wrapping and address label are the key to identifying the source of the publications.

ACQUISITION ROUTINES

Three of the state documents manuals that can be studied in the *Documents on Documents Collection* have sections on acquisitions routines: Louisiana, New Mexico, and Virginia. The Virginia list is an in-house list for the staff of the Virginia State Library, and the three procedures in that list that are of general application (recording in Kardex, date stamping, and recording statistics) are also included in the Louisiana and New Mexico lists. The lists of both Louisiana and New Mexico suggest that the library may choose to follow its general routines for handling new material. These two manuals suggest lists of possible procedures for those libraries without established routines and emphasize documents peculiarities. The procedures discussed here are based on Louisiana and New Mexico routines.

The first steps are the examination of the package as recommended above, the opening of the package, and separation of serials from monographs. Checking the publications against the shipping list, if the shipment is a depository one, is a necessary next step. Then, counting the publications received and stamping them as depository items, if appropriate, should follow. Recording the receipt of the items is essential. Several states (Mississippi, Missouri, and New Mexico, for example) require, by their rules and regulations, that a record of receipt be maintained. The Mississippi standard requires that a depository record its accessions and provide at a minimum a shelflist with holdings and call numbers. The Missouri standards read, "an orderly, systematic recording of receipt and subsequent arrangement of materials." Regardless of the status of the library, whether depository or not, it is prudent to keep a record of the receipt of library materials. As with an order file, such a record permits checking for duplicate holdings and follow-up on outstanding claims.

Both Louisiana and New Mexico procedural routines include rules for handling the receipt of catalog cards. Such rules are out-of-date because the advent of cataloging records in major bibliographic utilities has diminished the importance of the distribution of catalog cards with state documents, which has been discontinued in both Louisiana and New Mexico. Alaska still distributes cards because public libraries there do not subscribe to the OCLC card service. In Missouri, an OCLC main entry card is supplied for each new serial and monograph distributed. In Utah both OCLC and RLIN numbers are given on the checklist to accommodate libraries in the state using each of these bibliographic utilities.

The New Mexico routines suggest two additional steps, neither of which requires much additional time or effort and both of which serve to promote the collection: first, "Put popular documents on display [in] your new book section," and second, "Circulate shipping list to all reference staff as a current awareness tool."

The recording of holdings in the state checklist is inadvisable for several reasons. The California manual points out that the time lag in the receipt of the checklist necessitates a temporary record in the interval, a situation that might not occur in all states. However, even in the best administered programs, delays in publication of the checklist occasionally occur. The second caution, that when lists cumulate, the checking must be transferred, is the more serious and the more likely to result in problems later. Copying from one listing to another always produces the potential for error. The third reason given, that not all official publications had been listed in the past, may or may not apply in other states.

ACQUISITION RECORDS

Some of the information necessary in an acquisitions or holdings record is available on the shipping list. The more closely the check-in file conforms to the shipping list, the easier the check-in process. However, a caution must be given at this point. In making entries in an acquisitions or holdings record (the California manual calls it a "shelflist-checklist"), professional supervision is required.

> The fact that records in the shelflist-checklist are simple does not mean that they can be compiled by an untrained typist-clerk without assistance. Variations in names of agencies and serial titles, and vagaries in the num-

bering of serials make the supervision of a trained librarian imperative for the maintenance of adequate records.[3]

A number of state documents manuals list the necessary elements of an acquisitions record. The first four items are cited by all six manuals that have such lists. The requirements can be consolidated into a single list:

1. *Call number*. Two states with in-state classification schemes require the inclusion of that number in addition to the Dewey or LC number. Connecticut requires inclusion of the item number.
2. *Issuing agency*. Kansas refers to this as "author," which probably means corporate author.
3. *Title*. California and Nevada include for both issuing agency and for title the added requirement, "with notes of important changes."
4. *Frequency*.
5. *Number of copies received* (only required in California, Louisiana, and Nevada).
6. *Routing instructions* (required in four states and optional in a fifth).
7. *Shelf location*, if not indicated by classification number (required in four states).
8. *Retention policy*, if superseded portions are withdrawn or back file is discarded (required in two states).
9. *Title page*, table of contents, and index information (required in three states).
10. *Binding information* (required in four states; optional in one state).
11. *Source* (required in four states, with one providing specifically that depository and nondepository must be distinguished).

All of the manuals we are using as models provide sample checking cards. In most instances, these are standard 3x5 cards, permitting the interfiling of cards for monographs.

The acquisitions record described above is supplemented by a holdings record for all serials. The Virginia manual includes the standard serials procedure note—if the printed number is incorrect, add the correct number in brackets. A similar note on supplying information to complete the record relates to monographs—if the date is unknown, use the date received.

The California and Nevada manuals have a comment relating to check-in details: if a publication has both date and number, check in to reveal both. The section of the California manual on checking in a serial is given in outline form:

3. *California State Publications,* 2d ed. (Sacramento: dist. by Dept of Finance, 1961), section 4.131. Hereafter referred to as California manual.

Procedure for Checking in a Serial

1. Compare card with publication carefully to be sure that it is the correct one.
2. Enter publication on checking record.
    a. Use a hard pencil (no. 3 or 4) to prevent smudging when cards rub together.
    b. Make figures or checks smaller than squares on checking record—they are easier to read.
    c. Check in a publication that has both a number and date by both because it may be cited sometimes in one way and sometimes in another. A check mark (✔) may be placed beside the printed number on the checking card and the date written in the date box, depending upon the type of card used.
    d. Indicate additional copies by check marks.
    e. File-mark each piece (see Section 4.3) or write the call number in upper left corner.
    f. Attach routing slip if needed.
    g. Stamp each piece with ownership and date stamp.[4]

According to Paula Rosenkoetter, who referred to an earlier authority, Ellen Jackson, the minimum essential information for nonserials is "call number, corporate author, title, date of publication, and final paging."[5]

DATE STAMP

For depository libraries, a date stamp that identifies the publication as a depository item is a major convenience because it combines two necessary bits of information in one stamp: the word *depository* and the date. Such a stamp may also include the name of the library. When the collection is weeded, designation as a depository item serves as a caution that particular retention requirements must be followed; the date is an aid in observing those requirements. A number of states permit discarding of documents after a period of years. Nondepository libraries follow the usual practices of the library in identifying and dating newly received items.

STATISTICS

There are no nationally collected statistics on state documents distributed or state documents collections. For federal documents, for example, statistics based on both the number of documents distributed to the depository libraries and the number of documents listed in the *Monthly Catalog of United States Government Publications* (the items are numbered

---

4. Ibid., section 4.1343.

5. Paula Rosenkoetter, "Treatment of State Documents in Libraries" (Master's paper, University of Missouri—Columbia, Department of Library and Information Science, May 1973), 6.

sequentially by year as noted on the title page) are available from GPO publications. For state documents, no such figures are available because there are almost fifty distributing programs and checklists. The different state distributing programs distribute varying quantities of state documents. The individual state checklists differ in their scope of comprehensiveness.

No national agency is involved in the collection of statistics on state documents. At the Library of Congress, statistics are kept on the number of titles in the *Monthly Checklist of State Publications* (28,168 for 1985) and on the number of state documents received (120,101 for fiscal 1984).[6] These figures, however, are derived from the records of one library and depend upon the distribution systems discussed in Chapter 4.

Acquisition statistics are compiled as an indication of workload and as justification of internal library requests, as opposed to circulation and reference statistics which corroborate the need for the state documents program. The New Mexico manual suggests keeping a record of items received, divided into serials and monographs, with monthly and year-to-date totals. A special state documents rule is followed in Virginia for General Assembly materials. The instructions say:

> Do not count until the session is over. Then, make one count using check-in cards. Do not record this count in the above tallies. Put the entire count in the January–March quarterly report, as a separate count from other documents.[7]

State depository programs do not usually require the compilation of special statistics. The New Mexico manual suggests that state documents be added to the statistics forms already in use at the library. A simple form that can be used if the library does not have appropriate forms is given in Figure 8.

CLAIMING

Claiming, or requesting copies of publications expected, is important for documents librarians in general and in particular for documents librarians in depository libraries. Most document collections have a high proportion of serial publications published on a regular basis. Monitoring receipt and prompt claiming are necessary to keep these titles up-to-date. For depository libraries, which are responsible for all materials sent to them and which must be sure that all the items are actually received, claiming is vitally important.

6. *Monthly Checklist of State Publications* 76 (December 1985): facing 1202; U. S. Library of Congress, *Annual Report of the Librarian of Congress*, 1984 (Washington, D.C.: the Library, 1985), 62.

7. *Virginia Manual*, (n.p., n.d.) section I5.

ACQUISITIONS   MONTH of _____   Year to Date

State Documents

  Monographs   _____   _____

  Serials   _____   _____

Total   _____   _____

CIRCULATION
  State Documents

optional- In-house use
count before reshelving.   _____   _____

  Check-out
  monographs   _____   _____

  serials   _____   _____

REFERENCE

  State Documents

  in person   _____   _____

  phone   _____   _____

Figure 8. Sample statistics form. New Mexico manual, 1979, p. 17–18 in
Documents on Documents, 1973–1979, item NM:H1.

Claiming is often a less regulated activity for nondepository libraries than for depository libraries, although this should not be so. It is difficult to monitor the receipt of gifts, annual reports that are issued at varying intervals, and monthly magazines that have an irregular publishing history. All these items present claiming problems. One must remember that state agencies are not primarily publishers and that they issue their publications as time permits. Of course, a missing issue noticed when a subsequent issue is checked in can and should be claimed promptly.

Claiming in nondepository libraries must be done by surveying the check-in file to determine what should have been received. Two special cautions are pertinent for state documents. First, because state documents are often produced in limited quantities, claiming should be done promptly. Second, because numbered series do not always appear in exact sequence, claiming for very recent gaps should be approached cautiously. A note, "Not issued in numerical order," on the check-in card might serve as a warning not to claim too frequently in order to avoid a needless waste of time.

Claiming for depository libraries is usually a self-regulating activity. A shipping list notifies the library of the documents sent, and a designated time for claiming is specified. Shipping lists are prepared in most states that have depository programs. Ron Haselhuhn reported that twenty-one states had such lists.[8]

Shipping lists are intended as packing slips for checking the items received in the depository program. The Missouri manual suggests the procedure for checking the receipts against the shipping list, beginning with the marking of the list for all items in the depository selection list of the library.[9] It prescribes procedures for handling errors that might have occurred, such as missing documents or extra documents.

In most states, claims for depository items are directed to the distribution center. The criteria for communications in this instance are not critical because in almost all cases the messages are between two libraries, and both naturally place service ahead of formalities. If a library in a state where distribution is centralized in a distribution center makes a direct claim to a state agency, the agency might assume that the distribution center has not fulfilled its obligation to distribute the materials forwarded for distribution. A few words of explanation—"We received our depository copy but need another," "Our copy is defective," or "We lost our copy"— keep the channels of communication open and avoid later, perhaps awkward apologies or explanations.

If missing documents are identified, they must be claimed promptly. If claim forms are not supplied by the distribution center, an appropriate

8. Ronald P. Haselhuhn, "Bibliographic Control and Distribution of State Documents," *RQ* 20 (Fall 1980): 21.

9. *Depository Library Handbook* (Jefferson City, Mo.: 1980), 17.

wording of the claim is that recommended in the Nevada manual as shown in Figure 9 (the salutation might better read "Sir or madam" or something else non-sexist). This form is sent to a state agency that makes direct distribution to the depository libraries. The important words in Figure 9 are "should have been sent to us as a depository library." The relationship between state agencies and depository libraries is tenuous because many state agencies do not have a clear understanding of the role of libraries in the community; consequently, depository libraries should be particularly careful when communicating with state agencies for this reason. Mention should always be made of the fact that the library is aware of depository distribution requirements.

In a few states (Washington and Alaska are examples) depository libraries are enjoined by regulation from making direct contact with state agencies. Some state publications manuals recommend that a permanent member of the library staff sign all claims so that special rules about claiming when insufficient copies are received and special care with direct claims to state agencies can be observed.

Examples of shipping lists are found in the *Documents on Documents Collection*. Generally, lists are abbreviated entries, sufficient only for identification purposes. However, some are quite complete with full cataloging and availability information. Shipping lists include each individual issue for serials. The most abbreviated shipping lists include issuing agency, title, volume and number, and date. Some include the local classification number. Illinois marks ephemeral materials with an *E* and permits depository libraries to discard these items at will. Another feature of the Illinois list is the inclusion of OCLC numbers, a practice increasingly being adopted in other states. New Mexico has a supplemental list of the "for sale" items, with price and address for ordering.

The shipping list is sometimes distributed to nondepository libraries and serves as a selection guide for libraries not privileged to enjoy depository status as in Illinois.

BINDING

Library routines established for the binding of serials and separates should be sufficient for binding of state publications. Binding in libraries that have historical retention responsibilities should be encouraged by documents-oriented librarians in the state. Other libraries should bind documents in accordance with the policies established for other materials in the library. In a research library those items having lasting research value, such as annual reports, statistical compendiums, financial statements, blue books, and official bibliographies should be considered for binding. Suggestions for binding particular types of publications are found in the Louisiana manual:

```
                    LIBRARY
                    Address
                    Date


GENTLEMEN:

We have not received the following publication (s),
which we believe should have been sent us as a
depository library.  Can you supply it (them) to
complete our files.  Thank you.



                    Signature_____

                    Title_____
```

Figure 9. Sample claim form. Source: *Manual for Acquisition, Processing [and]
Use,* Nevada State Publications Depository System, Documents Section, Nevada
State Library, 1969, 17.

A. Periodicals—Bind complete volumes with title page, contents, and index.

B. Monographs issued in series, e.g. Agricultural Experiment Stations Bulletins and Circulars—collect consecutively numbered issues until a volume 2 1/2" to 3" in size is obtained. Bind as a serial with name of state agency, title of publication and inclusive numbers lettered on spine.

C. Monographs not in series. Bind separately if large enough. Otherwise place in pamphlet binders or retain unbound.

D. Annual publications superseded each year by new edition. Retain unbound, or if use justifies, place in pamphlet binders.

E. Miscellaneous folders, leaflets, mimeograph reports, etc. Retain in manila folders in vertical file or in pamphlet boxes on shelves.[10]

Binding problems created by monographic series that reuse the same number for revised editions or versions of a publication are difficult to handle. No recent author has given better recommendations for this unique problem than those made by Ellen Jackson years ago for federal documents. She says:

> The arrangement of revisions of series is often troublesome. If the files of the *Farmers' Bulletin* are bound, it is not feasible to withdraw superseded editions of individual bulletins as later editions appear . . . . A workable solution is to file the unbound later editions immediately following the bound volume that contains the original issue . . . . Some libraries prefer not to bind any of the file in permanent form, but to tie the series in groups of perhaps fifty numbers, between protective manila or other heavy paper covers, from which separate issues may be removed at will.[11]

Jackson's proposal addresses both the problem of revisions and the repetition of series numbers.

A similar problem with subseries within a series requires a decision based on user needs. The problem of handling a continuation that, if it were not in a series, would be handled in a straightforward fashion is caused by the need to tie together similar publications. A Louisiana example is the *Annual Report* of the superintendent of education, which is given a new number in the Department's Bulletin series each time a new report is issued. One solution is to acquire and bind a second copy; thus both the Bulletin series and the Annual Report file would be complete on the shelves. Although cataloging records can record the individual numbers for both the series and the subseries, the binding of the physical pieces (in the absence of a second copy) must be a judgment decision based on the perceived needs of the library in serving its patrons.

10. *Distribution of Documents to Depositories* (n.p.: Louisiana Library Association, 1972), 25.

11. Ellen Jackson, *A Manual for the Administration of the Federal Documents Collection in Libraries* (Chicago: American Library Association, 1955), 70–71.

The Hawaii manual makes a pertinent remark about binding in connection with its depository program:

> Documents will not be sent to the bindery before distribution. The documents are most useful soon after publication and the time spent at a bindery will delay them unnecessarily. Princeton files and pamphlet boxes work best for document storage.[12]

The use of Princeton files and pamphlet boxes is common in state document shelving. A unit on binding, covers, and pamphlet boxes in the California manual is the only known discussion of the ways to prepare documents for the shelves. Types of envelopes, loose-leaf binders, pamphlet binders, pamphlet boxes, and "tie-ups" are described. Although the manual is out-of-date (1961), no more recent information about the physical handling of state documents has been published.[13] The California pages were adopted for the Nevada manual in 1969.

Weeding and Deselection

Weeding, a topic which the state manuals include as part of the technical services routines, is today an integral part of collection development and is often referred to as "deselection." In depository manuals weeding provisions begin with the warning that specific retention periods must be observed. Specific items that may be discarded are listed. Federal documents librarians familiar with the list of the Superintendent of Documents for federal items will recognize the adaptation of that list to the state lists of items permissible for discard.[14]

Purging from depository collections can be more time-consuming than from other parts of the collection because of the need to consider any special rules that may have been established by the distributing agency. In addition to observation of specific retention periods and provisions for specific types of publications, a depository may also be required to offer the proposed discards back to the distributing agency.

Byron Stewart discusses retention and disposal issues, citing the Illinois regulations that require a five-year retention period except for superseded items. *Superseded* is interpreted liberally and includes items for which revisions and new editions are published. The problems Stewart cites include periodicals that have ceased and state agencies that have been abolished as well as publications of little value, such as "in-house" newsletters. As

12. Hawaii manual, (n.p., n.d.), 4.

13. "Binding, Covers, and Pamphlet Boxes: Description, Sources, and Use" in California manual, Appendix G.

14. "Disposition of Depository Publications," in U.S. Superintendent of Documents, *Instructions to Depository Libraries* (Washington, D.C.: GPO), loose-leaf, section 11.

possible solutions he suggests the Illinois plan, which is similar to that in other states (California was probably one of the first states to promulgate disposal policies), and the Louisiana filming plan undertaken as a pilot project in 1973.[15] The general subject of microreproduction of state documents is discussed in Chapter 4.

If a library is not a depository library and the state has a depository system, the library should rely on that system to maintain the historical collection for the state and should strive to have a "live" collection. A live, or current, collection contains only the latest edition of each directory or source book and only the most recent annual reports. Superseded materials are removed from the shelves so that the user or browser will pick up only the latest and most current information that the library has to offer. The assumptions are that current information is needed (an assumption confirmed by Hernon in his 1979 study [16]) and that it is a service to the library patron to avoid the confusion caused by out-of-date information. Much of the value of state documents lies in their currency, a feature that should be exploited by nondepository libraries. Removing out-of-date publications from the shelves is a service to the user, who might not notice the date, and a bonus for the librarian in providing space.

Depository libraries, on the other hand, do not always have title to the materials they receive as depositories and thus cannot discard them without following state regulations. Ownership may remain with the state library, as in Illinois. Thus, regulations frequently provide that documents may not be discarded unless a specified retention period has passed or the documents meet certain other qualifications. The usual requirements are that the publications be superseded by a later edition or by a cumulation or that they have only ephemeral value. Publications with an expired effective date, press releases, and pages from loose-leaf publications fall into the permitted disposal category. A few states, such as Hawaii, do not place any legal obligation on the receiving libraries.[17]

The date stamp with a depository designation on it, mentioned above, is a distinct advantage at weeding time. If actual publications are being handled, either in a vertical file or directly on the shelves, the convenience of determining immediately whether or not the publication meets the time limit for retention speeds the work appreciably. Color coding by year received has been used for the same purpose. For example, all publications received in the current year would receive a red mark, and the next year's receipts, an orange mark.

Depository libraries that receive copies of publications from sources other than the official distributing agency are not required to retain these

15. Byron Stewart, "Documenting Missouri," *Show-Me Libraries* 30 (September 1979): 33–35.

16. Peter Hernon, *Use of Government Publications by Social Scientists* (Norwood, N.J.: Ablex Publishing), 78–79, 112.

17. Hawaii manual.

extra copies when their usefulness has ended; only publications that the library receives as a depository are subject to depository library law.

Types of Publications Presenting Special Problems

Certain types of state documents present special problems because of their relationship to other publications (preliminary drafts and final editions, monographic serials, superseded publications), their format (loose-leaf), or intended permanence (advance sheets, press releases, daily legislative journals).

Again, whether individual handling or records are needed in a particular library depends on the organization of the library, the depository status of the library, and the number of documents acquired.

The 1961 California manual lists seven examples of publications presenting special problems and includes references to different library situations. The problem areas cited are preliminary editions, press releases, separates of regulations and decisions, frequently revised publications, cumulations, legislative publications, and loose-leaf publications.[18] In order to indicate the problems and provide some solutions, the following types of publications and formats are examined: preliminary editions; supplements, errata sheets, and addenda; advance sheets, slip laws and opinions; monographic serials; frequently revised publications; loose-leaf format; press releases; and bills and legislative materials. The discussion of these special types of publications, in a slightly different grouping, will indicate the problems and offer some solutions.

1. Preliminary editions in a historical depository library would be recorded and retained just as a final edition or report. In another library they might be discarded upon receipt of the final report. The California manual states correctly that, because the receipt of a final report is uncertain and unpredictable, generalizations are not possible. One reason for the establishment of the special state documents collection at the Library of Congress was to permit re-evaluation by the staff of such preliminary and draft reports.

2. Supplements, errata sheets and addenda are materials that appear after a report and must be recorded so that they will come to the attention of any user of the original report. Old fashioned "dashed-on" entries (that is, adding the new items to the catalog record for the principal work by using "en" dashes for the author and title that the two works have in common and then describing the second item) can be used on cards for monographs in a shelflist. In a visible file, a marginal note might be used;

18. California manual, section 4.136.

for example, a supplement might be entered at the edge or at the top of the card.

3. Advance sheets, slip laws and opinions contain information that is of such importance that it is published in a temporary format as soon as possible. Not all states have slip laws or advance sheets for laws. In some states promulgation of the new laws in a newspaper is the first form in which they are available. Libraries needing the text of new legislation promptly should acquire the advance sheets or preliminary copies, record their receipt in minimal fashion, and substitute the bound volumes when they are published.

Court opinions for most states are issued by commercial companies and not acquired for the documents collection. The advance sheets for court reports should be recorded in the serial record and discarded upon receipt of the bound volume.

4. Monographic serials with individual titles are a common type of state publication. Three important things to remember are (a) if the catalog record does not analyze these monographic serials, title entries in the documents shelflist are important; (b) if the state checklist does not list these publications in numerical order, a numerical list in the shelflist is useful; and (c) because monographic serials are prepared by individual authors, the series number may be assigned at the time publication is authorized, the numbers may not be published in strict numerical order, and some numbers may never be published.

5. Frequently revised publications are often retained in their latest edition only. Weeding advice or regulations for depository libraries may permit the discarding of a superseded edition immediately upon receipt of a new edition. The shelflist card can be marked, "Keep latest edition only." Often items that are revised are part of a bulletin series of which only certain numbers are periodically revised. Examples from the Louisiana Cooperative Extension Publications series include #1004 titled "Popular publications"; #1083, "Control cotton insects"; and #1185 "Vegetable planting guide for Louisiana." Some of these numbers are revised annually, so marginal notes on a checking card become confusing. One solution is to record all numbers that are reused on a separate card in the order in which they are received. This second card is not easy to decipher but does provide a record of the receipt of each individual number that can be consulted if necessary.

The California manual suggests inserting a colored flag in a number that supersedes an earlier one as a signal to the shelver to pull the superseded issue. For many public and nonresearch libraries, the removal of superseded publications from the shelves to maintain a current, live collection is one of the important conveniences offered by the library.

6. Loose-leaf format is occasionally adopted by a state agency for its publications. If the revision pages are issued with a numbered transmittal letter, these letters can be checked in by number. Often provision is made

for the transmittal or cover letter to be retained in the loose-leaf binder so that the user is apprised of the currency of the material.

If there is no formal transmittal or cover letter with the revision pages, the California manual recommends the insertion of a sheet in the front of the binder for recording the dates on which revisions are received.[19]

Pages withdrawn during the filing of a new release should be discarded except in unusual circumstances. A historical depository may elect to retain superseded pages; some law libraries do so for noncommercial publications.

Prompt filing of new pages in a loose-leaf service is essential because it is the timeliness of the information that originally dictated the loose-leaf format.

7. Press releases are another example of current information made available in a nonstandard format. Press releases are short statements on nonpermanent paper that may include information not available elsewhere. A complete depository may establish check-in records if multiple releases are received from particular agencies. Libraries with smaller collections or nondepository status may elect to file press releases in the vertical file by agency or subject. The New York guide to official publications prepared by Dorothy Butch mentions, in passing, that biographies of gubernatorial nominees which are originally published in press releases are not incorporated in the *Public Papers* series that reports the governor's activities and includes information from press releases. Butch recommends keeping the press releases with this biographical information in all libraries intending to maintain comprehensive collections.[20]

8. Bills and legislative materials distributed as part of a depository system may have a check-in card. Recording each bill number in its original and reissued forms is perhaps not necessary except in the historical depository libraries. Other libraries can merely put the bills on an open shelf in numerical order. Most states have a limited, designated time for the introduction of bills with the result that the printing and distribution of the bills are restricted to a short time. The Virginia library manual recommends that the bills not even be counted until the end of the session and that the count be recorded in the statistics as a separate line item.

Where all the procedures just discussed fit into the organizational structure of the library is a separate question. How the procedures are implemented as far as staff and budgets are concerned is another question. The topics of where within the library and how with respect to staff and budget conclude this chapter.

19. Ibid., section 4.1367.

20. Dorothy Butch, *Official Publications of New York State: A Bibliographic Guide to Their Use*, rev. August 1980 (Albany, N.Y.: New York State Library, Cultural Education Center, 1980), 12.

Place in Library Structure

The State and Local Documents Task Force study in 1980 showed such variation in the organizational place of state documents programs within the state libraries that no generalization is possible. In some situations the state documents service is directly responsible to the director of the library, and in others it is in a state government section or in the "services to state agencies" section. Placement seems to be about equally divided between technical services and reference services, and in some libraries personnel from both areas of responsibility work together without a separate state documents department. The checklist function is closely related to cataloging procedures.

Staff and Budgets

Staffing and budgets for state documents activities are interrelated problems. More staff and a larger budget can result in improved service, but many libraries operate with inadequate resources in both areas. Little quantitative research on these problems is available for federal documents and even less for state documents.[21]

For state documents, problems encountered in collecting data on staff and budgets are compounded by many factors: in-state and out-of-state questions, depository or nondepository status, various allocation of duties, and almost complete lack of budget figures.

STAFFING

Most libraries do not have special state documents personnel; many more assign state documents duties as only a part of a person's responsibilities; and some libraries have several professionals who contribute a small portion of their time to state documents functions. Reports on the number of staff may vary from less than one to as high as thirteen.

The kinds of libraries that typically have staff members whose primary responsibility is state documents are state libraries, state legislative reference libraries, and large research libraries. In state libraries, duties of state documents staff vary from those arising in a state with a comprehensive state documents program, such as Nebraska, to the duties in a state with a minimal program. In Nebraska, state documents librarians are responsible for the online checklist, the microfiche program, information service, and outreach. The Nebraska section in the *Documents on Documents Collection* illustrates the extent of this program.[22] At the opposite end of

21. Kevin L. Cook, "Varying Levels of Support Given to Government Documents Departments in Academic Libraries," *College & Research Libraries* 43 (November 1982): 460.

22. Lane, *Documents on Documents Collection,* 1973–1979 and 1980–1983.

the scale is the situation in Wyoming, where there is no depository program, an irregular checklist, and no legislation, and only a beginning has been made toward cataloging the state documents collection.

The 1980 survey by the State and Local Documents Task Force included a section on staff. A variance from a state documents staff of five in two states to less than one full-time equivalent (FTE) was revealed. Professional personnel varied from one-tenth of an FTE to three FTE. Some states did not include clerical personnel in their reports. In at least five states the support staff was one-half of an FTE or less.[23]

The situation is different in state legislative reference libraries where the entire staff is concerned with state problems and uses state documents on a daily basis. Documents of the home state, supplemented by out-of-state documents in subject areas, are the heart of a legislative reference library. The responsibilities of the staff may include indexing and calendaring of bills and assisting in bill drafting. Again, this diversity of responsibilities makes comparisons inappropriate.

In large research libraries documents may be completely integrated into the collection so that the entire library staff deals with them from time to time. In other libraries state documents may be handled in a separate documents department. In the documents department of more than one large research library, state documents responsibilities are assigned jointly with those for international and foreign documents. Meeting schedules of the ALA Government Documents Round Table are designed to accommodate members with dual state and international responsibilities.

College libraries, it was found in a 1981 survey, did not collect state documents on a large scale, nor did they systematically collect out-of-state documents. The survey report, which dealt largely with federal documents, found

> The amount of staffing devoted to documents varied. The general pattern of professional staffing was a reference librarian who devoted approximately 50 percent of his or her time to documents. The professional was usually supported by a half-time clerk and five to twenty hours of student help.[24]

The number of professional and support staff needed for state documents work in a library depends on too many factors to permit a gen-

23. Margaret T. Lane, comp., *State Publications: Depository Distribution and Bibliographical Programs*, State and Local Documents Task Force, Government Documents Round Table, American Library Association; Texas State Publications Clearinghouse, Documents Monograph Series, nos. 2 and 2A ([Austin]: Texas State Library, 1981). No. 2 is also in ERIC microfiche ED 195 283.

24. Kathleen Heim and Marilyn Moody, "Government Documents in the College Library: The State of the Art," in *College Librarianship*, ed. William Miller and D. Stephen Rockwood (Metuchen, N.J.: Scarecrow Press, 1981), 221–22.

eralized formula. The quantity of state documents issued by the state, the number of documents received, whether the library is a depository library, whether out-of-state documents are collected, whether the documents are in a separate collection or merged in the general collection, and finally, the level of reference service provided by the library all must be considered in determining the number of staff members needed in an individual library. The characteristics of a state documents librarian are discussed in the chapter on information services.

COSTS AND BUDGETS

Most states are not able to provide budget figures for state documents activities simply because no separate budget item or line exists at that level. Moreover, if the state documents staff and the state documents collection are not separately identifiable, there cannot be an identifiable budget item.

For state depository programs operated by state libraries, some figures are available in the 1980 survey by the State and Local Documents Task Force. Fourteen states were able to provide budget figures.[25]

A 1986 follow-up survey made for the present text queried only the states that were able to provide budget figures in the 1980 survey. The results of the 1986 survey are shown in Table 9. Eight responses were received, of which three—Alaska, New Hampshire, and New Mexico—reported that no budget figures were available. The New Mexico budget figures were available in 1980 because that year was the first year of the program; the appropriation was absorbed into the general budget after the first year.

Costs to a library to operate within a state depository program were studied by Jack Kranz in 1976. These costs are not comparable to those for operating a state distribution program. Kranz describes costs only in terms of staff salaries and the costs of cataloging.[26]

Conclusion

State documents librarians in a number of states are fortunate in having a procedure manual for handling state documents. Many librarians have used the California manual. No national guide, like Harleston and Stoffle for federal documents, is available for state documents.[27] The suggestions provided in this chapter are general and must be adapted to fit

25. Lane, *State Publications: Depository Distribution*, sections entitled "Budget."

26. Jack Kranz, "Cost Analysis of Selective (California) State Documents Depository" (Northridge, Calif.: California State University, University Libraries, 1976). ERIC microfiche ED 122 726.

27. Rebekah M. Harleston and Carla J. Stoffle, *Administration of Government Documents Collections* (Littleton, Colo.: Libraries Unlimited, 1974).

Table 9. Budgets for Handling State Documents

	CONNECTICUT	HAWAII	NEBRASKA	NORTH CAROLINA	TEXAS
Personnel	$49,860		$32,093	$45,000	$74,592
Postage			225	375	2,748
Communications			887	425	720
Checklist[a]			13,490	1,250	3,839
Travel			300		256
Equipment				300	
Data processing			4,000		
Rent			19,305		
Other			952		
Totals	—	$29,000[b]	$71,252	$47,350	$82,155

[a] Entered here are figures for Nebraska's "Publishing, printing," North Carolina's "Checklist printing," and Texas's "Paper."
[b] The Hawaii total is for 1985–87 and covers "microfilming the state documents, printing the *Hawaii Documents Cumulative Index*, maintenance of equipment, and processing supplies."

the situation in a particular state. The S&LDTF compilation has hints on handling state documents, such as the Kansas explanations on acquisition and receiving, and gives an indication of staff and budget figures for some states. Future surveys may provide more standardized data that may be used for comparisons.

10
CATALOGING AND CLASSIFICATION

All state documents librarians need to know something about the cataloging rules for state documents even though not all libraries have a cataloged collection.

State documents librarians must familiarize themselves with the problems of cataloging and classification because certain librarians in each state actually produce the necessary bibliographic records and because both librarians and patrons must use these records. Even administrators must know some of the conventions that are followed in cataloging state documents in order to evaluate the impact of new cataloging codes and new technology.[1] For all members of the library staff, but particularly for those who use the bibliographic records, some discussion of the basis for those records is important.

The major difference between cataloging of government publications and cataloging of trade publications is that government publications are issued by agencies of the government, that is, by corporate bodies, whereas trade publications are issued by commercial publishers. There are special sections of the cataloging codes for corporate names and government bodies. Corporate entries are a particularly difficult area of cataloging because choices must be made not only as to what entry should be used but also about the form of the entry.

Cataloging of state publications is not much different from cataloging of federal publications. In fact, the cataloging rules do not intend that the cataloging of government publications be different from cataloging trade books. One of the premises of both editions of the *Anglo-American Cataloguing Rules*, the standard guides to cataloging practices, is that "the rules cover the description and entry of all library materials commonly collected." All materials are treated the same regardless of the type of material.[2] Government publications are not accorded separate treatment as in the 1949 rules, which had a separate section on government publica-

1. Ronald Hagler and Peter Simmons, *The Bibliographic Record and Information Technology* (Chicago: American Library Association, 1982), 7.

2. *Anglo-American Cataloguing Rules*, 2d ed. (Chicago: American Library Association, 1978), 1.

tions.[3] The *AACR2* rules applicable to the cataloging of government publications are scattered throughout the rules, as illustrated by the table of contents of the manual, *Cataloging Government Documents*.[4]

Nevertheless, not all libraries catalog their state documents. Some libraries reason that the existence of a state checklist is an adequate substitute. The value of checklists as tools for controlling documents received in an individual library depends on (1) how current the list is, (2) whether it is indexed, (3) whether a classification scheme is indicated, and (4) even, in some cases, on the form of entry.

Reliance on a state checklist for bibliographic control requires study of the difference between catalog entries and checklist entries. In recent years, the form of entry is sometimes the same. This is obviously true in those states that produce a state document checklist as a product from entries in a bibliographic utility. The Kansas checklist is derived from OCLC tapes, the California documents list from RLIN data, and the Washington checklist from WLN cataloging. The *Monthly Checklist of State Publications*, however, constructs its own entries. Other states, such as Arkansas, use the cataloger's form of entry but do not produce the checklist automatically from the cataloger's data. Still other states construct the checklist entry by pragmatic principles that are unique to the particular state. The chapter on checklists comments on checklist entries and the checklist guidelines.

Changes in Cataloging Rules for Documents

Anglo-American Cataloging Rules, published in 1967, made major changes in the cataloging of state documents. These include changes in the choice of entry, the form of entry, and the linking of records. The previous rules were the 1949 rules for cataloging documents, based on the work of James B. Childs, documents specialist at the Library of Congress.

Before *AACR*, the name used for a government agency was the official name. The *AACR* codes require the name as found on the publications of the agency. This rule is stated very explicitly in *AACR2*:

> 24.17. General Rule
> Enter a body created or controlled by a government under its own name (see 24.1–24.3) unless it belongs to one or more of the types listed in 24.18. . . . Refer to the name of a government agency entered independently from its name in the form of a subheading of the name of the government (see 26.3A7).[5]

3. *A.L.A. Cataloging Rules for Author and Title Entries*, 2d ed. (Chicago: American Library Association, 1949), 126–48.

4. *Cataloging Government Documents: A Manual of Interpretation for AACR2* (Chicago: American Library Association, 1984), vii–x.

5. *AACR2*, 424.

AACR2 represents a change from a rule that listed types of corporate bodies that do not enter under jurisdiction (*AACR* 78, types 1–7) to a rule that lists the types of bodies that should be entered under jurisdiction (*AACR2*, Rule 24.18). The result is fewer entries under jurisdiction.

Acronyms have also been treated differently. Prior to 1967, cataloging rules preferred the full form; *AACR* permitted the use of the acronym if it was in upper and lower case letters, like "Unesco"; and *AACR2* says to use an acronym as found, whatever its form.[6]

A change affecting serials that was incorporated in *AACR* and continued in *AACR2* is the shift from the practice of using the latest entry to that of using consecutive entries (*AACR2*, Rules 21.3A1 and 21.3B). This change affects not only serials but also state agency names that change.

The adoption of the practice of superimposition (a policy followed by the Library of Congress of continuing to use previously established headings instead of creating new ones in accordance with *AACR*) lessened the impact of *AACR* changes for the Library of Congress and for all the libraries using LC cards.[7]

Factors Affecting Cataloging of State Publications

Several factors characteristic of state publications affect the creation of bibliographic records for state publications. Because a document is most valuable at the time it is issued, it becomes dated in a very short time. Documents should be made available to the public quickly; cataloging at the source is one answer to this need.

First, the need to create the record at the source, that is at the state level and ideally at the state capital, is a primary concern. The Library of Congress cannot be expected to catalog all state documents; it does not add every state document to its collections. The responsibility for cataloging the documents of a state is a state responsibility. This responsibility is affirmed in the S&LDTF guidelines and in the *Standards for Library Functions at the State Level*.[8] The advantage of cataloging at the capital city lies in the easy availability of additional information, if needed, and the local insights that can be applied.

Second, the importance of state agencies in the cataloging of state publications is inherent in the definition of state publications as "the publications of state agencies," and leads into the problem of corporate entries. State agencies change their names, sometimes use more than one

6. Hagler and Simmons, *Bibliographic Record*, 201.

7. Ibid., 225.

8. American Library Association, Association of Specialized and Cooperative Library Agencies, Subcommittee for Library Functions at the State Level, *Standards for Library Functions at the State Level*, 3d ed. (Chicago: ALA, 1985).

name, are related to other agencies in a hierarchical scheme, and may be referred to by acronyms. Cataloging at the state level and corporate names, including both choice of entry and form of entry, are the main focus of this chapter.

Another characteristic of state publications relevant to the bibliographic records created for them is their issuance by noncommercial publishers, which almost automatically puts them outside the cataloging in publication (CIP) program of the Library of Congress. CIP is for publications that will be cataloged by the Library of Congress and have national circulation. Because state publications are often a sideline activity in state agencies, locating the necessary data for the full bibliographic record can be difficult. Sometimes a formal title page is missing. Pagination may be irregular. Title changes and misnumbering are often problems with serials. Cataloging at the source is one solution to the problems that arise when agencies publish infrequently.

Many state publications are serials, requiring linkage to earlier and later titles. When state administrations change, the name of a monthly magazine may change to reflect the goals of the new administration.

Unconventional formats, errata sheets, and irregular supplementation, all requiring special notes, are other characteristics of state publications that plague the cataloger of state documents.

Finally, deciding whether a state publication is worth cataloging and adding to the collection is another of the problems faced by the state documents staff.

Corporate Names

A state documents librarian is often involved in establishing state agency names. This activity is sometimes formal cataloging, sometimes preparing checklist entries, and at other times establishing headings for acquisition or distribution files in a depository program.

This chapter deals principally with formal cataloging. State agency names for checklist entries are often the same as those used in cataloging, although there are some checklists that use the state agency name found on the piece without formally establishing it by research. The state agency names used in *Monthly Checklist of State Publications* are an example of this practice. State agency names used for internal office operations in a depository program may be either formal catalog entries or checklist entries. Such files usually include the names of many agencies that have no publications, for which the *AACR2* rule on variant names can be applied. The LC rule interpretation says:

> If a heading is needed for a proposed body, use the name found in the available sources. If the body is actually established later, and the estab-

lished name differs from the proposed name, use the established name in the heading and treat the proposed name as a variant form . . . .[9]

Establishing state agency names for state publications is an especially complex area of cataloging. Both corporate bodies and serials, according to a well-known text on bibliographic control, "attract bibliographic chaos by their very nature."[10] The other side of the picture is revealed by the doubt expressed by Catherine Carter that any library patron ever understood corporate entries.[11]

The optimum solution to this troublesome problem is given in the database guideline that requires the assumption of the responsibility for the quality of cataloging records by one institution in each state.[12] Then only fifty people or institutions would face and solve the problems for everyone else. But everyone else must know and understand the rules that those fifty hardy souls are following. The rules, of course, are *AACR2*. The problems are the choice of entry, the form of entry, and linking of entries.

CHOICE OF ENTRY

In the United States choice of entry has, since Jewett, included the possibility of a corporate entry.[13] Cutter's rules likewise recognized corporate entry, and after Cutter, corporate entry "has flourished like the green bay tree . . . ."[14] With the advent of *AACR* we see the retreat from the use of corporate entry (largely because of the Paris Principles and the compromises they embody).[15] Hagler and Simmons say, "The selection of the element under which to file a corporate name has been the single most troublesome problem in the entire history of cataloguing."[16] Nevertheless, corporate entries are a necessary access point for the publications of state agencies. Each state publication needs at least one corporate entry as an access point simply because the publication originates or has some relationship with a state agency. The importance of being able to recognize

9. *Cataloging Government Documents*, 191.

10. Hagler and Simmons, *Bibliographic Record*, 190.

11. Catherine Carter, "Cataloging and Classification of State Documents," *PLA Bulletin* 25 (March 1970): 95.

12. See Appendix A, "Guidelines for Inputting State Documents into Data Bases."

13. Charles Coffin Jewett, "On the Construction of Catalogues of Libraries, and Their Publication by Means of Separate, Stereotyped Titles. With Rules and Examples," in *The Age of Jewett: Charles Coffin Jewett and American Librarianship, 1841–1868*, ed. Michael H. Harris (Littleton, Colo.: Libraries Unlimited, 1975), Rule xxii.

14. Paul Dunkin, *Cataloging, USA* (Chicago: American Library Association, 1969), 39.

15. International Federation of Library Associations, "Statement of Principles adopted at the International Conference on Cataloging Principles, Paris, October 1961" (London: IFLA Committee on Cataloguing, 1971), 40.

16. Hagler and Simmons, *Bibliographic Record*, 201.

a state publication as a publication of state government lies in the authoritative, timely, and qualitative nature of these publications.

Choice of entry is not critical in a dictionary catalog because, by definition, this type of catalog includes many points of access. The same is true of a computer database, or online catalog. Choice of entry is vitally important in a main entry catalog, such as most union catalogs.

The cataloger's point of view is expressed by Duncan: "Few of the users of the catalog may be as interested in finding all the works of a corporate author entered together as they would be in finding all the works of a personal author listed together."[17]

Documents librarians, of course, do want to find all the works of a corporate author together. In "Rules for Preparing Check-List Bibliographies of American State Publications," A. F. Kuhlman states, "The entry of state publications or series of publications should be *corporate*" (italics in the original).[18] Kuhlman's example is a publication of the Alabama Geological Survey, "Report on the geology of the coastal plain of Alabama, by Eugene A. Smith, Lawrence C. Johnson . . . ."

For periodicals, the choice of entry is between title entry and corporate entry. Many catalogers believe that the user is best served if title entry is chosen. The reason documents librarians favor corporate entry was well stated in a report prepared for the GODORT representative to the Catalog Code Revision Committee:

> The importance of serial publications of government bodies lies in the fact that the contents contain various facts, regulations, explanations, and information that emanate from the mission of the issuing body. For this reason the Committee [Committee of *AACR* Revision, State Documents Task Force, Government Documents Round Table] recommends that the main entry be under the issuing body with added entry under distinctive title.[19]

Most documents librarians have no problem with choice of entry because their thinking is oriented to the organization of state government. Although documents librarians agree that the entry for state publications should be corporate, the Catalog Code Revision Committee did not adopt the proposal for a corporate main entry for all government documents.[20]

Choice of entry might seem to be a dead issue in these days of computer controlled files that permit access to individual records from many dif-

17. Dunkin, *Cataloging, USA*, 38.

18. A. F. Kuhlman, "Rules for Preparing Check-List Bibliographies of American State Publications," *Library Quarterly* 5 (January 1935): 52.

19. American Library Association, State Documents Task Force, Committee on AACR Revision, "Report to Bernadine Hoduski, GODORT Representative to the Catalog Code Revision Committee" (April 21, 1975).

20. *Cataloging Government Publications*, xii.

ferent points. The introduction to *AACR2* points out that this is not so.[21] The first edition of *AACR* discusses the issue in terms of dictionary catalogs and unit cards in contrast to the "access points" of *AACR2*. The reasons for the need for a main entry are essentially the same in both editions of *AACR*: for a single entry list or for a single citation as in a subject heading. Identifying a main entry also promotes standardization of bibliographic citation.[22]

In *AACR2* the general rule is, "Enter a body created or controlled by a government under its own name . . . " (24.17). The result is that the entry is not necessarily under the name of the state. An example, taken from *Cataloging Government Documents*, is: Geological Survey of Alabama. *AACR2* does, however, call for a cross-reference "in the form of a sub-heading of the name of the government"(24.17).

FORM OF ENTRY

What catalogers call "form of entry" answers the question, "Which name shall I use?" The possibilities include: (1) legal name, (2) full official name, (3) name on the publication, (4) popular name, or (5) most common form of name. The *AACR2* rule is: "the name by which it is predominately identified"(24.1).

The exact form that a corporate entry should take is fraught with problems. Librarians today are not faced with Rule 59 of the 1908 rules that recorded four different plans for entering the names of departments (the direct form, inverted, key word in brackets immediately after the state name, and distinctive words in a special type style).[23] Childs wrote the cataloging rules that were incorporated in the 1941 and 1949 rules. These rules specified the legal name of the agency. This was changed to the name used on the publication in the first edition of *AACR* and remains the same today.

During the 1940s, when use of the official or legal name was mandated by the rules, a considerable amount of work was done creating lists of the names of government agencies. A very active committee of the American Library Association, recognizing "the need for lists of state author headings as aids in the identification and checking in of state documents, because of the growing number of official agencies in each state, the frequent changes of title in those governmental bodies, and the tremendous increase in the amount of printed matter emanating from these sources" sponsored

21. *AACR2*, 2.
22. *Anglo-American Cataloging Rules* (Chicago: American Library Association, 1967), 2; *AACR2*, 2.
23. American Library Association, *Catalog Rules, Author and Title Entries* (Chicago:ALA, 1908), 17–18.

compilation and publication of state author heading lists.[24] These author heading lists recorded the name of the agency as it was to be used in the card catalog and any necessary cross-references. They also gave the citation for the creation and the demise of the agency, thus providing a capsule history of each government agency. The history of the ALA committees that worked in this area and a list of published works and completed theses for fifteen states are recorded in the literature. Since the adoption of the first edition of *AACR*, such lists can be at most suggested headings.

A 1970 survey on authority lists for names of state agencies made surprisingly little reference to the work done in the 1930s and 1940s on author headings.[25] Only four states cited published author heading lists. Some states with published lists of author headings and some for which theses have been prepared reported "no authority list" and cited state manuals or checklists of state documents. Thirty states referred to state manuals, registers, or rosters, and fourteen to state checklists of publications. Seven of these states referred to both types of publications.

A 1986 report indicates that work is still being done in this area. Work has been completed on the computerization of the New York documents authority file. The file has 4,185 entries, with cross-references and the New York classification number.[26]

Sources for establishing state agency names as listed by Catherine Carter, a Pennsylvania librarian, are: (1) Pennsylvania manual, (2) annual report (or other publication) of the department, (3) laws of Pennsylvania, (4) administrative code, (5) Pennsylvania author headings for older names, and (6) LC catalogs and *NUC*.[27]

LINKING ENTRIES

If there are variant forms of a name, changes of name, or hierarchical questions, links between the various access points are required.

It will be remembered that not all state publications are entered under the name of the state. *AACR2* Rule 24.17 says, "Refer to the name of government agency entered independently from its name in the form of a subheading of the name of the government (see 26.3A7)." The example is:

> **Task Force on Periodic Motor Vehicle Inspection** *see* **Maryland**. *Task Force on Periodic Motor Vehicle Inspection.*

24. American Library Association, Division of Cataloging and Classification, *In Retrospect; A History of the Division of Cataloging and Classification of the American Library Association, 1900–1950* ([Chicago: ALA, 1950]), 14–15.

25. Carol Krusinski, "Results of Survey Concerning Existence of Authority Lists for the Names of State Agencies" (Olympia, Wash.: Washington State Library, October 15, 1970).

26. Audrey Taylor, "GODORT State and Local Affiliates," *Documents to the People* 14 (June 1986): 56.

27. Carter, "Cataloging," 93.

Links between old and new names of an agency are an obvious need. If an agency has had several names, these should all be listed. Hagler and Simmons point out that "many governments restructure bureaucracies regularly and are ready to capitalize on the image fostered by new and progressive-sounding names."[28] Other examples arise from the need for cross-references from parts of the hierarchy.

NAME AUTHORITY WORK AND THE NACO PROJECT

"An important aspect of *AACR* in both its editions is the simplification of name authority work by reducing the reference search involved . . . and by removing inconsistencies in earlier codes."[29] Name authority work means establishing the form of the entry, ensuring consistency of the names, and deciding on cross-references. Name authority work is the most difficult part of cataloging and thus the most costly. For documents librarians, name authority work is particularly burdensome; state agency names are corporate, and corporate names are more complicated than personal names.

Nevertheless, corporate names must be established. The third guideline of the "Guidelines for Inputting State Documents into Data Bases" affirms this:

> 3. Each coordinating institution should compile, publish and maintain an authority file of state agencies citing the name of the agency as it is to be used for cataloging.

As often happens in documents work, the cooperative efforts in name authority work began at the national level. An arrangement between the Government Printing Office and the Library of Congress provided for the LC's acceptance of GPO cataloging. This cooperative effort was the precursor of the Name Authority Cooperative Project, known as NACO.

State participation in NACO began in 1979 as an outgrowth of suggestions made by an LC representative at a 1978 ALA GODORT program and a GODORT resolution adopted by ALA Council, which originated in the State and Local Documents Task Force:

> LIBRARY OF CONGRESS-STATE COOPERATIVE CATALOGING
> RESOLUTION
> WHEREAS, the Library of Congress has effectively demonstrated the feasibility of cataloging federal documents with the Government Printing Office on a cooperative basis, and
> WHEREAS, the Library of Congress has encouraged a library or agency within each state to act as the cataloging authority for publications of their respective states, and

28. Hagler and Simmons, *Bibliographic Record*, 210.
29. Ibid., 283.

WHEREAS, the Library of Congress has indicated the necessity for standardization of bibliographic records,

THEREFORE BE IT RESOLVED, that the American Library Association encourages the Library of Congress to establish a pilot project for the cooperative cataloging of state publications with several states representing various differences in population and geographical location, and

BE IT FURTHER RESOLVED, that the results of the projects be carefully evaluated and documented for implementation on a national level.[30]

The Texas pilot project in cooperative name authority work started with the training of a cataloger from the Texas State Library at the Library of Congress.[31] The original Texas agreement was for six months; then it was renegotiated for a twelve-month period and expanded to include all corporate names. Since August 1980 it has been enlarged to include personal names.

The procedure agreed upon was that the Texas State Library would first determine whether the Library of Congress had already established a heading; if not, the state library would establish the heading following LC practices, would use the LC worksheets, and then would forward the data to LC. LC would compare the heading with its files and report back to the state library that it had verified the record. This same procedure is followed today, except that LC does not report back after verification. A library can assume that the record has been verified if no message is received from the Library of Congress and the record appears in the online authority file.

Thirteen states are now doing state agency name authority work in the NACO program, as shown in Table 10. Other states are expected to join the program as their circumstances permit and as the Library of Congress is able to provide training. The State and Local Documents Task Force, in a report prepared by a committee appointed for the purpose, outlined the qualifications necessary for participation in the NACO project:

> The criteria for becoming a member of the Name Authority Cooperative Project (NACO) are as follows:
> a) Be a depository for publications of the area for which it is responsible.

30. "Library of Congress–State Cooperative Cataloging Resolution," adopted by State and Local Government Task Force, June 27, 1978; Government Documents Round Table, June 28, 1978; ALA Council, June 29, 1978 (Council Document 74), in *Documents to the People* 6 (September 1978): 207–8.

31. Carol Burlinson and Rowland Craig, "State Library and Library of Congress Begin Joint Cataloging Project," *Texas Libraries* 41 (Spring 1979): 3–5; "LC/Texas State Library Join in Authority Work Venture," *Library of Congress Information Bulletin* 38 (March 2, 1979): 70–72; "LC and Texas State Library Test Joint Cataloging Project," *American Libraries* 10 (April 1979): 217.

Table 10. NACO Participants and Items Contributed

LIBRARY	DATE JOINED	ITEMS COMPLETED		TOTALS TO DATE
		FISCAL YEAR 1985	FISCAL YEAR 1986	
Texas State Library	February 1979	189	252	2,039
Minnesota Historical Society	March 1980	578	507	2,736
Montana State Library	December 1980	37	96	1,439
New York State Library	February 1981	115	181	1,304
Louisiana State Library[a]	February 1982	422	185	1,666
Washington State University	February 1982	303	230	1,809
North Carolina State Library	April 1982	437	283	1,899
South Dakota State Library	April 1982	151	0	223
State Library of Ohio	May 1984	1,173	99	1,368
South Carolina State Library	May 1981	136	61	209
Utah State University	January 1985	19	51	70
Wyoming State Library	June 1985	43	139	182
University of Maryland	May 1986		182	182

[a]Louisiana State Library withdrew April 10 1986; Louisiana State University expects to participate.

Note: Numbers of items contributed to LC's automated files by participating state libraries and related institutions are arranged by dates of entrance into NACO.

Source: September 30, 1986 figures courtesy of Suzanne L. Liggett, Coordinator of Cooperative Cataloging Projects, Library of Congress.

b) Have the necessary tools required for research readily available (e.g., OCLC, NUC, Mansell, its own authority file, the statutes of the state, etc.)

c) Assign an experienced professional cataloger as the Library of Congress contact person, and sufficient staff to expedite the project. (The staff member actually doing the work must go to the Library of Congress for training and must be conversant with current cataloging rules.)

d) Have a commitment to quality cataloging and follow the latest cataloging code and Library of Congress practice.

e) Make adequate financial commitment to the project.

f) Have final authority in a written agreement with the Library of Congress.[32]

This last qualification has changed inasmuch as formal written agreements are no longer signed.

The S&LDTF committee report included informal comments from the Texas State Library when it was published by the Task Force in the guidelines booklet of October 1981. The five points made by the Texas cataloger can be summarized:

1. LC authority records require establishment of headings for related bodies and parts of the hierarchy and thus may require more work than the participating library is accustomed to doing. However, this additional work can be absorbed. One full-time cataloger should be able to produce between eighteen and twenty headings per month while meeting LC standards. The time per heading varies from five minutes to forty minutes.

2. The intensive training at the Library of Congress could only be appreciated by an experienced cataloger.

3. The Library of Congress originally verified headings by telephone but now notifies the cooperating library only if a change is necessary, which happens rarely.

4. Costs involved are significant; Texas spent $2,415 for the first six months.

5. Benefits include prestige for the library, training that will improve cataloging standards, and improved bibliographical access.[33]

Cataloging at the State Level

Universal Bibliographical Control, a program of the International Federation of Library Associations, has as one of its principal tenets that a

32. American Library Association, Government Documents Round Table, State and Local Documents Task Force, "Report of the Committee on Guidelines for Name Authority Cooperation" in "Guidelines Adopted by the State and Local Documents Task Force" (October 1981), 23.

33. Ibid., 23–25.

national bibliographic agency, not an international one, should work on the problems of authors' names.[34] As a practical matter, this principle can be extended to creating the entire bibliographic record as near the source as possible. In most states the majority of the principal state agencies and the state library are located at the state capital. If the state library creates the bibliographic records, its location near the issuing agency is an advantage. Accommodations can be made for the problems that arise due to location of state agencies outside the state capital.

S&LDTF Guidelines

The State and Local Documents Task Force of the ALA Government Documents Round Table, in its "Guidelines for Inputting State Documents into Data Bases," supports the principle of cataloging at the source:

> 1. To insure quality control, a single institution within each state should have sole responsibility for coordinating input of cataloging records for state documents into the data bases (e.g., OCLC, RLIN, WLN, etc.). . . . Cataloging role assignments may be made in selected areas.[35]

The commentary on this guideline recognizes the lack of a formal responsibility for state-level creation of bibliographic records for state documents and recommends the acceptance of such responsibility on a voluntary basis:

> Comment: At present, it is not possible for a state agency to have inputting authority, i.e., bump the records of other institutions. Any member of a utility is free to do original cataloging for any item not already in the data base. However, the depository agency, usually the state library, should *accept the responsibility* for the timely cataloging of the state's publications and for entering the records into a data base. Having accepted the responsibility, the cataloging agency should be committed to quality cataloging and have adequate staff and resources to perform the task. State depository centers unable to do the cataloging themselves may wish to reach an agreement with another institution to provide the cataloging.[36]

The mention of enlisting the assistance of another institution in the cataloging of state documents may be an acknowledgment of the problems that arise when state agencies are located away from the state capital. In several states there are state agencies that issue publications from offices in the largest metropolitan area of the state. For example, this is true in Chicago and in New Orleans, neither of which is a state capital.

34. Hagler and Simmons, *Bibliographic Record*, 191.
35. See Appendix A, "Guidelines for Inputting State Documents into Data Bases."
36. Ibid., no. 1.

"Cataloging at source" was the name of the precursor of the CIP program at the Library of Congress. Although the name was changed, the idea of the two programs—that cataloging should be done at the time of publication—is closely associated with the idea of cataloging at the state level. Louisiana participated in the cataloging at source project and was able to have cataloging information published in several state documents. One of the difficulties encountered was the need to predict when a publication was forthcoming. In the absence of a state printer, contact had to be made with the state printing procurement office and the particular printer who was the successful bidder. Another difficulty was the securing of permission from individual state agencies that did not understand the goals of the program.

An example of cooperation in Utah is the 1977 *Utah Authority File*. It serves as an example of the division of responsibility for one area of cataloging: name authority work. In the 1977 Utah list, the responsibility for the creation of state agency headings was divided by type of agency, with the Utah State Library acting "as the primary authority for all state executive, legislative, and judicial agencies, commissions and committees," and the colleges and universities within the state serving in the same way "for all agencies of their respective institutions."[37]

Classification Schemes

Libraries that have separate documents collections need special classification schemes, or at least a shelving notation system. The type of scheme needed depends on whether the separate collection encompasses state documents from more than one state and also on whether documents from other levels of government are included in the documents collection. In this chapter, after a brief background section, the discussion begins with classification schemes that are used for multistate documents collections. Some of these schemes are prepared to provide for more than state documents (other levels of government, for example) and some even include nongovernmental items. Classification schemes that provide for the documents of a single state are discussed last.

BACKGROUND

Classification schemes for state documents may some day be regarded as a phenomenon of the mid-twentieth century. They were not a concern of the early writers on state documents. Reece, writing in 1915, does not

---

37. Robert D. Woolley, ed., "Utah Authority File" (Salt Lake City: Utah State Library Commission and the Utah College Library Council Documents and Cataloging Committees, November 1977), Foreword.

mention classification schemes at all, although he does make a statement that "all state documents should be regularly classified."[38] By this he must have meant classified in the general classification scheme used for other library materials (probably Dewey in his day). This was actually a very progressive idea; today we would call it "mainstreaming." Even in 1940, Wilcox did not include discussion of classification schemes in the *Manual*, except for a few items in the bibliography.[39] The Swank and Jackson schemes, discussed in a separate section in this chapter, were created after the *Manual* was published.[40] The literature on classification examined in Lane includes the Louisiana classification scheme (Tilger, 1957), the Ohio schemes (Houk, 1962, and Lester, 1969), and the Maine scheme (Kirkwood, 1966), with all the remaining schemes dating from 1970.[41] The chart prepared by Russell Castonguay in his *Guide* is another convenient source for comparing state classification schemes.[42] It is adapted in Table 11. All the schemes Castonguay examines may be used for state documents except four, which do not extend to the state government level. Castonguay devotes several pages to the features, advantages, and disadvantages of each classification scheme and compares the schemes to one another.

Today classification schemes may no longer be needed for their primary purpose of keeping like things together because computers can handle this so easily. Furthermore, shelf arrangement is more a convenience for the library staff than a service for the library patron if stacks are closed. The thought that documents should be completely integrated with other library materials to avoid being overlooked and the increasing use of the computer as a tool for providing bibliographical access militate against the need for classification schemes as organizational devices. However, one attribute of classification schemes—the provision of a discrete number for each individual document in order to provide a shelf location symbol—remains essential. Probably classification schemes or notation systems to provide location symbols will continue to be used, even though bibliographic control is governed by a computer system. The need that classification schemes serve as logical arrangement tools will probably decrease because computer programs can provide multiple avenues for locating

38. Ernest J. Reece, *State Documents for Libraries*, University of Illinois Bulletin 12, no. 36 (Urbana, Ill.: University of Illinois, 1915), 70.

39. Jerome K. Wilcox, ed., *Manual on the Use of State Publications* (Chicago: American Library Association, 1940), 109–13.

40. Raynard Swank, "A Classification for State, County, and Municipal Documents," *Special Libraries* 35 (April 1944): 116–20; Ellen Pauline Jackson, "A Notation for a Public Documents Classification," *Library Bulletin* 8 (Stillwater, Okla.: Oklahoma Agricultural and Mechanical College, 1946).

41. Margaret T. Lane, *State Publications and Depository Libraries* (Westport, Conn.: Greenwood Press, 1981), 214–15.

42. Russell Castonguay, *A Comparative Guide to Classification Schemes for Local Government Documents Collections* (Westport, Conn.: Greenwood Press, 1984), 21.

Table 11. Classification Schemes

NAME OF CLASSIFICATION SCHEME, YEAR OF PUBLICATION	ARRANGEMENTS		USE WITH FOLLOWING TYPES OF DOCUMENTS						
	SUBJECT	ARCHIVAL	LOCAL	STATE	COUNTY	REGIONAL	NATIONAL	TERRITORIAL	NONGOVERN- MENTAL
DDC, 1894									
19th ed., 1976	X		X	X	X	X	X	X	X
LC, early 1900s	X		X	X	X	X	X	X	X
Glidden, 1942	X		X	X	X	X	X	X	X
Swank, 1940		X	X	X	X			X	
Jackson, 1941		X	X	X	X	X	X	X	
Plain "J", 1972		X	X	X	X	X	X	X	X
CODOC, 1974		X	X	X	X	X	X	X	X

Source: Adapted from Russell Castonguay, *A Comparative Guide to Classification Schemes for Local Government Documents Collections* (Westport, Conn.: Greenwood Press, 1984), 21. The abbreviated names for the classification systems are those used by Castonguay.

documents, and reliance on shelf arrangement as a means of access is no longer necessary.

SUBJECT ARRANGEMENT OF STATE DOCUMENTS

Both the LC and the Dewey classification schemes arrange publications according to subject.[43] Although subject arrangement is not a common practice for documents collections, it is possible to incorporate documents within the Dewey or the LC classification schemes.

Yuri Nakata, in her book on organizing local documents collections, suggests a means of achieving a subject arrangement merely by assigning the appropriate Dewey number and writing above it a code for the state or city. Under her plan, all Illinois documents would have "Ill." above the classification number.[44] This suggestion and another somewhat more complicated idea, called classification by attraction ("a microscopic subject arrangement" within an appropriate Dewey classification number), are explained in Castonguay's Guide.[45]

Castonguay also discusses the possible use of the LC classification system, concluding that "when used for a local government documents collection, [it] does not fare much better or worse than the DDC."[46] An interesting adaptation of the LC classification scheme puts all documents into the "J" schedule, which is for political science. This plan, called "Plain 'J'," was proposed by Mina Pease, then at Pennsylvania State University. It enlarges the Library of Congress J schedule to allow for the inclusion of publications from different levels of government.[47]

In a 1973 research paper, Paula Rosenkoetter reported that of 73 libraries responding to her question on classification, 25 used Dewey in a separate documents collection, and 17 used LC. Some of these libraries used more than one scheme concurrently.[48]

Almost all classification schemes limited to government publications follow the archival principle of provenance. The aim of the classifier applying this principle is to base the arrangement on the issuing agency, subdividing along hierarchical lines for subordinate bodies. Subject arrangement, as used in the LC and Dewey classifications, is not the objective, and subject access must be accomplished by other means, such as the

43. Library of Congress, *Classification: Class J, Political Science*, 2d ed. (Washington, D.C.: Library of Congress, 1924; reprinted, 1956); Melvil Dewey, *Dewey Decimal Classification and Relative Index*, Edition 19, ed. Benjamin A. Custer, 3 v. (Albany, N.Y.: Forest Press, 1979).

44. Yuri Nakata, Susan J. Smith, and William B. Ernst, Jr., *Organizing a Local Government Documents Collection* (Chicago: American Library Association, 1979), 29–32.

45. Castonguay, *Classification Schemes*, 22–25.

46. Ibid., 27.

47. Mina Pease, "The Plain 'J': A Documents Classification System," *Library Resources and Technical Services* 16 (Summer 1972): 315–25.

48. Paula Rosenkoetter, "Treatment of State Documents in Libraries," *Government Publications Review* 1 (Winter 1973): 126.

analytical subject indexes of the *Monthly Checklist of State Publications*. A limited subject access is built into the system insofar as state agencies function within particular subject areas.

SWANK AND JACKSON

Among the well-known classification schemes developed to accommodate state documents of all the states were Swank in 1941 and Jackson in 1946.[49]

Raynard Swank was the first documents librarian at the University of Colorado and developed his scheme for that library. According to Catharine Reynolds, later documents librarian there, the Swank system is "easy to follow, easy to remember, and a quick, inexpensive notation system which essentially is an arrangement by issuing office, subordinate bureau and title . . . ."[50]

The Swank classification scheme has provision for state, county, municipal, and territorial documents. The states are numbered; the original scheme included only forty-eight states, necessitating the addition of Hawaii and Alaska at the end of the sequence. Nevada, in its adoption of the scheme, was able to incorporate the new states in their alphabetical place.

The Jackson classification scheme, on the other hand, includes not only the levels of government provided for by Swank, but also provision for regional, national, foreign, and international levels. Neither Swank nor Jackson provides for nongovernmental items related to documents collections.

Swank and Jackson are based first on a geographical division, then level of government, issuing agency and subdivisions thereof, and finally, an individual item number. In Swank this number is a form subdivision and a date; in Jackson, a Cutter number for the title. The similarity between the two can be attributed to the fact that Swank began the system that Jackson finished. Both are expandable, flexible, and easily applied and understood. Both have a philosophy similar to that of the Superintendent of Documents classification scheme, and the principle of provenance.

A minor comment, pertinent at the time, by Catharine Reynolds about the Swank system was that lower case letters, superior numbers, and colons presented problems in the computer adaptation of the system.[51]

GLIDDEN-MARCHUS

As indicated above, for documents librarians "classification scheme" usually means a system based on jurisdiction and issuing agency. Subject

49. Swank, "A Classification for State, County, and Municipal Documents"; Jackson, "A Notation for a Public Documents Classification."
50. Catharine Reynolds, response to questionnaire in files of S&LDTF.
51. Ibid.

classification is not customary. The one subject classification cited in the literature is the Glidden-Marchus system prepared for political science collections.[52] It is based in part on a scheme developed in 1928 and was published in 1942. One of the reasons the Glidden-Marchus scheme was created was because the Dewey and LC systems did not provide adequately for public administration materials.[53] The Glidden-Marchus system accommodates all levels of government, and nongovernmental publications as well.

The Glidden-Marchus notation starts with a breakdown into classes. It begins with general reference and continues through the constitution, three branches of government, and the functions of government (planning through agriculture). Subclasses are provided for. Level of government is the next major breakdown, followed by form subdivisions, such as accounting, administration, appropriations, maps, reports, and surveys. The form subdivisions are numbered in alphabetical order.

Glidden-Marchus has a subject index, which serves as a key to the classification schedules. This index is also designed to serve as a subject heading list.

Glidden-Marchus has been used in a number of special libraries, but the printed version, issued in 1941, is out-of-date. A reproduction of the 1941 version, with additions, deletions, and cross-references made by the Joint Reference Library, Public Administration Service in Chicago, was published in 1975.[54] The changes, which are numerous, are those made by the library that developed the classification scheme in 1942.

CODOC

The notation system that originated at the University of Guelph is known as CODOC, a name adopted to indicate the use of the system at a consortium of Canadian universities.[55] CODOC is a software system that provides classification numbers for documents from all levels of government and also for nongovernmental publications. It is a computer program designed for clerical input. Entering data for a particular document requires identification of (1) jurisdiction (for example, US for United States); (2) level of government, followed by numbers and letters designating the name of the unit (that is, 2 for state and IL for Illinois); (3) agency name (which might be U for University of Illinois and 40 for Cooperative Extension Service); and (4) title or series ("Circular," for example, might be

52. Sophia H. Glidden and D. G. Marchus, *A Library Classification for Public Administration Materials* (Chicago: American Library Association, 1942).

53. Castonguay, *Classification Schemes*, 31.

54. Sophia Hall Glidden and D. G. Marchus, *A Library Classification for Public Administration Materials* (Chicago: American Library Association, 1975).

55. Margaret Beckman, *Automated Cataloging Systems at the University of Guelph Library*, Computerized Cataloging Systems Series (Peoria, Ill.: LARC Press, 1973).

19C). The resulting CODOC number would be US2ILU40-19C32, with 32 being the particular circular number. For monographs, the final segment of the code begins with the year and is followed by a Cutter number from the title: for example, 72C59 for a publication titled "Care for Your Trees," issued in 1972.

The advantages of CODOC are the ease of entering new documents into the system, the lack of dependence on professional librarians for input, the speed with which the documents can be entered, and the multiple access points for the data. Virginia Gillham reported that the procedure for entering documents into the system "is so fast . . . that it is cheaper to code an item than to take the time to make the decision not to code it."[56] The CODOC computer programs produce five separate indexes: corporate author, personal author, title, series, and serials, and also a keyword-out-of-context (KWOC) report. A shelflist can be produced as a supplementary tool.

On the other hand, critics of the CODOC system point to the need to enhance the subject access because reliance on the words in a title often fails to reveal the contents of a publication. A title such as "Confidentially Speaking" gives no indication that this Louisiana publication deals principally with nutrition. Another disadvantage of relying on titles alone for subject approach is the lack of coordination for synonyms. One title may use the word "forage" and another "pasture," and the user may be left with only half of the pertinent literature. As a practical matter, adoption of the CODOC system is no doubt often ruled out because of the cost of the software. This expenditure would be justified only for a large research library or a network of cooperating libraries. Virginia Gillham, University of Guelph, has compiled a complete bibliography of articles about CODOC.[57]

CLASSIFICATION SCHEMES FOR A SINGLE STATE

Examination of the many classification schemes devised for the documents of a single state is a project beyond the scope of this text. Many states have such schemes, and some states have more than one. Illinois, New York, North Carolina, Ohio, and Texas are examples of states with several schemes. The minutes of a 1974 State and Local Documents Task Force meeting indicated that efforts were underway to use a unified system

56. Virginia Gillham, "The Guelph Document System," *Government Publications Review* 7A, no. 3 (1980): 211–16.

57. Virginia Gillham, "CODOC as a Consortium Tool," *Government Publications Review* 9 (January–February 1982): 52–53; Virginia Gillham, "CODOC in the 1980s: Keeping Pace with Modern Technology," in *New Technology and Documents Librarianship. Proceedings of the Third Annual Government Documents and Information Conference* (Westport, Conn.: Meckler, 1983): 89–98.

in North Carolina, Ohio, and Texas.[58] The State Library in North Carolina published a classification scheme in 1983 and a supplement six months later. The Texas State Library puts classification numbers into the OCLC records in the 086 field.[59]

In several states the local classification scheme is used in the state checklist. Examples are California, Louisiana, and Texas. While adoption of the checklist classification scheme is not mandatory in these states, libraries have the option of using it.

Another reason for forgoing a detailed discussion of individual state classification schemes is that the states tend to borrow from one another. Pennsylvania State Library's system is said to be based on Houk's Ohio scheme; Missouri is similar to the Florida Atlantic scheme; and five states report that their classification scheme is based on the California scheme.

Sources for information on individual state classification schemes include: (1) the State and Local Documents Task Force materials, which include a preliminary 1973 report by Elizabeth Maine and the *Documents to the People* bibliography and its supplement; (2) the literature survey in Lane; (3) Rosenkoetter's discussion based on her 1973 survey; and (4) Castonguay's *Guide*.

The State and Local Documents Task Force has had a continuing interest in classification schemes. Some classification schemes are in the *Documents on Documents Collection*, described in Chapter 9. However, at the time that collection was first organized, many classification schemes were withdrawn and sent to a S&LDTF ad hoc committee. The information assembled by that committee was the basis for the *Documents to the People* (*DttP*) bibliographies. A thirty–seven–item bibliography in *DttP* listed both classification schemes and articles about them and was followed by a thirteen-item supplement.[60] Source notes for additional information were included. The committee working in this area had as its goal the publication of abstracts of the schemes. Six, for Pennsylvania, Glidden, Nebraska, New York, and Texas, as well as one by Alderman, were published.[61] Over half the classification schemes listed are in the committee files and are available on interlibrary loan.[62]

58. Ruth Hartman, "Classification Committee," in "GODORT Conference Report—Part I," *Documents to the People* 3, no. 1 (September 1974): 17.

59. Dan Havlik, "Texas Documents Classification Numbers in OCLC Records," *Public Documents Highlights for Texas* 5 (Spring 1985): 7.

60. Ruth D. Hartman, comp., "Bibliography of Classification Schemes Used for State Document Collections," *Documents to the People* 3, no. 4 (March 1975): 23–25, and Supplement Number 1, *Documents to the People* 4, no. 5 (September 1976), 23–24.

61. George Bordner, "Pennsylvania," *Documents to the People* 4, no. 4 (June 1976): 15–17; "Glidden," *Documents to the People* 3, no. 5 (May 1975): 36–38; "Nebraska," *Documents to the People* 3, no. 5 (May 1975): 38–41; "New York," *Documents to the People* 3, no. 5 (May 1975): 41–43; "Texas," *Documents to the People* 4, no. 6 (November 1976): 28; Alice Alderman, "Classifying State Documents," *Documents to the People* 4, no. 3 (May 1976): 58–63.

62. The classification schemes are available from Lauri Sebo, University Research Library, University of California, Los Angeles, CA 90024.

The literature survey in Lane notes that classification schemes that encompass different levels of government are not indexed under the word "state," with the result that the "Plain 'J'," or the CODOC system might escape the attention of the state documents librarian. Doris C. Dale's historical article and articles on the nature of classification are cited, along with six articles on individual state schemes.[63]

Rosenkoetter discusses the responses to her survey beginning with DDC, LC, Swank, and Houk and then comments on the replies from thirty-four libraries that reported using another classification device. Her conclusion was:

> In summary, those libraries which use original, unpublished classification systems are generally satisfied with their own ways of doing things. Most of the systems are at least partially agency-based. The major problem facing state documents librarians is the constantly-changing nature of state governments. Subject-based or accession-based classifications avoid this problem but require more indexing. None of the respondents claimed to have found the perfect system.[64]

Conclusion

The need for greater control at the state level (because the diversity of issuing agencies precludes the possibility of handling at the Library of Congress and because not all state publications are of national interest) and the higher quality of the bibliographic record when produced at the state level (at least theoretically) make cataloging of state publications an important part of a national bibliographic network.

63. Lane, *State Publications and Depository Libraries*, 214–15.
64. Rosenkoetter, *Treatment of State Documents in Libraries*, 129.

11
CONCLUSION

The most important characteristic of state documents, their origin in a governmental agency, is one that they share with all documents. The first part of this chapter is a recapitulation of the significant factors relating to state publications and their use by the public, and the end, a look at potential trends.

State documents differ from other documents because of the level of government in which they originate. They stand between publications of the U.S. government (federal documents) and those of counties and municipalities (local documents). They deal with subjects that affect people directly in their daily lives: health practices, environmental quality, roads and highways, and state officials.

Most of the characteristics of state documents—their official issuance, their relationship to archival records, their nature as primary source materials, their issuance in series—are common to all official publications. However, at the state level, some of these characteristics have special significance.

One difference between publications emanating from the different levels of government is the timeliness of state publications, which often are issued prior to federal compilations on the same topic. Timeliness is one of the most important attributes of state publications. Vital statistics are the prime example. Statistics on births, deaths, and diseases, on crime and criminals, and on employment and wages are all collected and published by state agencies and only later made available in federal publications. In addition to being more timely, the presentation of the information and the details supplied in the state version may differ from those in the federal version. For example, Louisiana publications use the correct designation, "parish," for the governmental units that in other states are called counties. More detail is possible at the state level. This locally specific presentation of state information is a special characteristic of state publications.

State publications begin with the date the state entered the union; thus, the time span of state publications varies from 1789 to date in the thirteen original states to 1959 to date in our two newest states. Territorial publications are sometimes included in state documents collections and bibliographies, thus making state publications predate federal publications. Detailed and explicit definitions of the terms *state agency* and *state documents* (or *state publications*) have been created as a necessary element of depository distribution legislation. Definitions are also useful in library situations where state documents are separately acquired, shelved, or serviced. The definition of state agency varies from state to state, and depending on the purpose of the definition, may or may not include all three branches of government, state institutions of higher education, or agricultural experiment stations. State documents librarians must also recognize the existence of documents that span more than one level of government: state and federal, state and local, intrastate regional, and interstate regional publications. The definition of state agency does not necessarily include these fringe areas, and it behooves state documents librarians to recognize the value of these publications and ensure that they come under bibliographic control. The *Monthly Checklist of State Publications*, for example, has a separate listing of regional publications.

The definition of state publications may be broad enough to include reports produced under a research grant and publications issued in nonprint formats, or it may be narrow and limited to printed publications issued directly by executive department state agencies.

Libraries are critical to both the use of state publications and their preservation. Because state publications are issued for various purposes, their availability in libraries is an advantage that exploits the full value of the publications. State publications are issued in small quantities by noncommercial publishers and go out of print quickly, making it difficult for individuals to determine their existence and use them to their full potential. Libraries, which exist to serve as a general information source, also provide information for the areas in which state agencies function and should have state agency publications available. Educators need the studies made by state departments of education as well as independently published materials. Conservationists can find much useful information in state publications. Libraries are also an appropriate source for information that is available only in official publications of the state. Individuals seeking information on nursing homes, environmental quality, roads and bridges, or recreational possibilities may find the answer at the local library. Although state agencies want their publications to be used, state officials do not always know all the people who might want to use them or all the needs which the publications can meet.

State depository library systems are a means of providing access to state publications on a statewide basis. A trip to the office of a state agency at the state capital should not be necessary. Citizens who live far from the state capital should not be at a disadvantage in acquiring state information merely because of a geographical happenstance. Library collections of state publications have been even more necessary in recent years with the trend toward more limited distribution to individuals.

The preservation function of libraries meets the needs of those people who need noncurrent state information. Journalists seeking to detect trends in the treatment of mental illness find answers in library collections of reports from state institutions and state departments of hospitals. Historians and social scientists value research based on original sources.

Although each state has its own constitution and government, there are many areas in which the states cooperate and look to each other for models. The field of state documents is one such area. Legislation relative to state documents not only includes recent depository legislation but also goes back to much earlier times when attempts were made to encourage the states to establish collections of the documents of all the states and to achieve bibliographic control of the documents within the state in which they originated. The documents exchange of the early 1900s resulted in major collections of state documents in many state libraries. Such exchanges, however, benefited only one library in each state.

Bibliographic control, partially achieved on a national level by the *Monthly Checklist of State Publications*, was a goal of state documents librarians in the 1930s. Only limited gains were achieved. Some states were able to prepare checklists that expanded the coverage of the *Monthly Checklist*, and others were not. The 1975 "Guidelines for Minimum State Servicing of State Documents" broadens the goals of state documents librarians by addressing both out-of-state collections and comprehensive in-state collections.

The important collections of state documents at the Library of Congress, the Center for Research Libraries, the New York Public Library, and a few other major libraries must be remembered when access to all-state collections is needed. For the documents of a single state it has always been true that the best collection is found in the state in which the documents originated. It is significant that collections of in-state documents are now distributed throughout the individual states, thus lessening the dependence of the end user on one or two libraries in the state. Equitable availability on a geographical basis throughout the state is one of the principal objectives of state documents depository legislation.

State documents issued as microforms, audiovisual tapes, or computer disks are not essentially different from other materials in these formats. Certain types of state publications have been converted to microformats by commercial publishers. Some republishing for distribution is done by libraries or archives agencies. Many state publications are best used in a microfiche.

Computers and the vast amounts of information which they can accommodate are widely used at the state level. However, the hardware and software may not, in many states, be compatible from agency to agency, much less from state to state. In most states computerization of legislative activities has been one the first areas brought under control. Bill status reporting is available not only within legislative agencies but also in many states to the general public. Administrative units concerned with state finances and budgeting have also used computers to control information; in this area, however, general public access is not available.

Librarians who acquire and make state publications available to the public should be aware of the need for an understanding of the organization and structure of state government, the advantages of state depository systems, the usefulness of a carefully prepared and indexed state checklist, and the need for state documents librarians committed by training and desire to public service. They must know what information is available in state documents -and must make it available to all.

Today the emphasis in state documents work is on making state information easily accessible and readily available to the general public. State publications in hard copy are being used together with state information in various physical forms. Online databases, such as OhioPi, are merging data from official as well as unofficial state publications in the same system. Some state information is no longer available in hard copy but only online. This accords with the trend in libraries toward incorporating all government publications into the information resources of the library and exploiting those resources without reference to their origin.

The advent of computer-based cataloging records, with their standardized data elements and format, is bringing bibliographic access to state publications into the larger library picture. The cooperation of catalogers and checklist editors in producing state document checklists with full cataloging information is becoming more frequent, with resulting reduction both of duplication of effort on the part of librarians and, it is hoped, of confusion of the library patron. With the increased access to state publications made possible through computer searches, libraries can make documents more easily accessible to the end user.

Availability is increasing as distribution patterns are expanding. The realizations that depository distribution need not be limited to hard copies and that the responsibility of a depository librarian extends beyond the confines of the library collection to encompass all state government information are concepts gaining increasing acceptance in state documents work. Distribution in microfiche is an element of a depository program that not only makes copies of publications more widely available but also decreases costs to state agencies. Linda Feist, in describing the developments in state document control in Minnesota, emphasizes this dual benefit that accrues both to libraries and to state agencies.[1] Referring users to sources not immediately at hand, whether those sources be state agencies or other libraries, is becoming increasingly recognized as a responsibility

1. Linda S. Feist, "The Evolution of Access to and Control of State Documents in Minnesota," *Government Publications Review* 13 (July–August 1986): 465–71.

of the state documents librarian. The full value of state publications as an expansion of library resources then becomes available to citizens of the state and to all who might have occasion to use them.

GUIDELINES FOR
STATE DOCUMENTS WITH
SELECTED COMMENTARY

American Library Association
Government Documents Round Table
State and Local Documents Task Force

INTRODUCTION

The guidelines collected in this compilation were drafted by the State and Local Documents Task Force of the Government Documents Round Table, of the American Library Association (ALA), to make state publications more easily accessible and more widely available to the general public. This recognizes that an informed electorate forms the basis of a democratic society. They were reviewed and approved by appropriate units of the American Library Association and adopted as ALA documents. This course of events is in accord with the statement of purpose of the Government Documents Round Table and also with the priority placed by ALA on access to publications.

The text of the guidelines was adopted by ALA Council and represents ALA policy. This introduction and the commentaries accompanying the guidelines are official GODORT policy.

These guidelines focus on the responsibilities that should be assumed at the state level by the library community of each state. The first guideline, Minimum State Servicing, is the most general. The Checklist, Inputting into Data Bases, and Depository Legislation guidelines address specific areas of activity pertinent to state documents within the state. The fifth guideline, Distribution Center Activities, supplements the first four guidelines by listing additional activities appropriate for state-level action.

Although the guidelines might seem to be quite general, they were drafted as minimum statements so that all states would accept them. The endorsement by COSLA (Chief Officers of State Library Agencies) is an indication of their credibility.

The underlying purpose of the guidelines, although it is not stated explicitly, is to bring state documents into the mainstream of the information flow. Peter Hernon says, "increased access will not occur by accident or serendipity; only with direct involvement, commitment, and planning can government publications be 'mainstreamed' with other library/information services" (*Public Access*, p.404). The State and Local Documents Task Force guidelines are a step in this direction.

Access and availability encompass the idea that publications should be at hand in the place where they are needed, in a format that permits appropriate use, at the time they are required.

Definitions for terms used in the guidelines are given here for convenience. Earlier versions of the guidelines included definitions in the servicing and checklist commentaries and references to the checklist definitions in both the database and legislation guidelines. In order to reconcile the definitions, they have been rewritten and are to be used in all State Documents Task Force guidelines.

State Agency—A corporate body created by the state legislature, or governor, or another state agency under the authority of the legislature, acting as the state's agent and/or being funded partially or wholly by state funds, or operating at the direction of the state.

State Document/Publication—Information intended for public distribution by or for a state agency in any format.

This definition includes the words, "intended for public distribution," which was a last minute amendment in ALA Council and was designed to assure that archival records were not included. The targeted audience for a publication is not relevant to the status of the material as long as such publications are distributed outside the agency. The breadth of circulation afforded state information can be used as an indication of intent to make public distribution.

Printed informational matter may include any document, report, directory, statistical compendium, bibliography, law or bill, rule, regulation, newsletter, pamphlet, brochure, map, or serial. Also included are publications issued by private bodies, such as consultant or research firms, even though they may not have been financed by any state funds, when the publications have been issued under contract with and/or supervision of a state agency. Nonprint informational matter may include machine-readable data files, microforms, or audio or visual presentations. State-supported college and university publications with the exception of copyrighted university press publications are also included within the definition.

State Depository Agency—An agency designated by law to fill one or more of the following basic functions: to maintain a collection of state publications, to distribute copies of state publications within the state and/or to exchange copies with other states.

Normally a state depository agency will receive publications directly from the issuing agency, but might also receive them from a state printer. There may be more than one depository agency in a state, each filling limited functions.

Depository Library (In-state Depository)—"A library legally designated to receive . . . state government publications supplied by the state agencies of a particular state for distribution by the state library." A depository library may be either a full depository or a partial (selective) depository.

The quoted definition is from the *ALA Glossary*; the words, "without charge" are omitted from the definition. The Servicing guidelines use the term, "in-state depository."

Authority File—"A set of authority records establishing the authoritative forms of headings to be used in a set of bibliographic records and the references to be made to and from the headings."

This definition is taken from the *ALA Glossary*. The Servicing guidelines use the term, "authority list."

State Document Checklist—A regularly published bibliographic list of all current state documents (as defined in the scope of the publication) identified to have been published by the state.

Two terms, National Depository and Professional Person, formerly defined in the Servicing commentary have been dropped from this commentary. The earlier comment on the term, National Depository, was that there is no national depository. The comment on the term, Professional Person, was that library school education was an essential factor in what constitutes a professional staff. Both these comments are true today, but need not be stressed.

GUIDELINES FOR MINIMUM STATE SERVICING OF STATE DOCUMENTS

1. In each state an agency or agencies should be designated by law to act as the depositories for the documents published by the state to maintain a collection of and to distribute copies of such documents within the state and to exchange copies with other states. The functions of such depository should be adequately defined and determined in legislation.

2. The appropriate state agency should maintain a list of in-state depositories to which it regularly sends some or all state documents, and should receive a sufficient number of copies to serve those depositories.

3. The appropriate state agency should be prepared to exchange documents with other states, or at least to have an adequate supply of copies available to meet out-of-state requests. What is an adequate supply will depend on the nature of each document and its potential interest to persons in other states.

4. The appropriate state agency should compile and distribute a checklist and/or shipping list of its state publications.

4a. Such a list should appear at least quarterly.

5. The appropriate state agency should deposit at least one copy of all its state's publications with the Library of Congress, and send at least one copy to an additional designated national depository, if and when one is created.

6. The appropriate state agency should maintain and have available for distribution an authority list of state agencies.

7. In the appropriate state agency at least one professional person (full time or equivalent) should be assigned to the state documents function, and that person should have adequate supportive staff.

GUIDELINES FOR STATE DOCUMENTS CHECKLISTS

WHEREAS, the ALA has adopted "Guidelines for Minimum State Servicing of State Documents" which states: "(4) The appropriate state agency should compile and distribute a checklist and/or shipping list of its state publications. Such a list should appear at least quarterly"; and WHEREAS, the Library of Congress *Monthly Checklist of State Publications* is selective and does not purport to be a comprehensive state bibliographic tool; and WHEREAS, checklists of state publications are necessary for bibliographic control; now, therefore be it RESOLVED that each state must assume primary responsibility for bibliographic control of its own publications in order to provide access to state documents, and, be it further RESOLVED that Guidelines for checklists of state publications are hereby promulgated.

Comment: This second set of guidelines was prepared by the State Documents Task Force in 1977 to assist in the bibliographic control of state documents. The checklist guidelines provide an opportunity for all states to cooperate in achieving uniformity in reporting the existence of state documents—furthering the goal of nationwide bibliographic control.

The most comprehensive bibliographic source for identifying state documents, the Library of Congress' *Monthly Checklist of State Publications*, is an accession list of state publications received by the Library of Congress; therefore, any state publication not received is not listed.

Only the state agency responsible for identifying and collecting the state's publications is in a position to report fully to the document user on its state's publishing activities.

1. *Legality.* A checklist of state documents should be required by statute.

Comment: A legal mandate is necessary to ensure continuity and to designate the agency responsible for compiling and publishing the list. The legislation should indicate the purpose of the checklist, the authority for its preparation, publication and distribution, and the funding source.

2. *Scope.* This official state document checklist should provide the most complete listing of the state's documents possible.

Comment: Diligence should be exercised to discover and list all works. An effort should be made to make the checklist comprehensive and to include all known documents whether received by the agency preparing the checklist or not. The more complete the coverage, the more significant and useful the checklist will be.

A checklist is primarily current in nature, listing those documents published or received by the agency preparing the checklist during the specified time period. However, the inclusion of "older" titles not previously listed should be considered, particularly if the state already has a comprehensive bibliography and there are only occasional newly discovered titles.

3. *Format.* The checklist publication should follow the American National Standards Institute, Inc. *American National Standard for Periodicals: Format and Arrangement.* 1967 (11 p.) (ANSI Z39.1-1967).

Comment: Reference to the ANSI Standard should be construed as referring to the latest edition. The more important provisions of the *Standard* which pertain particularly to checklists are:

1. A periodical should have a distinctive title;
2. Volume number, issue, number, date, and frequency should be stated;
3. Availability information should include price (if priced), publisher, and address.

4. *Frequency.*

    A. The checklist should be published at least quarterly (ALA Guidelines for Minimum State Servicing of State Documents, 4a).

Comment: For acquisition and reference use of the checklist, timeliness is extremely important. State publications are often limited in quantity, become quickly out-of-print, and are seldom reprinted. The checklist's usefulness as an acquisitions tool is directly correlated to its frequency of issue.

    B. A cumulative index should appear at least annually.

Comment: The minimum requirement is an annual index. If the individual issues of the checklist are indexed (a commendable practice followed in some states), those indexes should be cumulated into an annual index. The minimal index is a KWIC or KWOC index. It is desirable that additional points of access be afforded by the indexing of subjects, titles, authors, corporate authors, series, etc.

If the list itself is a dictionary catalog and does not have an index, it should be cumulated annually. The publication of cumulated lists helps the user by reducing the number of lists to be consulted and provides an opportunity for editorial corrections and re-arrangement of titles.

5. *Distribution.* Adequate in-state and appropriate out-of-state distribution should be provided.

Comment: The checklist should be sent automatically to all depository libraries in the state. In recognition of the state's responsibility in the national bibliographic control of state documents, the list should be available to out-of-state libraries (including the Library of Congress, the Center for Research Libraries, and the Council of State Governments Library) and to other libraries and individuals on a complimentary basis or by subscription. Before resorting to subscriptions, exchange arrangements should be considered.

6. *Preparation.* Preparation of the checklist should be by, or supervised by, professional library personnel.

Comment: Professional supervision is necessary to ensure proper bibliographic citations, to identify incomplete and inaccurate bibliographic information and to prepare a quality index.

7. *Checklist Content.*

A. Full statement of the scope of the checklist consisting of a policy statement developed by the responsible agency:

Comment: A statement should appear in the foreword of each issue outlining the policies adopted by the publishing agency. In addition, the arrangement of the checklist must be carefully explained including choice of entry, arrangement by agency or author, series arranged by title of series or individual title or author, etc.

1. Agencies & types of publications excluded from the list.

Comment: Specifically, the omission of any of the following types of agencies should be noted: regulatory bodies, interstate commissions, the state bar, universities, institutions, agricultural experiment stations, the courts and other judicial bodies, and the legislature and legislative bodies.

Any of the following categories of publications that are not included should be mentioned: research reports, ephemeral materials, college catalogs and newspapers, announcements, press releases, mimeographed materials, films, tapes, data bases, and sale items.

2. Period covered (publication date or receipt date of publications listed).

Comment: Indicate whether rule for inclusion is imprint date or date of receipt. If the period covered is determined by date of receipt, the need for a cumulation of entries is greater than if the period covered is determined by the imprint date.

3. Inclusion policy for "older" publications.

Comment: The practice of including all older publications that are not included in the state's retrospective bibliographies is strongly recommended.

4. Treatment of periodicals (listed each issue, semi-annual, annual, etc.).

Comment: New periodicals should be reported when issued as well as in the periodic listing, if any. Periodicals can be listed annually if inclusive volumes and numbers and also dates of issues are given.

B. Information on how to obtain copies of listed publications.

Comment: Because the checklist will be used as an acquisitions tool, the availability of publications listed should be noted. The availability of microforms should be indicated. Symbols, for which there must be a key, may be used, or a general statement on availability may be made. Depository libraries should be listed at least annually to assist checklist users in locating library copies of publications.

C. Cross-references.

8. *Bibliographical Content of Entries.*

A. Issuing agency.

Comment: The geographical entity is understood to be that of the issuing agency; therefore the state name preceding the agency may be omitted. The form of agency name to be used is not specified because the variance is so great. However, it is agreed that divisions of an agency should be listed following the agency; that is, the full hierarchy should be given.

B. Full title.

Comment: Cover title should be included if prominent and at variance with title page.

C. Author(s).

Comment: Individual as well as corporate authors should be given.

D. Dates and numbering for serials.

Comment: The beginning and ending date of the report period for annual reports should be given.

E. Imprint (including copyright date, if applicable).

Comment: Place of publication may be omitted if it is the state capital. Copyright should be included to alert the librarian and the user that the material has restrictions on duplication and reproduction of content.

F. Collation.

G. Series.

Comment: Series may be listed as analytics under the series title or by author with a series note. It is important that the series information be included.

H. Price.

Comment: The inclusion of the price, when known, reduces inquiries.

I. Restrictions on distribution and availability.

Comment: This requirement is included to reduce needless correspondence.

J. Other identifiable information such as ISSN, ISBN and stock numbers.

9. *Mailing Addresses.* The mailing address of each issuing agency should appear either as an adjunct to the entry, at the end of the checklist, or as a reference to a separate publication.

10. *Mailing Lists.* Notification should appear in the checklist to alert recipients prior to updating the mailing list.

11. *New Agencies.* When the first publication of a new agency is listed, the legal authority for the agency's creation and a brief history should be included.

Additional features that a checklist could display, although they could not be called minimum standards, are:

1. Addition of classification number and subject headings.
2. Full cataloging data, including all tracings.
3. Special notation for reference tools.
4. Historic cumulations for agency names.
5. Holding symbols.

GUIDELINES FOR INPUTTING STATE DOCUMENTS INTO DATA BASES

The purpose of this document is to establish policies for the creation of state bibliographic records which are compatible with the developing national bibliographic networks.

Comment: The "Guidelines for Minimum Servicing of State Documents" do not require either the full cataloging of state documents or the entry of their records into data bases, however, these procedures are strongly recommended. Some reasons for this are:

1. When fully cataloged and entered on-line, bibliographic data become immediately available to all utility members. This can mean almost national access to information about a state's publications.

2. Interlibrary loan is greatly enhanced.

3. Subject access to publications is possible on the bibliographic utilities. Archival tapes can now be used to produce author, title and subject indexes.

1. To insure quality control, a single institution with each state should have sole responsibility for coordinating input of cataloging records for state documents into the data bases (e.g., OCLC, RLIN, WLN, etc.). State documents should be considered as any information intended for public distribution produced by or for a state agency in any format (Guidelines for State Documents Checklists, Checklist Commentary, p.1). [Editor's note: All definitions are now in the introductory commentary.] State supported college and university publications will be considered as state publications with the exception of copyrighted university press publications. Cataloging role assignments may be made in selected areas.

Comment: At present, it is not possible for a state agency to have inputting authority, i.e., bump the records of other institutions. Any member of a utility is free to do original cataloging for any item not already in the data base. However, the depository agency, usually the state library, should *accept the responsibility* for the timely cataloging of the state's publications and for entering the records into a data base. Having accepted the responsibility, the cataloging agency should be committed to quality cataloging and have adequate staff and resources to perform the task. State depository centers unable to do the cataloging themselves may wish to reach an agreement with another institution to provide the cataloging.

2. Each coordinating institution should input full original cataloging in MARC format, according to the latest edition of *AACR*.

Comment: Since January 1, 1981 members of OCLC, RLIN, and WLN have been required to catalog according to *AACR2*. The appropriate MARC format must also be chosen since state publications can include maps, recordings, films and other media, as well as books and serials.

The rules for cataloging serials are of particular concern to catalogers of state publications since many documents are serials. The rules call for successive entry cataloging requiring a new entry for each title change. Ephemeral items with frequent title changes may therefore require work out of proportion to their worth. A library may choose to create uniform titles to reduce this problem.

OCLC, RLIN and WLN recommend that member libraries be aware of Library of Congress rule interpretations and follow LC practice. LC decisions are published in the *Cataloging Service Bulletin* available by subscription from the Library of Congress. Also suggested is the ALA publication, *Cataloging Government Documents*.

3. Each coordinating institution should compile, publish and maintain an authority file of state agencies citing the name of the agency as it is to be used for cataloging.

A. The authority file should be based on the latest edition of *AACR*.

Comment: Name authority for state agencies involves determining the form of name that should be used consistently for a heading. *AACR2* and the *Cataloging Service Bulletin* have much to say on the form of name to be used for government bodies and their subordinate agencies. LC name authority records are now available on tape and on microfiche, and through OCLC. Copies of the LC card authority file for a state are available from LC with price depending on the size of the file.

Use LC headings when they are available. Under the new rules parts of the hierarchy of an agency are more often omitted than under previous rules.

B. The authority file should include a history of each agency, its position in the governmental structure and any necessary cross references.

Comment: It may not be possible, given the time it takes, for the cataloger to provide a complete history for each agency he or she establishes for cataloging purposes. Give the date of establishment and/or the statutory citation when possible. Where the position of the agency in the government structure is not represented adequately in the heading or cross-references, make appropriate clarifications in the name authority record.

GUIDELINES FOR STATE PUBLICATIONS DEPOSITORY LEGISLATION

State publications depository legislation should provide for:

1. Definitions of a state agency and state publication. The definition in "Guidelines for State Documents Checklists" should be followed.

Comment: The definitions referred to appeared in the commentary for the checklist guidelines. In this compilation, all definitions have been moved to the introductory section.

2. A specific administering agency designated by law to carry out depository legislation. Authorization to the administering agency to adopt rules and regulations.

Comment: While most states designate this responsibility to a library body within the state, there are others that place the responsibility in branches of government such as an archives unit. However, there should be one single overall agency designated for carrying out the depository program. For instance, in some states the responsibility for maintenance of a state documents collection is carried out by one state agency while the distribution of state documents is handled by another. Unfortunately, in such instances, many items are lost to the depository system because they are either identified too late or not identified at all. There are also instances where certain classes of publications, such as legal compilations, are distributed, solely by the issuing agency, thus by-passing the depository system. Centralized coordination in the authorizing legislation together with responsibility for promulgation of rules and regulations would eliminate some of these difficulties.

3. A requirement that state agencies must supply sufficient copies of all their publications to meet distribution needs.

Comment: This is the basic provision in the depository legislation—a depository program cannot exist without publications to distribute. This is also the weakest area in most depository legislation, and the one which gives depository librarians the most problems. Almost all state legislation has a phrase which states that agencies shall provide the distribution unit with copies of the publications sufficient to meet the needs of the depository libraries. However, since most systems rely on the good will of agencies, which are, in turn, subject to increasing cutbacks, enforcing this requirement is a problem. In an effort to secure cooperation, one state included in its legislation a requirement for an affidavit showing delivery to the library distribution unit before the printing account is paid. Another state required that there be a designated state person within each agency responsible for sending publications to the library distribution unit. Still other states require the printer to send copies of state publications directly to the library distribution unit.

A related problem sometimes arises over the number of copies. In states where different quantities are required, distribution centers often find it difficult to institute a coordinated policy for distribution.

Guidelines are helpful, but they still require explanation. In states where the legislation specifies the number of copies needed, this problem is solved to some extent. These states also usually include a provision for acquiring additional copies when they are needed. Some sample terminology might be:

Each agency shall furnish the library . . . twenty-five copies of each . . . public document. However, if the division shall so request, as many as twenty-five additional copies of each public document shall be supplied

or

Each agency which issues public documents shall furnish the State Library fifty copies of all publications . . . . However, if the library requests, as many as twenty-five additional copies of each public document shall be supplied.

4. Authorization for the administering agency to use micrographics or other means of reproduction to meet the needs of depository distribution.

Comment: With the rapid development of the micropublishing industry and subsequent public acceptance of microforms, inclusion of such authorization is essential for the future growth of the depository distribution system. The saving both in terms of production cost and storage expense of microprint government publications have effectively been demonstrated by the Government Printing Office. Microreproduction of state publications will result in their widespread accessibility.

5. Systematic and automatic distribution of state publications from the administering agency.

Comment: In most states, the authorizing legislation mentions the creation of a system for the orderly distribution of documents. It does not specify the operational aspects other than the designation of a responsible agency. Typical statements are:

The state publication library distribution center shall promote the establishment of an orderly depository library system

or

It shall be the duty of the division to . . . provide a system for distribution of the copies furnished it

or

The center shall promote the establishment of an orderly depository system.

The specific operational elements such as frequency of a shipment and the method of delivery can be identified later in the agency's rules and regulations.

6. Distribution to a system of designated depository libraries—to ensure easy availability to the public. Such a system should include full and partial depository libraries. Distribution should include the Center for Research Libraries and the Library of Congress.

Comment: This element is at the core of any depository legislation since it identifies the method of public access to state publications. Most state legislation includes:

1. The type of library that is eligible (municipal, university, college or public library, library association, state library agency, Library of Congress).

2. The eligibility requirements (ability to preserve publications, ability to make publications available, adequate geographic distribution, adequate staff for servicing the publications, etc.).

3. The method of forming the system (depository library contracts, agreements among the participants, etc.).

The inclusion of two classes of libraries, full and partial (or selective), in the legislation allows the widest participation by libraries. Following the federal depository system, full depositories usually receive one copy of all publications either produced or sent to depository libraries. The use of the term "partial" allows each state to set up its own system for distribution to the libraries which cannot handle the full load of state publication distribution. In some cases, partials can select which items they wish to receive. For example:

A selective depository shall be sent one copy of every publication from the specific state agencies it designates.

In other cases, the partials receive a core collection of documents from selected areas as agreed to by the depository librarian.

Specific retention schedules need not be mentioned in the legislation but could be outlined either in the agency's rules and regulations or as guidelines to the depository libraries. Specifying distribution to the Library of Congress and the Center for Research Libraries in the legislation assures that those agencies will receive the publications automatically. Distribution to other states can be accommodated by the inclusion of a reciprocal agreement section, such as:

. . . may exchange copies for the publications of other governments

or

The center may also contract with public out of state libraries for exchange of state and other publications on a reciprocal basis

or

The . . . library may enter into agreements with appropriate state agencies of each of the forty-nine other states of the United States to establish a program for the exchange of publications.

7. A provision for the maintenance of a complete permanent historical collection.

Comment: As part of the depository legislation, it is essential that some provision be made for the permanent retention of a historical collection. Most states require that some copies (usually three) be sent to the library or other appointed agency for permanent retention. It is also helpful to specify in the legislation the type of retention. For instance, archival retention is far different from library retention and some provision should be made for easy public access to this material. The problem of the completeness of the collection will probably always remain, despite the excellence of the state agency publication definition. The solution probably lies in a good public relations campaign and continued persistence in contacting state agencies.

8. Bibliographic control of state publications compatible with national developments and preparation of a checklist in accordance with "Guidelines for State Documents Checklists."

Comment: The growth of bibliographic control for state publications via cataloging networks is perhaps the most striking development of the past few years. It is for this reason that acceptance of national bibliographic standards (such as cataloging according to *AACR2* with MARC level records) should be included in the depository legislation. Such acceptance would result in a nationwide consistency of state document bibliographic records, which would then be compatible from data base to data base. Such a system is not as far in the future as we might think as libraries throughout the United States are cataloging their state agency publications online.

GUIDELINES FOR STATE DISTRIBUTION CENTER ACTIVITIES

These Guidelines supplement and expand the Guidelines on servicing, checklists, data bases, and legislation already adopted by S&LDTF. Items relating to the distribution centers which are outlined in the existing Guidelines are not repeated, e.g., the duty to issue a checklist, to provide for out-of-state libraries, etc.

The state distribution center should:

1. Coordinate state agency efforts to comply with the law, and educate and advise state agencies on library and user needs through training sessions, manuals and brochures, and personal contacts.

2. Follow an intensive, systematic program of document identification and acquisition and encourage libraries throughout the state to assist in identifying documents to be acquired.

3. Encourage the acceptance of depository library responsibilities in all appropriate areas of the state.

4. Prepare and promulgate standards for depository libraries.

5. Send documents promptly to the depository libraries, with shipments at least once a month.

6. Prepare a shipping list for the depository library packages.

7. Make available to the depository libraries a manual containing legal and administrative documents related to the depository program and recommendations on the handling of documents in various kinds of libraries.

8. Insure through provision of variant formats and through appropriate duplication processes that sufficient copies of publications are available to meet the needs of the depository system.

9. Consider the establishment of a microform program by the distribution center to satisfy the storage needs of depository libraries.

10. Maintain records on the distribution to the depository libraries.

11. Visit and inspect depository libraries on a regular basis.

12. Hold workshops and training sessions for depository librarians.

13. If state has a statewide classification scheme, maintain the scheme, supplying new numbers as required.

14. Prepare and distribute a current list of state agencies with addresses, telephone numbers, contact persons, etc.

15. Prepare brochures, posters, news releases, radio spots and other publicity that can be used throughout the state.

16. Promote state documents as reference and information sources through annotated bibliographies, workshops, etc. for depository and non-depository libraries.

17. Administer an exchange program or a warehouse for duplicates and encourage state agencies to list or deposit their surplus publications with the program.

18. Consider establishing a depository library council with a representative from each depository library.

19. Consider establishing an advisory board with membership from publishing agencies, the legislature, the budget office, depository and other libraries.

Approvals and endorsements : The *Servicing* Guidelines were approved by the American Library Association (ALA) Council in 1975, after receiving prior approval by the Government Documents Round Table (GODORT), the Reference and Adult Services Division (RASD), the Library and Information Technology Association (LITA), the Resources and Technical Services Division (RTSD), and the now defunct ALA Interdivisional Committee on Public Documents.

The *Checklist* and *Data Base* Guidelines were approved by GODORT, RASD, Association of State Library Agencies (ASLA), and LITA in 1978. They were amended by the State and Local Documents Task Force (S&LDTF) in 1979 and as amended were approved by the Cataloging and Classification Section (CCS) of RTSD, RTSD (in principle), and the State Agency Section of the Association of Specialized and Cooperative Library Agencies (SLAS), (the section is the successor to ASLA), in 1981.

The *Legislation* Guidelines and the *Activities* Guidelines were approved by GODORT, RTSD (in principle), and SLAS in 1980 and 1981. In addition, the *Legislation* Guidelines were approved by the ALA Legislation Committee in 1980.

All five Guidelines were approved by the Chief Officers of State Library Agencies (COSLA) in April, 1981 and were accepted by the LITA Board for information in July, 1981.

Checklist, Data Base, Legislation, and *Activities* Guidelines were adopted by ALA Council as amended, January 26, 1982.

Commentary for all Guidelines was approved by S&LDTF, June 29, 1986, and by GODORT on July 1, 1986.

Publication data : ALA Council, *Minutes,* 1975 (Midwinter) includes *Servicing* as 1974-75 ALA Council Document #21 (Exhibit 27) and ALA Council, *Minutes,* 1982 (Midwinter) includes the remaining four guidelines in 1981–82 ALA Council Document #12 (Exhibit 9).

APPENDIX B
SUGGESTED READINGS

The suggested readings are limited to articles and books of national interest. Articles relating to a particular state are not included. The few exceptions are major articles, such as those by Shaffer on Nebraska and Stewart on Missouri. The following paragraphs serve as a topical guide to the readings.

A number of sources should be consulted for historical background. The serious searcher should look at the proceedings of the National Association of State Librarians, an organization that, from the time it was organized, had a continuing interest in state publications. A number of articles on state documents were included in the Public Documents series of the ALA Public Documents Committee in the 1930s. Kuhlman, Wilcox, Childs and other leaders all contributed articles to this series. In 1940 the *Manual on the Use of State Publications* appeared. It has excellent essays on the importance, character, and use of state publications. A bibliography compiled for the *Manual* includes the significant articles published up to 1938.

Historical recapitulations were written by Blasingame (a now-is-like-then theme), Cohen (the Information Handling Services story), Dalton (government publishing), Libbey (the *Research Design* of the ALA Inter-divisional Committee on Public Documents), Jenkins (early state records), Kuhlman (the state documents centers, and bibliographic control), and Brigham (state documents clearing house).

The articles on acquisition and collection building include those by Erlandson, Moody, two by Parish, Weech, and Welsh. Boyer's thesis on checklists measures the checklist issued in the late 1970s against the ALA GODORT S&LDTF "Guidelines for State Documents Checklists" (Appendix A). Also recommended on checklists is the Ferruso article on the *Monthly Checklist of State Publications*. Of historical interest are the comments by Hardin, Lane, and Lloyd and the Kuhlman proposal of the 1930s with his suggested rules for compilation.

Depository legislation is the topic of the articles by Shaffer on Nebraska and Stewart on Missouri. Lane's *State Documents and Depository Libraries* includes both a general discussion of depository legislation provisions and a state-by-state section giving the legislation, rules and regulations, contracts, and other documents relating to depository programs. The article by Gaines reports the status of depository programs in 1978; the article by Nakata and Kopec is 1980. Haselhuhn's article compares depository programs over a ten-year period.

For reference and information services, the March-April 1983 issue of *Government Publications Review* (a theme issue, "State Government Information Sources," edited by Terry L. Weech) is recommended. It includes articles by Weech, Lane, Purcell, Ford and Nakata, Johnson, and Parish, all listed in this suggested reading list. Also suggested is the Weech article, "New Technology and State Government Information Sources."

Reference and information services have been the subject of articles by Hernon, Ford, Purcell (two articles), and White. Hernon ("State 'Documents to the People' ") looks at documents from the reference point of view. Ford and Purcell are companion studies for reference use—Ford on academic libraries and Purcell on public libraries. Purcell also reported on a user survey on state document use in Tennessee. White's state/federal analogy was designed as a means of improving reference use.

The two texts on subject compilations have excellent guides on research techniques for locating the state laws on particular subjects. The Foster and Boast volume covers statutory laws, and the Nyberg and Boast, administrative law.

Classification writings on the list are those by Dale (not limited to state documents but an important historical survey) and the book by Castonguay on local classification schemes, many of which encompass state documents. Rosenkoetter has details on cataloging and classification and handling procedures. Carter's article is easy to read, practical, and encouraging. On CODOC read the article by Gillham, which incidentally has an extensive bibliography.

Articles limited to a particular type of state document include Faull (maps), Riche (statistical abstracts), Ronen (microform collection at Harvard), Schmidt (agricultural publications), and Ternberg (regional publications). Weech has an extensive article on the characteristics of state publications.

Blasingame, Ralph. "Public Documents of the States: Their Collection, Listing, Distribution and Value." *Proceedings of the Second Assembly of State Librarians, 1960*, 1–8. Washington, D.C.: Library of Congress, 1961.
    A retelling of the 1930s project for state documents centers, with the conclusion that not much had been accomplished then but that the proposals were still valid and the need for action still existed.

Book of the States. Lexington, Ky.: Council of State Governments, 1935+. Biennial.
    "Each volume contains selected bibliographies concerning the problems of state governments" (Palic).

Boyer, Yvonne. "State Checklists: A Survey." Master's paper, University of North Carolina, 1981.

Examines the effect of the S&LDTF "Guidelines for State Documents Checklists" by comparing checklist issues from 1977 and 1979. Some improvements were found, but an average of 56.71% of the guidelines were currently met. Areas in need of improvement were frequency and indexing.

Brigham, H. O. "Public Document Clearing House and Its Activities." American Library Association, Committee on Public Documents. *Public Documents, 1936,* 146–49. (Also appeared in National Association of State Libraries, *Proceedings and Papers* 39 (1936): 25–27.)

Plans for the Public Document Clearing House.

Carter, Catherine. "Cataloging and Classification of State Documents." *Pennsylvania Library Association Bulletin* 25 (March 1970): 86–97.

A readable analysis of *AACR* changes for state documents.

Casey, Genevieve M., and Edith Phillips. *Management and Use of State Documents in Indiana.* Research Report no. 2. Detroit: Office of Urban Library Research, Wayne State University, 1969. 75 p. Also published as Indiana Library Studies Report 17 [Bloomington, Ind.]: Indiana University, Bloomington, Graduate Library School, 1970, 68 p. ERIC ED 046 473.

Chapter 3 analyzes the responses of 39 states to a questionnaire on laws governing state documents and practices in cataloging, listing, and distributing documents. Later untabulated data on the same topics are available in the ALA GODORT S&LDTF publication, *State Publications.*

Castonguay, Russell. *A Comparative Guide to Classification Schemes for Local Government Documents Collections.* Westport, Conn.: Greenwood Press, 1984.

Most of the classification schemes described accommodate state as well as local publications. Comparisons between the various schemes together with explanations and examples of the notation systems make this a handy reference.

Cohen, Herbert C. "An Immodest Proposal: State Publications When and Where You Want Them (Almost)." *Illinois Libraries* 58 (March 1976): 200–4.

Describes the plans of Information Handling Services for checklists and microfiche as envisioned by the IHS editorial director. Before its demise, the project included online access to the checklist data.

Dale, Doris Cruger. "The Development of Classification Systems for Government Publications." *Library Resources and Technical Services* 13 (Fall 1969): 471–83.

Not limited to state publications and historical in approach, but important as background information.

Dalton, P. I., et al. "Government and Foundation Publishing." *Library Trends* 7 (July 1958): 116–33.

Covers a wide range of topics relating to state publishing, including financial backing, editorial control, copyright, distribution, sales, and advertising.

Erlandson, John, and Yvonne Boyer. "Acquisition of State Documents." *Library Acquisitions: Practice and Theory* 4 (1980): 117–27.

Suggests that the causes for underutilization are limited bibliographic access, lack of centralized publication and distribution facilities, and confusion about the structure of government. Estimates that 88% require no payment. Sources for identifying and ordering: *Monthly Checklist of State Publications,* various checklists, various departmental checklists, *Public Affairs Information Service,* advertisements, LC cards with a state as the main entry, patron requests, bibliographies, and library staff orders.

Faull, Sandra K. "State and Local Map Publishing in the United States." *Government Publications Review* 10 (July-August 1983): 375–80.

Results of a survey on state and local government map publishing. A beginning effort; little research in this area.

Ferruso, Agnes. "Monthly Checklist of State Publications." Washington, D.C.: Library of Congress, 1974. ERIC ED 095 891.

Detailed discussion of the production of the *Monthly Checklist* and its characteristics by the editor.

Ford, Barbara J., and Yuri Nakata. "Reference Use of State Government Information in Academic Libraries." *Government Publications Review* 10 (March-April 1983): 189–99.

Based on questionnaire covering staff, value of various sources and types of publications, bibliographic control (including online sources). Concludes that reference librarians need to take the initiative in expanding services, particularly for online sources.

Foster, Lynn and Carol Boast. *Subject Compilations of State Laws: Research Guide and Annotated Bibliography.* Westport, Conn.: Greenwood Press, 1981. 1–59.

Supplement issued by Nyberg and Boast.

Gaines, Robert F. "Recent Developments in Depository Systems for State Government Documents." *Documents to the People* 6 (November 1978): 229–30.

A report on the states having depository library systems, using microforms, or having computerized bibliographic control. Access through OCLC and the possibility of using OCLC records for checklists are noted.

Gillham, Virginia. "CODOC in the 1980's: Keeping Pace with Modern Technology," in *New Technology and Documents Librarianship. Proceedings of the Third Annual Government Documents and Information Conference.* Ed. Peter Hernon. Westport, Conn.: Meckler, 1983. 89–98.

Explanation of this notation system with comprehensive bibliography.

Goodsell, Charles T., et al. "Bureaucracy Expresses Itself: How State Documents Address the Public." *Social Sciences Quarterly* 62 (September 1981): 576–91.

A study of the "communication effectiveness" and "tone of voice" of a sampling of state publications. Finding that great variation exists and a vast improvement is desirable.

Hardin, A. R. "United States State Publications." *College and Research Libraries* 12 (April 1951): 160–63.

Includes charts analyzing the 19 state checklists being issued.

Haselhuhn, Ronald P. "Bibliographic Control and Distribution of State Documents." *RQ* 20 (Fall 1980): 19–23.

Detailed analysis of Texas Documents Monograph no. 2; compares it to Casey's Indiana study (ERIC microfiche ED 046 473).

Hernon, Peter. "Exploiting State and Local Information Resources." In *Public Access to Government Information: Issues, Trends and Strategies*, by Peter Hernon and Charles R. McClure. Norwood, N.J.: Ablex Publishing, 1984.

Includes brief literature survey, bibliographical control and collection development, and ends with look at the future, concluding that the greatest need is for librarians to become more knowledgeable about state government resources.

————. "State 'Documents to the People'." *Government Publications Review* 3, no. 4 (1976): 255–66.

A major article emphasizing the reference use of state publications and suggesting areas in need of research.

————. "State Reference Sources." *Government Publications Review* 7A (1980): 47–83.

Bibliographic listing of general reference sources, with mention of depository programs and microformed publications; arranged by state.

Hubbard, Abigail. "Online Research for a State Legislature." *Online: The Magazine of Online Information Systems* 6 (July 1982): 27–41.

Describes and gives sample searches for Legislex, ELSS, and Legi-Slate.

Jenkins, William S. *Collecting and Using the Records of the States of the U.S.: 25 Years of Retrospection*. Chapel Hill, N.C.: University of North Carolina, 1960.

Jenkins, a political science professor, recounts the evolution of public documents from the time of the American colonies, beginning with manuscript records. The filming of the early state records is described and the contributions of persons associated with the project, Hasse and Childs among others, noted.

Johnson, Nancy P. "Providing Reference Service Using State Documents." *Reference Service Review* 9 (January-March 1982): 89–91.

A list of 18 titles useful as reference sources and a list of selected state microform collections.

————. "Reference Use of State Government Information in Law Libraries." *Government Publications Review* 10 (March-April 1983): 201–12.

State government information constitutes a major portion of a law library collection. Acquisition discussion is accompanied by a list of tools for current and retrospective acquisition. Good discussion of new technologies: microforms, computerized legal research, legislative information systems, and video.

Kessler, Ridley R., Jr. "State Documents, an Expanding Resource." *Southeastern Librarian* (Fall 1971): 172–75.

An essay on the kinds of state documents and their importance.

Kuhlman, A. F. "Preserving Social Science Source Materials." *ALA Bulletin 27* (March 1933):128–32.

Describes the launching of the state public document center plan by the Social Science Research Council. Includes a listing of the types of materials to be covered and the programs of action to be followed in the states.

——. "Need for a Comprehensive Check-list Bibliography of American State Publications." *Library Quarterly* 5 (January 1935): 31–58.

Existing bibliographical aids and the need for more effective tools are given, together with a suggested plan of procedure and rules for preparing the checklists.

Lane, Margaret T. "The 'Documents on Documents' Collection." *Microform Review* 13 (Fall 1984): 250–53.

Explains the origin of the collection, the preparation of the guides and the availability of the ERIC microfiche.

——. "Distribution of State Government Publications and Information." *Government Publications Review* 10 (March-April 1983): 159–72.

Methods of distribution of paper publications are both statutory and voluntary. Availability in microformat, in computer databases, through telephone lines, and from state information centers is increasing.

——. "State Documents Checklists." *Library Trends* 15 (July 1966): 117–34.

Checklists before cataloging records were available in the bibliographic utilities.

——. *State Publications and Depository Libraries: A Reference Handbook.* Westport, Conn.: Greenwood Press, 1981.

Heavy emphasis on depository legislation.

Libbey, Miles A. "Development of a Research Design for a Comprehensive Study of Government Publications." *Illinois Libraries* 53 (June 1971): 412–25.

Describes the research design prepared for the ALA Interdivisional Committee on Public Documents at the Indiana University Research Center for Library and Information Science.

Lloyd, Gwendolyn. "Status of State Document Bibliography." *Library Quarterly* 18 (July 1948): 192–99.

Supplements the list in the *Manual on the Use of State Publications.* Text discusses history of bibliographic publications listing state documents.

Moody, Marilyn. "Developing Documents Collections for Non-Depository Libraries." *RQ* 25 (Winter 1985): 185–89.

Section on state documents (p. 187) says for smallest libraries state and local documents may be more needed than federal documents.

——. "State Depository Microform Publications." *Microform Review* 14, no. 4 (1985): 232–36.

States with strongest depository programs have been the first to use microfiche for the program. Iowa program described.

——. "State Documents: Basic Selection Sources." *Collection Building* 7 (Spring 1985): 41–44.

Concise statement on acquiring state documents, with comprehensive annotations of the principal tools.

Nakata, Yuri, and Karen Kopec. "State and Local Government Publications." *Drexel Library Quarterly* 16 (October 1980): 40–59.

An in-depth study of depository libraries, based on Texas Documents Monographs nos. 2 and 2A.

Nyberg, Cheryl, and Carol Boast. *Subject Compilations of State Laws, 1979–1983: Research Guide and Annotated Bibliography*. Westport, Conn.: Greenwood Press, 1984.

Continues compilation by Foster and Boast.

Parish, David W. "Considerations in State Document Collection Building." *Documents to the People* 10 (March 1982): 34–36, 39.

Based on a request to each state for five to ten state reference titles, Parish establishes a dozen "worthwhile state documents categories," on which 75% of the respondents agreed. The list begins with state blue books and state checklists. The official budget of the state was a 100% selection item.

———. "Into the 1980s: The Ideal State Document Reference Collection." *Government Publications Review* 10 (March-April 1983): 213–20.

Describes the 11 "most important," that is, most useful, categories of state reference sources, as reported by documents specialists in the 50 states. Although Parish suggests these categories for collection building, he believes it impractical to define an ideal collection.

———. "Some Light on State Bibliographies." *Government Publications Review* 12 (January-February 1985): 65–70.

The utter disregard for the value of state bibliographies is attributable to lack of knowledge of their existence, their specialized nature, and the difficulty of learning about their existence, in determining access, and in acquisition. Subject coverage is as broad as that for federal documents. The article is based on the research for the author's *A Bibliography of State Bibliographies*.

———. "State and Local Byways." *Government Publications Review* 11 (March-April 1984): 192–94 and subsequent issues in July-August and November-December.

Part of the Information Update section of *GPR*. Discusses developments in state documents programs, reviews new titles and lists new publications.

Purcell, Gary R. "Reference Use of State Government Information in Public Libraries." *Government Publications Review* 10 (March-April 1983): 173–88.

Based on survey of 125 libraries in 10 states. Found a contradiction in level of state commitment and implementation of policies that support that commitment. Also found that libraries are meeting only a portion of the needs of persons requiring state government information and that libraries are particularly remiss with respect to machine-readable numeric data.

———. "The Use of Tennessee State Government Publications." *Tennessee Librarian* 32 (Spring 1980): 20–32.

User survey made by ten libraries is analyzed for frequency of library use, reasons for use and non-use, occupations of respondents, and methods of identifying and locating state publications. Recommendations: (1) an agency to acquire, distribute, and publicize, (2) library association to work for legislation, (3) a list of publications and centralized cataloging, and (4) libraries to make a greater effort to acquire.

Riche, Martha F. "State Statistical Abstracts." *American Demographics* 3 (July-August 1981): 38.

Discusses types of agencies issuing statistical abstracts and the frequency of issuance, and lists the primary statistical reference work for each state.

Ronen, Naomi. "Creating a Micropublishing Project: A Non-Commercial Perspective." *Microform Review* 11 (Winter 1982): 8–13.

The Harvard Law School project—6,000 volumes from the state documents collection in areas of banking, insurance, labor, public utilities, and taxation, principally annual reports—its inception, planning, filming, and marketing.

Rosenkoetter, Paula. "Treatment of State Documents in Libraries." *Government Publications Review* 1 (Winter 1973): 117–34.

Extensive survey of cataloging, classification, and handling of state documents based on questionnaire with 125 responses representing all the states.

Schmidt, Fred. "State Agricultural Documents." *Documents to the People* 2, no. 1 (October 1973): 15, 20.

Announces and reproduces the "Memorandum of Understanding Between the Land-Grant College and University Libraries and the United States Department of Agriculture (National Agricultural Library)."

Shaffer, Dallas. "State Document Legislation: Nebraska, a Case Study." *Government Publications Review* 1 (Fall 1973): 19–27.

The full story of how one state secured new depository legislation, with budget figures for the new program.

The State of State Documents: Past, Present, Future. Ed. Brenda F. Shelton Olds. Austin, Tex.: Legislative Reference Library, November 1976. ERIC ED 142 174.

An overview of state documents activity in 14 southwestern and mountain plains states together with background materials on documents planning nationwide. Includes a comparative chart of federal/state sources.

Stewart, Byron. "The Development of the Missouri Documents Depository System: 1971–1977." *Government Publications Review* 12, (July-August 1985): 321–44.

Historical account of the six-year process of setting up a state documents program. Examples of primary source documents and other reference material from Missouri are given.

Ternberg, M. G. "Regional Government Organizations and Their Publications." *Government Publications Review* 9 (September-October 1982): 493–98.

Describes the growth and function of regional government organizations, illustrates the types of publications issued, and suggests how to locate the publications.

Tseng, Henry P., and Donald Pedersen. "Acquisition of State Administrative Rules and Regulations—Update, 1983." *Administrative Law Review* 35 (1983): 349–89. (Earlier editions in *Administrative Law Review* 28 (1976): 277–98 and 31 (1979): 405–42.)

The 1982–83 survey reported in this article generated data on "the status of state administrative code and register projects, trends in the availability of such materials in microform, options in printed format, the emergence of state administrative law reporters, and the state administrative law holdings of several major U.S. law libraries."

Weech, Terry L. "Characteristics of State Government Publications, 1919–1969." *Government Publications Review* 1 (Fall 1973): 29–51.
  Based on Ph.D. dissertation. Reviews bibliographic tools for state publications. Compares listings in *Monthly Checklist of State Publications* by subject and by functional characteristics decade by decade for 50 years.

———. "Collection Development and State Publications." *Government Publications Review* 8A (1981): 47–58.
  Comprehensive article on selection, acquisition, selection tools, bibliographic control and depository systems.

———. "New Technology and State Government Information Sources," in *New Technology and Documents Librarianship. Proceedings of the Third Annual Government Documents and Information Conference*, Ed. Peter Hernon, Westport, Conn.: Meckler, 1983. 77–87.
  Reviews status of availability of government information in print and more particularly, the newer sources of information, electronic data. Stresses need for public access: "On the whole, the sources based on new technology are even less accessible to the public than those in traditional print formats." Sees need for a "government information specialist" with expertise at all levels of government.

———. "State Government Publications in Microform." In *Microforms and Government Information*, by Peter Hernon. Westport, Conn.: Microform Review, 1981.
  Topics include retrospective and current collections and current programs.

Welsh, Harry E. "An Acquisitions Up-Date for Government Publications." *Microform Review* 6 (September 1977): 285–98.
  Discusses recent developments that have affected acquisition of government publications. Limited number of state titles cited.

White, Marilyn Domas. "Drawing Analogies between State and Federal Documents: A Method for Increasing Access to State Publications." *Government Publications Review* 2 (Spring 1975): 111–25.
  Compares federal and New York publications as information sources, most of which are legislative or judicial.

Wilcox, Jerome K., ed. *Manual on the Use of State Publications*. Chicago: American Library Association, 1940.
  "Includes a bibliography of bibliographies of state publication (p.75–91), legislative digests and indexes (p. 125-31), law compilations (p. 139–49)" (Palic).

DEPOSITORY AND
STATE AGENCY MANUALS

This appendix includes the more substantial manuals in the *Documents on Documents Collection* (ERIC ED 247 940 and ED 263 923) and in current materials of the collection available on interlibrary loan. Some of the manuals are loose-leaf, and one even lacks a title page; the informal type of listing used in the guides to the *Documents on Documents Collection* is followed here. The *Documents on Documents Collection* identification number is given as an aid to locating the manuals on the microfiche or requesting interlibrary loan.

Also recommended is the 1985 *Federal Depository Library Manual*. Section 6, "Technical Processing," poses a long list of questions that must be answered as one decides upon proper handling procedures.

California
California State Publications: Manual for Acquisition, Processing, Use. Second ed. rev. by California State Library. Distributed by Department of Finance, Organization and Cost Control Division. Various pagings. 1961. CA:H.
Comprehensive, widely cited. First edition was 1957.

Colorado
Manual of Guidelines for Colorado State Agencies. August 1981. 22 p. CO85:H.
Covers who shall deposit, what shall be deposited, and how to deposit state publications. Appendixes include laws and regulations.

Connecticut
Manual for Depository Libraries. 1980. Unpaged. CT:H.
Loose-leaf. Includes "Basic Reference Sources for State" and shelving requirements.

Hawaii
To: Director, Hawaii State Library; Director, Public Libraries Branch; Director, School Library Services; Subject: Publications Distribution Center, July 23, 1969. 14 p. HI:H.
Memorandum outlining the procedures of the distribution center.

Kansas
State Documents of Kansas: Handbook. Rev. 1980. 17 p. KS:H.
Discusses advantages and disadvantages of using Kansas documents classification in a separate collection and interfiling using Dewey.

Louisiana

Distribution of Documents to Depositories. Documents Committee, Louisiana Library Association. June 1972. 48 p. LA:H.
Includes background documents for depository program.

Minnesota

Minnesota State Documents: A Guide for Depository Libraries. 1984. 23 p. MN84:H.
The most recently issued manual. Prepared for a state without a depository system. Good section on "Encouraging Use."

Mississippi

State Depository for Public Documents: Handbook for State Agencies and Depository Libraries. Prepared by Gerald Buchanan. January 1978. 13 p. MS:H.
Addressed to both state agencies and depository libraries.

Missouri

Depository Library Handbook. January 1980. 28 p. MO:H4.
Lists "Publications Contacts" for state agencies and "Core Documents."
State Agency Handbook, prepared by Maggie Johnson and Barbara Klempke, January 1980. 26 p. MO:H5.
First prepared in 1977 (MO:H); has been revised several times.

Nevada

Nevada State Publication Depository System: Manual for Acquisition, Processing, Use. Compiled by Documents Section, Nevada State Library, May, 1969. iii, 65 p. NV:H.
Like California.

New Mexico

Depository Library Manual. Prepared by Sandra K. Faull. 2d ed. August 1985. 23 p. NM85:H.
First edition was 1979. Detailed procedures for handling documents in the library; bibliography of coverage of state publications; and list of articles and publications about state publications.
State Agency Manual. Prepared by Sandra K. Faull. February 1979. Various paging. NM:H1.

North Dakota

Administrative Manual for North Dakota State Document Depository Libraries. 1977. 8 p. ND:H.
Very brief.

Oklahoma

Manual for Publications Officers. November 1984. Includes appendixes. 31 p. OK85:H.
Comprehensive guide; includes section on standard format for publications, tables of examples of publications required or not required for deposit, and many forms.

Virginia

[Manual] Received 1980. 37 p. Loose-leaf. VA:H.

Wisconsin

Manual for Wisconsin Document Depositories. Guidelines for Standards and Procedures of the Wisconsin Document Depository Program. January 1975. 10 p. WI:H.
Guidelines and standards more than procedures.

AALL STATE DOCUMENTS BIBLIOGRAPHY SERIES

The following twenty-three titles, arranged here by state, are available as of January 1, 1986. Bibliographies for states not yet reported on are added to the series at the time of the annual meeting of the American Association of Law Libraries (AALL), usually for states in the area of the meeting. New titles are reported periodically in *Jurisdocs*, the newsletter of the Government Documents Special Interest Section of American Association of Law Libraries. The address for ordering is: American Association of Law Libraries, 53 West Jackson Boulevard, Chicago, IL 60604.

Alaska
Ruzicka, Aimee. *Alaska Legal and Law-Related Publications: A Guide for Law Libraries.* 1984.

Arizona
Teenstra, Richard, Susan Armstrong, and Beth Schneider. *Survey of Arizona State Legal and Law-Related Documents.* 1984.

California
Ranharter, Kathryn. *The State of California: An Introduction to Its Government Publications and Related Information.* 1979.

Connecticut
Voisinet, David, Dennis J. Stone, and Judith Anspach. *Connecticut State Legal Documents: A Selective Bibliography.* 1986.

District of Columbia
Ahearn, Carolyn, Barbara Fisher, Betty Gellenbeck, and Carolyn Whitman. *Selected Information Sources for the District of Columbia.* 1981.

Indiana
Fariss, Linda, and Keith A. Buckley. *An Introduction to Indiana State Publications for the Law Librarian.* 1982.

Kansas
Wisneske, Martin E. *Kansas State Documents for Law Libraries: Publications Related to Law and State Government.* 1984.

Louisiana
Corneil, Charlotte, and Madeline Hebert. *Louisiana Legal Documents and Related Publications: A Selected Annotated Bibliography.* 1984.

Maryland
Davis, Lynda C. *An Introduction to Maryland State Publications for the Law Librarian.* 1981.

Massachusetts
McAuliffe, Leo, and Susan Z. Steinway. *Massachusetts.* 1985.

Michigan
Yoak, Stuart D., and Margaret A. Heinen. *Michigan Legal Documents: An Annotated Bibliography.* 1982.

Missouri
Aldrich, Patricia, Kit Kreilick, and Anne Maloney. *A Law Librarian's Introduction to Missouri State Publications.* 1980.

Nevada
Henderson, Katherine. *Nevada State Documents Bibliography.* 1984.

New Jersey
Senezak, Christina M. *New Jersey State Publications: A Guide for Law Librarians.* 1984.

New Mexico
Wagner, Patricia. *Guide to New Mexico State Publications.* 1983.

New York
Dow, Susan L., and Karen L. Spencer. *New York Legal Documents: A Selective Annotated Bibliography.* 1985.

Oklahoma
Corcos, Christine. *Oklahoma Legal and Law-Related Documents and Publications: A Selected Bibliography.* 1983.

Oregon
Buhman, Lesley Ann, Bobbie Studwell, Cynthia A. K. Romaine, and Katherine Faust. *Bibliography of Law Related Oregon Documents.* 1984.

Pennsylvania
Fishman, Joel. *An Introduction to Pennsylvania State Publications for the Law Librarian.* 1986.

Texas
Allison, Malinda, and Kay Schueter. *Texas State Documents for Law Libraries.* 1983.

Virginia
Aycock, Margaret, Jacqueline Lichtman, and Judy Stinson. *A Law Librarian's Introduction to Virginia State Publications.* 1981.

Washington
Burson, Scott F. *Washington State Law-Related Publications: A Selective Bibliography with Commentary.* 1984.

Wyoming

Greene, Nancy S. *Wyoming State Legal Documents: An Annotated Bibliography.* 1985.

INDEX

Washington (state), 24
Weech, Terry L., 4, 45, 75, 84, 89
Weeding and deselection, 179–81
WESTLAW, 145, 149
White, L. D., 20, 74n
White, Marilyn Domas, 16n
Wilcox, *see Manual on the Use of State Publications*

Wisconsin, 81, 93, 123–24
Woolley, Robert D., 124, 133, 202
Workshops, western librarians, 24–25

Zink, Steven D., 144, 164

Margaret T. Lane is a law librarian with the firm of Lane, Fertitta, Lane, and Tullos, in Baton Rouge, Louisiana. She was formerly recorder of documents in the Louisiana Secretary of State's office. Lane is an active member of ALA's Government Documents Round Table (GODORT) and in 1981 was awarded GODORT's James Bennett Childs Awared for "exceptional contributions" to the field. Lane is the author of *State Publications and Depository Libraries* (Greenwood Press, 1981).